Schizophrenia

A Developmental Analysis

SCHIZOPHRENIA
A Developmental Analysis

Sidney J. Blatt

Departments of Psychiatry
and Psychology
Yale University
New Haven, Connecticut

Cynthia M. Wild

Department of Psychiatry (Psychology)
at The Massachusetts Mental
Health Center
Harvard University School of Medicine
Boston, Massachusetts

ACADEMIC PRESS   New York   San Francisco   London   1976

A Subsidiary of Harcourt Brace Jovanovich, Publishers

ACADEMIC PRESS, INC.
111 Fifth Avenue, New York, New York 10003

United Kingdom Edition published by
ACADEMIC PRESS, INC. (LONDON) LTD.
24/28 Oval Road, London NW1

Library of Congress Cataloging in Publication Data

Blatt, Sidney Jules,   (date)
    Schizophrenia: a developmental analysis.

    Bibliography: p.
    Includes index.
    1.   Schizophrenia.   2.   Developmental
psychology.   I.   Wild, Cynthia M., joint author.
II.   Title.   [DNLM: 1.   Schizophrenia.   WM203
B644s]
RC514.B56   616.8'982   75-3963
ISBN 0-12-105050-5

To our parents:
Fannie and Harry Blatt
and
Catherine and John Wild

Contents

Preface

This book systematically examines the hypothesis that schizophrenia involves developmental disturbances in the capacity to establish and maintain boundaries. Numerous reports of boundary disturbances in schizophrenia have been made by clinicians of different theoretical persuasions; and many of the impairments in cognitive, perceptual, and interpersonal functioning reported in research investigations of schizophrenia can be understood as manifestations of boundary disturbance.

We first considered the development of boundaries as discussed in developmental psychology and psychoanalytic theory to derive an integrated formulation covering the cognitive, affective, and interpersonal dimensions of boundary development. We then applied this formulation to a wide range of empirical and clinical data in the literature on schizophrenia. We found that our conceptualization of the development of boundaries based on an integration of developmental research and theory (e.g., Piaget and Werner) with psychoanalytic formulations provided us with a model that facilitated an integration of a wide array of sometimes unrelated and even contradictory findings in the research on schizophrenia. This formulation permitted a fuller understanding of some of the ambiguities and paradoxes of the cognitive and interpersonal aspects of this most troubled psychological state.

We also applied our formulation to clinical data gathered on a group of psychotic patients in an intensive inpatient treatment program to examine different levels of boundary disturbance in a series of patients. Finally we considered the limitations of our formulation of boundary disturbances in schizophrenia and its implications for further research. While we believe that this formulation also has important implications for the treatment of schizophrenic patients and their families (Blatt, Wild, & Ritzler, 1975), such considerations were beyond the scope of our primary focus in this book on research issues.

ix

Our understanding of the matters discussed in this book are in large measure due to the opportunities we have had to work at the Yale Psychiatric Institute (YPI)—a long-term, intensive inpatient facility for the treatment of severely disturbed adolescents and young adults. Independent of any consideration of the therapeutic efficacy of intensive, long-term inpatient treatment for seriously disturbed patients, a treatment facility such as YPI provides clinicians and researchers a unique opportunity for intense involvement with and careful observation of patients. Only a setting such as YPI can provide the depth and range of clinical observations necessary for a detailed analysis of psychotic states. We are indebted to our colleagues at YPI and to the patients who gave us the opportunity to try to understand some aspects of the profoundly painful and troubled state called schizophrenia. We are particularly indebted to Dr. Theodore Lidz and Dr. Stephen Fleck whose pioneering research in the psychological and social aspects of schizophrenia and whose devotion to clinical research influenced and aided our thinking and work in numerous ways. Our formulations have been influenced by Dr. Lidz's observations of boundary disturbances in schizophrenia which began as early as 1952 when Dr. Ruth Lidz and he discussed the mutuality of boundary disturbances in schizophrenic patients and their mothers.

We are grateful to the director of YPI, Dr. Charles Gardner, and to the YPI clinical staff for permission to use the clinical files, and to the therapists, nurses, social workers, teachers, aides, and activity workers whose sensitive observations contributed to the richness of the clinical material. We are also indebted to these staff members and other members of the faculty of the Yale Department of Psychiatry for their thoughful comments and observations in discussions of our formulations. We are particularly indebted to Drs. Arthur S. Blank, C. Brooks Brenneis, Steven Feinstein, George Gallahorn, David Glass, Richard Isay, Dorothy Lewis, Florence Levy, Harriet Lutsky, Richard Munich, Barry A. Ritzler, Samuel Roll, Jean G. Schimek, and John Shershow and to Skip Atkins, Harris Baderak, Jean Brenner, Ann Chambers, Karen Cronan, Jim Ellis, Iza Erlich, Gail Evans, Gloria Hankin, Michele Remus, Julia J. Rothenberg, Susan Suskind, and Anita Ward. We are also indebted to the graduate students, psychiatric residents, and psychology trainees and fellows whose perceptive and thoughtful insights and comments in seminars over the past decade have aided us in refining our formulations. We would also like to acknowledge our debt to Drs. Jean G. Schimek, Frances Kaplan Grossman, C. Brooks Brenneis, Donald M. Quinlan, Patrick O'Neill, and Theodore Lidz for their helpful comments on early drafts of the manuscript, to Mollie Nelson, Chris Durang, and Susan Blatt for editorial assistance, and to Sandy Rabinowitz for the jacket illustration. We want to express our gratitude to our spouses, Ethel S. Blatt and George L. Cowgill, for their understanding, concern, and sensitive observations and comments which have contributed to this book in manifold ways.

Quotation Credits

Permission to quote from the following works is gratefully acknowledged.

p. 110. Allison, J., Blatt, S.J., & Zimet, C. *The interpretation of psychological tests.* New York: Harper & Row, 1968. p. 101.

p. 37. Bleuler, E. The basic symptoms of schizophrenia. In D. Rapaport (Ed.), *Organization and pathology of thought.* New York: Columbia University Press, 1951. pp. 589-590.

p. 48. Brown, R.W. *A first language, the early stages.* Cambridge, Massachusetts: Harvard University Press, 1973. p. 200.

p. 87. Burnham, D., Gladstone, A., & Gibson, R. *Schizophrenia and the need-fear dilemma.* New York: International Universities Press, 1969. pp. 31-32.

p. 70. Federn, Paul, M.D. *Ego psychology and the psychoses.* Edited and with an Introduction by Edoardo Weiss, M.D. © 1952 by Basic Books, Inc., Publishers, New York. p.61.

pp. 52, 74, 77. Flavell, J.H. *The developmental psychology of Jean Piaget.* Princeton: D. Van Nostrand-Reinhold, 1963. pp. 160-161, 152-153, 156-157.

pp. 39, 76. Freeman, T., Cameron, J.L., & McGhie, A. *Studies on Psychosis.* New York: International Universities Press, 1966. pp. 81, 91.

pp. 3. Freud, S. *Civilization and its discontents* (1930). Standard Edition, Vol. XXI. London: Hogarth Press, 1961, 57-145. p. 66. Also W. W. Norton & Co., 1962.

p. 243. Garmezy, N. Children at risk: The search for the antecedents of schizophrenia. Part 2. Ongoing research programs, issues and intervention. *Schizophrenia Bulletin,* 1974, 9, 55-125. p. 92.

p. 58. Holt, R.R. *Manual for the scoring of primary process manifestations in Rorschach responses.* Unpublished 9th draft. New York University Research Center for Mental Health, 1963. P. 21.

Schizophrenia

A Developmental Analysis

1 / *Introduction*

Schizophrenia is one of the most extensively studied clinical phenomena. Endless numbers of case reports and theoretical formulations, as well as volumes of research data about the psychological, interpersonal, and physiological aspects of schizophrenia, are testimony to the numerous attempts to understand some of the paradoxes and contradictions surrounding this most severe form of mental disorder.

In attempting to review and integrate the extensive and diverse literature on schizophrenia, a number of methodological problems become apparent. One major problem is the lack of any consistent definition of schizophrenia (Pious, 1961). Relatively few research publications indicate how schizophrenia was defined, how it was differentiated from other psychoses, what criteria were used, who made the judgments, and with what degree of reliability (Blatt & Allison, 1968). Thus it is difficult to evaluate, contrast, or integrate findings from various studies, since it is unclear whether the samples are comparable. Differentiation of subgroups, such as chronic-acute, process-reactive, and delusional (paranoid)–nondelusional (nonparanoid) patients, reflects recent efforts to achieve greater precision in defining schizophrenia. Contributions made by many studies using these distinctions suggest that a good deal of the earlier confusion and contradiction in the literature may be a function of imprecise definition of the clinical disorder. These studies also suggest that further conceptualization and differentiation of the clinical phenomena may lead to greater clarification of some current ambiguities.

We should make it clear that we do not regard schizophrenia as a nosological label for a disease entity with a specific causative agent and a rigid,

1

fixed course. We do not consider schizophrenia to be a hopeless, deteriorative illness occurring in a closed system. Rather, we consider it to result from multiple causal factors, including serious disturbances in the early interpersonal transactions of parents and child and genetic and biological factors, which interact in complex ways to produce serious disruptions of some of the most fundamental and rudimentary psychological processes. These disruptions include profound disturbances of perceptual and cognitive functions, sense of self, and capacity for interpersonal relationships. Fuller consideration of early normal developmental processes and their possible disruptions may contribute to a more precise definition of schizophrenia and further delineation of subtypes. Such a developmental approach may also help to integrate the vast amount of clinical and empirical data gathered on this subject and to diminish some of the negative historical associations attached to it, leading to greater understanding and more effective treatment of schizophrenics. In addition, this approach may suggest further directions for research on schizophrenia.

From a number of divergent areas and points of view, there is agreement that one of the earliest and most basic steps in human development is the evolution of a capacity to experience, perceive, and represent a sense of separation, or boundaries, between objects. Psychoanalytic theorists and developmental psychologists have both used the concept of boundaries to describe very early developmental sequences in the neonate, early ego development, and the formation of psychic structures. Numerous authors have also pointed to boundary problems as a primary disturbance in schizophrenia. An inability to differentiate, articulate, and represent boundaries can be seen as a common factor in the profound disturbances in cognition, sense of self, and interpersonal relationships often observed in schizophrenia.

The purpose of this book is to consider the various conceptualizations of the development and impairment of boundary differentiation, to integrate concepts from developmental psychology with concepts from psychoanalytic theory, and to examine whether this integrated conceptualization of the development of boundaries can be useful in organizing the diverse clinical and experimental literature on schizophrenia, in understanding the confusing and bewildering experiences reported by psychotic patients, and in suggesting further directions for research on schizophrenia.

The concept of boundary was first introduced in the study of schizophrenia by Tausk (1919) in his paper on the influencing machine. Tausk ascribed the changes in schizophrenia, specifically the development of a delusional formation of an "influencing machine," to a projection of the patient's own body accompanied by a loss of the boundary between self and objects. Freud (1930) also referred to the role of boundaries in psychopathology when he commented in *Civilization and Its Discontents* that:

Pathology has made us acquainted with a great number of states in which the boundary lines between the ego and the external world become uncertain or in which they are actually drawn incorrectly. There are cases in which parts of a person's own body, even portions of his own mental life—his perceptions, thoughts, and feelings—appear alien to him and as not belonging to his ego; there are other cases in which he ascribes to the external world things that clearly originate in his own ego and that ought to be acknowledged by it. Thus, even the feeling of our own ego is subject to disturbances and the boundaries of the ego are not constant [p. 66].

Federn (1952) has made the most extensive contributions to the concept of boundary; in contrast to Freud, Federn viewed psychosis as a withdrawal of cathexis from the ego boundary, rather than as a withdrawal of cathexis from object relationships leading to a state of primary narcissism. For Federn, one of the primary tasks in the treatment of psychosis is the consolidation of ego boundaries. He saw the impairment of the capacity to establish and sustain ego boundaries as a fundamental issue in the psychotic experience (Bergmann, 1963).

Cameron (1951) has discussed the schizophrenic's impairment in cognitive processes and concept formation as a boundary defect. Fenichel (1945) also commented on boundary incompleteness as permitting a fusion of ego with the outside world. Lidz and Lidz (1952) described the mutuality of boundary disturbances in the schizophrenic patient and his mother. Searles (1965) illustrated with vivid clinical examples the struggle around fundamental interpersonal boundaries and symbiotic relationships in schizophrenia. Jacobson (1964) has also discussed the pathological fusion of self and object representations in schizophrenia.

There are numerous other references to boundary formation in the literature, such as Fisher and Cleveland (1958), who studied barrier and penetration themes in body image, and Landis (1970), who studied the dimension of permeability–impermeability of ego boundaries. These authors developed systems for scoring Rorschach responses in terms of "boundaries," and their criteria cover a very wide spectrum. Fisher and Cleveland as well as Landis comment on the unique penetration or permeability responses of schizophrenics, which indicate "radical boundary changes" (Landis, 1970) that are highly discontinuous with the types of boundary disturbances found in neurosis. Rorschach responses of schizophrenics reflected disruptions of boundaries that were substantially different from the penetration or permeable responses found in neurotic and normal subjects.

Thus, the concept of boundaries has been used to describe a wide range of phenomena. The concept has often been loosely defined, and theoretical conceptualizations have often been at varying levels of abstraction. There is a need for a more limited and specific formulation of boundary development and disturbance, particularly when considering these issues in psychosis.

Early normal development has been discussed in terms of establishing boundaries. Psychoanalytic theorists have considered the development of reality testing and the capacity to discriminate what is inside from what is outside the self as aspects of the development of boundaries. Initially, the infant is seen as devoid of a sense of reality or a knowledge of external human, animate, and inanimate objects as separate from each other and from the self (e.g., Décarie, 1965; Escalona, 1953). Mahler (1968) distinguished an early autistic stage of development, where the child is unable to differentiate objects, and Pious (1961) discussed this timeless, objectless state in psychosis as the nadir. Freud (1914) conceptualized this objectless, undifferentiated condition as a stage of primary narcissism. As suggested by Fenichel (1945), Hartmann, Kris, and Lowenstein (1949), Jacobson (1964), Kernberg (1966, 1972), Loewald (1951, 1960, 1973), Mahler (1968), Parens (1971), Schafer (1968), and others, separation and individuation from external objects and the formation of internal psychic organization and structures develop in a reciprocal way, and a lack of differentiation of the external world may be paralleled by a lack of internal differentiation. The nature and importance of initial differentiations, the establishment of boundaries between self and external objects in normal development, and the role of these differentiations in the formation of psychic structures have also been discussed in social psychology (e.g., Parsons & Bales, 1955).

Mahler (1968) considered early difficulties with internal and external differentiations to result from the child's inability either to form, or later, to break, a symbiotic fusion with the mother. This initial separation of self from the mothering figure can be seen as a necessary experience in developing the most rudimentary differentiations in external reality and internal psychic structures. Freud pointed out in *Civilization and Its Discontents* (1930) and in his earlier papers on *Negation* (1925) and *Instincts and Their Vicissitudes* (1915) how difficulties in the feeding relationship can affect ego development, the articulation of boundaries, and the evolving capacity for reality testing. In *Instincts and Their Vicissitudes*, Freud also elaborated how early self–other discrimination is determined by the capacity for muscular action, which is only one of several ways in which self–object differentiation seems to be facilitated. Mahler (1968) and Bettelheim (1967) conceptualized that locomotion and action, as well as normal negativism, are critical in the child's ability to continue to make further differentiations in reality and to separate physically and psychologically from the mother.

According to Mahler (1968), there is initially in development a lack of differentiation; people and the mother are not represented as separate and external objects. Without this fundamental differentiation, there is also difficulty in distinguishing between human, animate, and inanimate objects. In the second, symbiotic phase of development, there is some awareness of the self and of the mother as separate; but temporary loss of the mother is reacted to with intensity and, as a defense against that experience of loss, there is a tendency toward experiences of fusion, merging, and attempts to minimize any differentiation between the self and nonself. The development from primary narcissism to a symbiotic fusion with the need-gratifying object to separation, individuation, and the beginning of mature object relationships is conceptualized in part as the capacity to perceive and represent the boundaries between self and the external world, between other people, and between human, animate, and inanimate objects. Without this critical developmental achievement, Mahler (1968) believes that psychosis is likely to occur. She further suggests that this conceptualization, partly based on the study of childhood psychosis, has important implications and potential for differentiating levels of psychopathology in adults.

In developmental psychology, the evolution of a capacity to experience, perceive, and represent a sense of separation between objects is also considered to be one of the earliest and most basic developmental steps. For example, both Piaget (1954) and Werner (1948) discuss the first perceptual–cognitive differentiation as the experience of a boundary occurring in an initially undifferentiated perceptual field. Clinical data (Roth & Blatt, 1974), the study of perceptual processes subsequent to the removal of congenital cataracts (von Senden, 1932; cited by Osgood, 1953), and recent studies of the development of perception in infants (Kagan, 1971) all indicate that high contrast at contour edges is ontogenetically one of the earliest factors influencing visual orientation. As early as the first two days of life, an infant is most attentive to movement or to a high degree of black–white contrast (Berlyne, 1958; Carpenter, Tecce, Stechler, & Friedman, 1970; Fantz, 1963, 1966; Fantz & Nevis, 1967; Haith, 1966; Karmel, 1969; Salapatek, 1968; Salapatek & Kessen, 1966; Wilcox, 1969). The infant's early attraction to highly contrasting contours is consistent with neurophysiological studies that indicate very early neurological and perceptual responses to contrast (Hubel & Wiesel, 1959, 1962; Karmel, Hoffman & Fegy, 1974; Kuffler, 1952, 1953). These studies all suggest that a differentiation of boundaries is one of the earliest developmental processes.

Piaget and Werner, based on different observations and using somewhat different terminology, both discuss the development of boundaries. Piaget's sensorimotor period (1954) and Werner's undifferentiated "syncretic" phase of mental development (1948) describe a period of mental processes that occurs before the child develops a concept of the object as existing independent of himself and his action upon the object. The differentiation between independent objects or events is considered by Werner (1948) as the first step beyond the blurred, diffuse syncretic orientation of the most primitive level of mental development. Piaget (1954) considers the earliest sensorimotor stages of mental development as beginning with the infant's differentiation between the object and his action upon the object. The concept of the object, including the capacity to appreciate the presence and displacement of objects not directly perceived, requires a separation between the object and the self. It is primarily in the sixth stage of sensorimotor development that the child first becomes capable of maintaining a stable mental representation of an object when it is not immediately present in the sensory field. According to Piaget, this level of the concept of the object and of object constancy is a prerequisite for the subsequent development of the representational and symbolic functions. Other boundary distinctions occur at later levels of cognitive development, including the capacity to differentiate the object from its mental representation and verbal signifiers. Thus, to use the example of the concept "mother," the child must first be able to recognize the mother in different contexts and situations when she is physically present (object concept) and then to have a stable mental representation of her when she is absent (object constancy) before being able to maintain a differentiation between the actual mother and the mental image and verbal signifiers used to represent her. If these realms are confused, as when the word becomes equivalent to the actual object, further disturbances in language, concept formation, and other symbolic processes occur (Werner & Kaplan, 1963).

By boundary differentiation we mean the capacity to maintain a separation between independent objects and between representations of independent objects. Perception is sufficiently articulated and attention sufficiently focused so that ordinary segments of reality are perceived and represented as separate from other segments of reality that have similar properties or that are temporally or spatially contiguous. We also mean the maintenance of a separation between an object and its representation, as well as between self and nonself, and between internal experience and external objects and events. We also use the term to refer to the capacity to maintain a stable representation of the self as separate and distinct from representations of others, so that interpersonal relationships are not disrupted by extreme wishes for, or fears of fusion and merging, or both.

A formulation of boundary problems in schizophrenia from a developmental perspective suggests some specific hypotheses. Numerous theoretical, empirical, and clinical statements have suggested that there are significant relationships among the cognitive and interpersonal disturbances observed in schizophrenia. Even further, these statements have suggested a similarity between the disturbances observed in schizophrenia and aspects of early development. Thus Freeman, Cameron, and McGhie (1966) have suggested that the degree and nature of cognitive disturbance may be associated with the extent of disruption of human relationships.

They have postulated that there is a reciprocal and complex intertwining of the development of the child's cognitive–perceptual capacities to identify and represent external objects and events as separate and his ability to establish basic differentiation and separation from his family. Thus it can be hypothesized that in psychosis there are important relationships between the degree and type of disruptions of various cognitive–perceptual functions, the level of definition of self and others, and the level and nature of interpersonal relationships. Understanding of the interrelationships among the disruptions of these various functions in schizophrenia may be facilitated by a developmental approach that emphasizes different levels of boundary differentiation and articulation.

Studies of infant development suggest that there are important relationships between the quality of the caring relationship and disturbances in cognitive development. Infants raised in institutions (Freud & Burlingham, 1944; Provence & Lipton, 1962; Spitz, 1946; Spitz & Wolf, 1946) have been found to suffer developmental impairments because of a lack of adequate interpersonal stimulation. Clarke-Stewart (1973), in an extensive review of the child development literature, found consistent evidence indicating a significant relationship between the quality of the mother–child relationship and the infant's cognitive development. The mother's positive attitudes about child rearing and her capacities to enjoy the relationship and to provide frequent and diverse stimulation were related to the infant's cognitive development. Clarke-Stewart, in a study of the mother–child transaction, found a significant parallel between the mother's modes of stimulation and the infant's development of specific cognitive skills. Also, there was a significant relationship between the degree of the infant's responsiveness and the subsequent affection and responsiveness of the mother. Clarke-Stewart's (1973) findings stress the transactional quality of the mother–child relationship and how the quality of this relationship significantly affects the infant's cognitive development. S. Bell (1968, 1970), investigating the development of object and person permanence, found that quality of the mother–child interaction was related to the development of the concept of the object. Infants who were able to establish and maintain interaction with their mothers developed the concept of the object more rapidly. Infants who were developmentally slower usually achieved object permanence before they developed person permanence and they often had mothers who were more disapproving and rejecting.

Based on the theoretical formulations of Piaget (1954) and Werner and Kaplan (1963), four basic levels of boundary differentiation can be delineated: the development of the concept of the object, the development of object constancy, the differentiation of the object from its mental representation, and the differentiation of the object from its verbal signifiers. Diffi-

culties with these differentiations can be postulated to occur in schizophrenics to varying degrees, reflecting greater or lesser boundary disturbance. Such disturbance can range from difficulty in distinguishing self
from nonself and inside from outside to difficulty in maintaining a separation between an actual object and its representation and between representations of different objects, including the representation of the self and
representations of other people.

There is ample evidence of a wide variation of disturbance in subtypes of
patients considered to be schizophrenic. In comparison with more reactive
(or good premorbid) patients, more process (or poor premorbid) schizophrenics with long-standing histories of difficulties and withdrawal have
fewer developmental achievements (Phillips, 1953, 1966; Zigler & Phillips,
1962). Differences in level of disturbance have also been noted between
paranoid and nonparanoid subgroups. Marked subgroup differences have
been observed in the degree of disruption of attention and of cognitive
functions. Wynne and Singer (1963a, b) noted a similar range of differences
in individual patients and their families, whom they classified into "amorphous" and "fragmented" subtypes on the basis of characteristic problems
with sharing foci of attention. Likewise, Searles (1965) has observed differences between patients he described as "nondifferentiated" and "nonintegrated." The process, nonparanoid, amorphous, and nondifferentiated
subgroups of patients appear to function at more primitive developmental
levels, with greater boundary disturbance, less self–other differentiation,
and less capacity for object constancy than the reactive, paranoid, fragmented, and nonintegrated subgroups. While the distinctions between process–reactive,   nonparanoid–paranoid,   amorphous–fragmented,   and
nondifferentiated–nonintegrated patients are valuable, these subtypes are
not dichotomous but rather represent the polarities of continua.

The differences in levels and types of functioning between the paranoid
and nonparanoid subgroups suggested one of the major hypotheses to be
presented in this book: that in some instances, certain paranoid characteristics appear to be attempts to maintain boundaries, particularly self–object
differentiation. Projection requires, and at the same time reinforces, such a
differentiation. Paranoid organization seems to involve a greater degree of
differentiation between self and others than is found in other forms of
schizophrenia. In many ways, the excessive suspiciousness and guardedness
and the use of projection can be seen as desperate efforts to fortify and
maintain boundary distinctions in an exaggerated form and to keep interpersonal relationships distant in order to prevent experiences of fusion and
merging and feelings of dissolution and of loss of the sense of self.

It should be stressed that this formulation of the importance of boundary
disturbance in schizophrenia does not assume that boundary disturbances

are omnipresent in schizophrenia. Quite to the contrary, we assume that schizophrenic patients can range considerably in their functioning from effective and appropriate responses to severe disruptions. But we assume that a fundamental dimension in schizophrenia is an instability in the concept of the object and that there is a particular vulnerability to situations, such as intense interpersonal interactions, which stimulate fears of rejection and abandonment and threaten the tentative concept of the object that has been established. There are considerable individual differences among schizophrenic patients in the degree of vulnerability, the extent or severity of the disruption of the object concept, and the capacity to re-establish more effective modes of functioning. While we assume that all schizophrenic patients have a vulnerability in the stability of the concept of the object, individual differences in vulnerability allow for the consideration of a schizophrenic spectrum ranging from severe and chronic schizophrenia to subtle, mild and transient borderline phenomena.

This developmental view of schizophrenia poses many questions. For example, is schizophrenia a regression to or a fixation at a particular level of development? Inconsistencies are found if either hypothesis is adopted, for the impairments associated with schizophrenia occur in contexts very different from normal developmental sequences and most schizophrenics do not function consistently at an early developmental level. Individual patients may shift in their level of functioning, depending, in part, on variations in context. For instance, borderline patients typically regress only in ambiguous and unstructured situations. Schizophrenics also vary in the amount of stress necessary to precipitate regression. Some patients may experience boundary difficulties only in stressful circumstances, while others may experience them even in relatively neutral situations. It seems most reasonable to assume that when an acute psychotic break occurs, there is some lack of resolution of earlier developmental stages and also some regression from previously attained levels. We have no answer to this controversial question of fixation versus regression, but we hypothesize that schizophrenic subtypes with more intact functioning are more likely to have reached a relatively higher developmental stage from which they have subsequently regressed, while those subtypes with more primitive functioning have made less developmental progress (Lidz, 1973). In part, the severity of psychosis may be defined by the degree of stress necessary to precipitate regression, the degree and extent of regression, and the resiliency to cope with the regression.

There are also difficulties with this developmental formulation of boundary problems in schizophrenia. Often the theoretical statements have been based on clinical case material from severely disturbed children and psychotic adults and extrapolations have been made to aspects of normal development. Such attempts to reconstruct normal developmental processes from the study of serious disturbances have been very useful. But this approach has inherent limitations. Recently, there has been a marked increase in research on the development of the concept of the object, including the evolving capacity to establish boundaries and object constancy (e.g., Kagan, 1971), which suggests the importance of boundary differentiation as an early developmental achievement. But much more research on normal development is needed. Another problem with the concept of boundaries is that it has been used and defined in many different ways. When defined at a high level of abstraction, it seems too broad and vague to be useful; its behavioral referents cannot be specified. Also, some of the behaviors it refers to are very difficult to operationalize. For example, tendencies toward fusion in interpersonal relationships are extremely hard to measure in terms of actual behavior with other people. Thus, there is a need to review systematically the various definitions and measures of boundary differentiation to see whether the formulation of differing levels of boundary disturbance in schizophrenia can be tested in research.

Although this book deals only with psychological functions and the family environment in schizophrenia, we realize that other factors such as neurophysiological, genetic, and sociocultural may have crucial etiological importance. For example, evidence from recent twin (Gottesman & Shields, 1972) and adoption (Heston, 1966; Kety et al., 1968; Rosenthal et al., 1968; Wender et al., 1968) studies leaves little doubt that genetic factors have an important role in the etiology of schizophrenia. Heston (1966), for example, studied 47 children of schizophrenic mothers who were permanently separated from their mothers shortly after birth. While, in comparison to a control group, a significant proportion of these children developed schizophrenia or sociopathic personalities and had a "significant excess of psycho–social disability" (see also Rieder, 1973), approximately one half of the 47 children became "notably successful adults" who "possessed artistic talents and demonstrated imaginative adaptations to life which were uncommon in the control group [p. 825]." In an analysis of the data on the genetics of schizophrenia, Kidd and Cavalli-Sforza (1973) conclude that the data indicate that "both genetics and environment contribute in an important way to the manifestations of the disease [p. 263]." They state that diagnostic uncertainties, variability of symptoms, and important, but uncertain environmental factors, make it difficult to decide among different genetic hypotheses. A developmental approach to schizophrenia, however, easily allows for an interaction between hereditary factors, prenatal difficulties, and specified environmental conditions. For instance, a developmental approach is congruent with authors (e.g., Bergman & Escalona, 1949; Fish, Wile, Shapiro, & Halpern, 1966; Rosenthal, 1970) who hypothesize a genetic predisposition, such as impaired stimulus barrier or other very early developmental dysfunctioning, that interacts with environmental stress.

Although formulations of boundary disturbance in schizophrenia have a long history and there have been frequent references to boundary disturbances in the clinical, theoretical, and research literature, few attempts have been made to review this literature systematically. While we recognize that there are numerous other ways in which the various disruptions of psychological functions in schizophrenia could be conceptualized, we hope to demonstrate in this book that a conceptualization of levels of boundary disturbance, based on developmental theory and research, can be of value in organizing and integrating the diverse clinical observations and research findings on schizophrenia. Since the literature on normal developmental processes and schizophrenia is enormous, our review is not comprehensive or exhaustive. Rather, we have intentionally selected aspects of the literature that seem most relevant to a developmental formulation of boundary disturbance in schizophrenia. We believe that this formulation is very valuable in studying clinical data, such as data from projective techniques, leading to greater understanding of the experience of schizophrenic patients. Most importantly, we also believe that it can suggest further directions for research. Despite the many references to boundary disturbance in the literature, very few empirical studies have been directly concerned with this topic. Therefore, our major goal in presenting this developmental formulation and reviewing the various definitions and measures of boundary difficulties is to suggest further hypotheses to be tested and methods for testing them.

In the chapters that follow, we shall discuss various disturbances in schizophrenia as manifestations of boundary problems and consider paranoia as a series of compensatory mechanisms for coping with the threat of loss of boundaries. We shall then present some clinical examples to show how a developmental formulation of boundary problems can be applied to clinical data and, finally, discuss the research implications of this formulation.

In Chapter 2 we shall discuss schizophrenic disturbances in perceptual and cognitive processes, including reality testing, perception, attention, concept formation, language, and thinking. Disruptions of perceptual and cognitive processes will be considered as a function of a relative lack of subject–object differentiation expressed in a diminished capacity to differentiate between internal and external reality, a tendency toward perceptual fusion, and difficulty in establishing and maintaining focused attention. We shall also consider boundary disturbances manifested in the more symbolic processes of concept formation, language, and thinking, which are characterized by an interpenetration of themes and difficulty with using connectives. The more intact cognitive processes and sharper cognitive focusing of paranoid patients will be considered as compensatory attempts to defend against a loss of boundaries, with its accompanying threat of feelings of disintegration and annihilation.

In Chapter 3 we shall consider the expressions of boundary disturbance in the sense of self and in interpersonal relationships, and the role of the family in the etiology and maintenance of boundary disturbances. We shall discuss the view that fundamental identity problems involve the lack of a distinct sense of self and of stable self representations, as well as a diminished capacity for self-awareness, reflection, empathy, and interpersonal relationships. These difficulties can also be seen as reflecting degrees of loss of the discrimination between self and others and between self and object representations, manifested in experiences of merging, inappropriate interpersonal distance, sex role disturbances, and a loss of generation boundaries between parents and children. While we have separated our review of the theoretical, clinical, and research literature into two chapters—one covering cognitive and perceptual processes, and the other interpersonal relationships and sense of self—it should be stressed that we have organized the material in this way for clarity of presentation. Given the hypothesis of the complex interrelationships among these various functions, this is an artificial and arbitrary division. In fact, our approach leads to the conclusion that all of these aspects of functioning are interdependent and influence each other in complex ways. Therefore, we shall make frequent references back and forth throughout the discussion in these chapters.

In Chapter 4 we shall present five extensive clinical examples to illustrate how boundary disturbance can be shown in various aspects of the clinical material, including the case history, the therapeutic process, and psychological tests. In presenting clinical examples, we also hope to demonstrate how various levels of boundary disturbance are expressed simultaneously in a variety of spheres and functions. While it is very difficult to enter the world of a person functioning at such levels—perhaps comparable in some respects to the difficulty in understanding the experience of the infant and young child—clinical material provides some opportunity to understand the experiences of people with these problems.

In Chapter 5 we shall critically evaluate the concept of boundaries. We shall also attempt to specify further directions for research that are suggested by the hypothesis that a variety of disturbances in schizophrenia are manifestations of problems in boundary differentiation.

2 / Cognitive Processes

Introduction

In this chapter, we shall consider how various disturbances of cognitive and perceptual processes observed in schizophrenia can be viewed as expressions of deficits of the rudimentary capacity to experience, perceive, and represent boundaries. The development of cognitive and perceptual processes depends, at least initially, on the establishment of primary boundary distinctions. These distinctions include the differentiation between various objects and events, between self and nonself, between inside and outside, and between objects and their mental representations. The capacity for subject–object differentiation and the establishment of independent mental representations of self and of objects are crucial steps in cognitive development. A grasp of the permanent existence of external objects distinct from the self and a capacity to establish stable mental representations of these objects are essential for the development of cognitive functions such as reality testing, concept formation, and thinking (Piaget, 1954; Werner, 1948).

Sequences of frustration and gratification are primary experiences considered to facilitate the differentiation between self and nonself and a sense of continuity and permanence of objects (Jacobson, 1964; Mahler, 1968; Schafer, 1968). The gratification of needs by a consistent figure provides the child with repeated experiences of the appearance and disappearance of a need-gratifying object. According to many theorists, it is these experiences with the object, centered around the fundamental dimensions of pleasure–pain and hunger–satiety, that enable the child to develop a sense of the object as separate—leading to attainment of the concept of the object and

13

of object constancy. Once subject and object are differentiated and the capacity to represent the absent object is established, the child can begin to distinguish between the actual object and its mental representation. Not only do sequences of frustration and gratification enable the child to develop the concept of the object; they also facilitate the development of the concept of the self, as will be discussed in Chapter 3. Self-initiated action resulting in a need-satisfying response from an external object leads to the distinction of self from responding figure. This process also enables the child to articulate his needs more fully and to distinguish among the experiences that gratify various needs. The more frequently the infant's actions produce satisfying results, the more he learns how to adapt his actions to the environment and to develop a sense of trust and reciprocity in relation to the environment. Bettelheim (1967) attributes the development of infantile autism in part to "the conviction that one's own efforts have no power to influence the world, because of the earlier conviction that the world is insensitive to one's reactions [p. 46]." Tentatively, Bettelheim suggests that this conviction stems from the cumulative effect of experiences of frustration during three stages: before 6 months; from 6 to 9 months, when other persons and the self begin to be recognized as individuals and the child reaches out to others; and from 18 months to 2 years, when the child makes major efforts to master the world physically and intellectually.

Lack of consistent and satisfying relationships with need-gratifying figures disrupts the infant's evolving capacities to develop adequate concepts of the object and the self, and a sense of trust and security in relation to the external world. Disruptions in the concept of the object can affect a wide range of functions, including those involved in reality testing—such as sense of time, perception, and attention—and symbolic processes—such as concept formation, language, and thinking. One of the earliest and most fundamental steps in the development of the concept of the object is the articulation of boundaries between objects, including the distinction of self from nonself and inside from outside. Disruptions in the early development of the concept of the object involve, at least in part, impairments in boundary distinctions. The unarticulated perception, diffuse attention, disordered concept formation with interpenetration of themes, and contaminatory thinking with merging of independent perceptions and concepts that are frequently observed in schizophrenia can be viewed as expressions of impaired and unstable boundary differentiation. A consideration of degrees of impairment in boundary differentiation may provide a framework for conceptualizing types of difficulties in a wide range of fundamental cognitive–perceptual functions and symbolic processes, such as concept formation, language, and thinking.

Not only can a conceptualization of levels of disruption of boundary differentiation provide a basis for evaluating disturbances in a wide range of functions and processes; it may also provide a way of evaluating severity of psychosis. In this chapter, we shall consider the hypothesis that different subtypes of schizophrenia, such as process and reactive, paranoid and non-paranoid, show varying degrees of boundary disturbance. For instance, we shall attempt to show how the relatively more articulated but fragmented functioning of paranoid schizophrenic patients can be viewed as involving an emphasis on part properties and an exaggeration of differences, serving to fortify and sustain boundary distinctions in order to prevent experiences of merging and fusion. The heightened sense of cognitive focusing and control and the highly articulated perception and attention of paranoid patients suggest a desperate struggle to keep experiences separate and discrete.

In this chapter, we shall consider how the disturbances in cognitive processes in schizophrenia can be understood as reflecting degrees of instability in the capacity to establish and sustain boundary distinctions. We shall examine the manifestations of various levels of disruption of boundary differentiation in reality testing, perceptual articulation, attention, and the more symbolic processes such as concept formation, language, and the nature and quality of thought. We shall also consider how a formulation of levels of disturbance in boundary differentiation can aid in distinguishing levels of psychosis. We believe that this formulation leads to the further understanding of some of the dynamic issues in psychosis such as the wish for and fear of merging and fusing and primary identification (Rosenfeld & Sprince, 1963, 1965; Rosenfeld, 1972; Searles, 1965; Burnham, Gladstone, & Gibson, 1969) often observed in borderline and psychotic states.

Reality Testing

Introduction

The processes through which reality is accurately assessed are complex and involve many fundamental ego functions, including perception, memory, concept formation, reasoning, and the ability to direct and focus attention on both internal experiences and external events (Bellak, 1958). The capacity for reality testing requires a differentiation of self from the object world: the establishment of stable boundaries between self and nonself. The development of ever-increasing capacities for differentiating the boundaries between self and nonself and inside and outside the self is fundamental to the achievement of reality testing. As indicated by developmental research, the sense of reality begins with an initial awareness of a separation between objects at points of marked contrast (Kagan, 1971; Roth & Blatt, 1974).

This separation between objects includes the differentiation between self and nonself. Inadequate or unstable boundary differentiation results in confusion of what is self with what is nonself, of what is real with what is unreal. When boundaries between the self and the object world are inadequate, distorted internal experiences of the self can occur, and external events can be misperceived and become infused with personally determined, drive-laden meanings. As discussed by Schafer (1968), an important developmental step in the establishment of reality testing, including the crucial capacity for distinguishing reality from fantasy, is for the child to locate the idea of an external object as inside and the object to which the idea pertains as outside. When objects are first recognized by the infant, they have no definite location in psychological space. The inside–outside location is another, partly independent differentiation.

> To begin with, recognized objects possess no index of internality or externality—they just exist or they appear or disappear. . . . as the boundary between inside and outside develops, objects may be located primarily inside, outside, inside and outside, or their location may be unspecified or indeterminate; the fluidity of the inner–outer boundaries during the earliest phases of development, and at later times of crisis and regression, makes it possible for the primary location of the same object to be different at different times or under different conditions; and it is only after the inner–outer boundaries exist as reliable aspects of experience that the concepts introjection and projection are applicable to psychic processes, for these concepts make sense only with respect to the crossing of established boundaries, that is, the at least temporarily clear perception of alternative locations [Schafer, 1968, pp. 74-76].

The process of establishing the differentiation between self and nonself depends in part on repeated sequences of frustration and gratification in which a consistent external object repeatedly appears, disappears, and reappears, particularly at moments of considerable discomfort. This process of rediscovery of the gratifying object at moments of discomfort and frustration enables the child, at a time when his perceptual experiences are becoming more differentiated, to recognize and establish the existence of an object external to and distinct from the self (Schafer, 1968).

Initially, repeated sequences of the alleviation of need states by a consistent object facilitate the differentiation between aspects of external objects and between the child's representation of an external object and the object itself. The repeated appearance, disappearance, and reappearance of a consistent need-gratifying object fosters the individuation of self from object, the differentiation of the actual object from the child's memory and image of the object, and the child's emerging capacity to establish some consistent representation of the object, which persists when the object is unavailable, that is, object constancy. Subsequent experiences, such as effective motor activity and consistent and differentiated response patterns of an external object to various need states, facilitate further differentiation. These consistent patterns of gratification of the infant's intense needs by an external object lead to a sense of basic trust and a general sense of time, including an emerging capacity for anticipation and planning and an emerging under standing of causality and continuity (Erikson, 1959).

Consistent sequences of interaction with an external object that provide varying experiences in the gratification of different needs also foster the child's differentiation between bodily experiences of comfort and discomfort and between aspects of the object providing gratification. There seems to be a constant interaction between the establishment of internal cognitive structures and the consistency of the structure provided by the environment. Stability and consistency of the external environment facilitate the child's capacity to establish basic differentiations in reality; and the child's capacity to establish these basic differentiations in turn facilitates his ability to organize and understand subsequent experiences. Loewald (1951) comments that the psychological constitution of ego and reality go hand in hand and that the infant's repeated experience of something that was originally felt to be part of him as not always available leads to the development of the ego and to the differentiation of reality. Ego development initially requires a move away from primary narcissistic union between mother and child and from the infant's experience of a lack of boundaries between himself and the outer world. According to Loewald, the father interferes with the libidinal ties to the mother and helps the infant to modify his narcissistic union with her. The father provides a powerful force that stands against "the threatening possibility of remaining in or sinking back into the structureless unity from which the [ego] has emerged [p. 15]." The role of the father in providing structure against the symbiotic union with the mother furthers understanding of the nature of libidinal attachments in schizophrenic patients struggling with boundary issues. Loewald's formulation offers a possible explanation for the role of homosexual attachments in paranoid males and of sexual promiscuity in schizophrenic females; that is, the search for a male figure to interrupt the union with the mother. The father, as a positive identification figure, facilitates the articulation of reality and provides support against the primary narcissistic union with the mother in which there is a loss of the boundaries between ego and reality, between self and object (Loewald, 1951). Loewald considers that his formulations about the role of the father have particular relevance to understanding schizophrenia. As will be discussed in Chapter 3, greater disturbances would be expected in patients whose fathers, as well as mothers, failed to provide the support and structure necessary for interrupting the basic fusion with the mother. These patients would be expected to show less subject–object differentiation, more poorly articulated and stabilized boundaries, and greater impairment of reality testing.

As Federn (1952) stated, once ego boundaries are developed, the basic sense of reality is established. Later development, such as remembering and learning, serves to enrich reality testing and make it more complex so that the individual can experience varying degrees of certainty and doubt and begin to respond to degrees of subtlety. If the boundaries between self and other and between inside and outside are not firmly established in early development, it is difficult for advancements in the level of reality testing to occur. Patients with disturbances in boundary differentiation whose interpersonal relationships are confused or threatened by wishes for merging and fusion will have difficulty in maintaining adequate levels of reality testing. These disturbances may be expressed in hallucinations and delusions and in the impairment of a number of functions necessary for reality testing, such as perceptual articulation, focused attention, sense of time, and sense of the constancy of objects, including the self. In reviewing some of the literature on disturbances of reality testing and some of the part functions involved in this process, we shall examine the findings in terms of our basic conceptualization that one of the basic issues in schizophrenia is the difficulty in establishing and sustaining boundary distinctions. The literature on the various aspects of reality testing is diverse and ranges from clinical reports of hallucinations and delusions to more behaviorally oriented research on perception and attention. While our review will not be exhaustive, we shall attempt to consider a wide range of reports and findings that are available on reality testing in schizophrenia.

Hallucinations and delusions

Impaired reality testing has often been considered as one of the primary features of schizophrenia. Most basic to reality testing is the ability to distinguish self from nonself and inside from outside. Without these fundamental distinctions there is confusion between thoughts, fantasies, and actual events. Without the establishment of fundamental boundaries between self and nonself and between inside and outside, it is difficult, if not impossible, to differentiate fantasy from reality, to maintain a differentiation between thoughts and actions, and to distinguish between independent and separate events and perceptions. Feelings and thoughts can easily distort the perception of reality, and subjective reactions can be confused with events in the environment. Thought can become confused with action so that an individual, for example, can believe that his aggressive thoughts will, or have, destroyed an aspect of the world. Hallucinations and delusions are prime examples of the failure to maintain an adequate differentiation between internal experiences and the perception of events and experiences occurring outside the self.

Carney Landis (1964) cites a vivid example of the sense of boundary loss in hallucinatory experience. A very articulate young woman who was nearly blind and knew braille, with sufficient intactness to take distance from her experience, reported that she was hearing voices accusing her of being a "defense plant whore." After being alone for half an hour, she said:

> You know, it seems to come from within my head and the lettering in braille lettering. It doesn't come out in handwriting or print. It seems to come out in braille lettering, like in front of my forehead, in front of my eyes. I see the words "defense plant" as I think of it. . . . What I actually thought in my mind would sort of flow out of my mind and seem to focus in front of it. And it comes out in braille writing. At the same time I think of it—both together [p. 137].

This young woman obviously has some ability to discriminate thought from perception, yet she expresses her sense of thoughts "flowing" out of her mind. This example also serves to illustrate the confusion of inside and outside and the fusion of sense modalities, for she seemed to "see," hear and touch the words and the braille letters simultaneously.

One issue in evaluating hallucinatory experiences is to distinguish hallucinations from images. Sedman (1966a) makes this distinction on the basis of the location of the perception—whether it is internal or external. He considers imagery to be an experience of "inner subjective space," lacking the concrete reality of a perception. True hallucinations appear to come through the senses as perceptions of external events. As E. Bleuler (1911) stated, "Often the hallucinations are simply fitted into the surroundings [p. 104]." Patients vary in the degree of conviction they maintain about a hallucinatory experience. Bleuler (1911), Sedman (1966b), and Strauss (1969) use this dimension to differentiate levels of hallucinations. "True hallucinations" are those maintained with a high degree of conviction (Sedman, 1966b) and those that occur independent of any situational factors (Strauss, 1969). Thus, one of the primary criteria for "true hallucinations" is loss of the distinction between inner experiences and external events. Patients experience hallucinations as ". . . something divorced from their ego; despite the inner location they were really arising in external subjective space. They were certain that they were not responsible for conjuring up the thought or voice, and were either at a loss to explain how it came about or put a delusional interpretation on the event [Sedman, 1966a, p. 489]." In studying auditory hallucinations, Alpert and Silvers (1970) found that schizophrenics, in contrast to alcoholics, usually only hallucinated voices that were highly intelligible—like thoughts that had become audible.

Freeman et al. (1966) also view hallucinations as an inability to discriminate between thoughts and perceptual experience, involving a regression to earlier developmental levels of functioning. They distinguish two categories of hallucinations, differing in the degree to which the patient has maintained reality contact and a capacity for object relations. Hallucinations occurring in patients at a higher developmental level are apt to involve real people who have meaning to the patient. The second, more regressive type of hallucination is not anchored to real objects in the environment, but is concerned with the construction of a new reality which substitutes for the real world. Freeman et al. provide clinical evidence indicating that the first type of hallucination is associated with greater capacity for interpersonal relationships than the second type, which is associated with minimal capacity for maintaining object cathexis. The latter type of hallucination is probably also associated with less differentiation between objects, including self and others.

Federn also distinguishes between various gradations of loss of reality contact, depending on the degree of regression. For Federn, the schizophrenic is engaged in false reality production, while the more paranoid person has a false certainty about reality. "False reality means substitution of a false world for the real one, while false certainty merely means changes in judgments about the world [1952, p. 232]." It has been repeatedly observed on the Rorschach, for example, that schizophrenics tend to misperceive and distort the reality of the blots. In nonparanoid patients this reality distortion is often manifested in inaccurate and unjustified perceptions, while in more paranoid patients the basic perceptions are likely to be accurate and the distortions usually occur in elaborations of the initially accurate perception. Thus, the nonparanoid may respond with a percept that bears little relation to the form of the blot (reality), such as "an open mouth with fangs." In contrast, the paranoid patient is more likely to give an accurate response, such as "two figures," which conforms to the configurations of the blot, but shows reality distortion in the meaning attributed to the perception, as in describing the figures as "menacing and sinister."

There have been a number of attempts to distinguish hallucinations from delusions as well as to distinguish levels of hallucination and delusion. Generally hallucinations are considered to reflect distortions of basic perceptual processes, while delusions involve associative distortions of initially accurate perceptions. Delusions are considered an "ideational" distortion (Strauss, 1969), a "false belief *not* subject to correction by experience, reason, or logic [Small, 1971, p. 4]," "a disorder of interpretation [Cameron, 1943, p. 220]." Federn (1952), in his distinction between "false reality" and "false certainty," suggests that false certainty precedes the creation of a false world: "The first delusions which replace real facts . . . happen long before external reality is lost [p. 187]." While there are different opinions about whether delusions precede or follow hallucinatory experiences, there seems to be agreement that generally hallucinations reflect more severe psychopathology than delusions.

Delusions are experienced as basically ideational rather than perceptual, and are primarily "a disorder of interpretation [Cameron, 1943]." While there are occasional misunderstandings and misinterpretations in everyday life, the delusion is monothematic, final, and without alternative. Delusions serve to isolate the individual from others and enable him to maintain distance and a high level of vigilance for threatening situations. A delusion not only serves to maintain the boundary between self and others but also reduces ambiguity and doubt; and in the false certainty, the patient feels a sense of closure and clarification (Cameron, 1959). The intensity and severity of delusional thinking is reflected by its extent and by the degree of conviction with which the delusion is held. A middle-aged woman was hospitalized a few months subsequent to the sudden and unexpected death of her teen-age daughter from a congenital heart defect that had gone completely unnoticed. On admission, the patient was intensively involved in an extensive delusion of how each person evolves from a different species of animal and that one has to be careful of certain "animal types." After some months of treatment, she disavowed any belief in the prior delusional thoughts; but during a predischarge evaluation interview, a clinician familiar with only the general facts of the case inferred correctly that the patient must have previously believed she was descended from tigers because she continued to prefer to wear a dress with narrow, yellow and green, horizontal stripes. While the intensity of the delusion had diminished considerably, a degree of delusional thinking seemed to have persisted.

Though there seem to be several types and degrees of hallucinations and delusions, hallucinations generally appear to reflect distortions of the basic perceptual process, while delusions generally seem to involve associative distortions of reasonably accurate perceptions. There is evidence suggesting that delusional patients function on a higher level than those with hallucinations (e.g., Shakow, 1962). Hallucinatory schizophrenic patients are less likely to be able to distinguish between what is inside and outside the self, between a thought and a perception of the external world. Their impairments in reality testing can be seen as an inability to preserve boundaries at several different levels. Delusional thinking, on the other hand, often seems to serve to isolate the individual from others and to support the maintenance of rigid boundaries in exaggerated form.

Sense of body

The relative instability of maintaining boundary distinctions between self and nonself can not only seriously impair the accurate perception of external reality but can also seriously distort internal experiences such as the experience of one's body. Federn (1952) has commented extensively on the importance of the body experience in schizophrenia. Federn views schizophrenia as involving regression to an infantile level due to a diminution or partial loss of cathexis for the ego boundary, which may even reach a totally narcissistic level, in which the ego and the outside world are not separated. Federn stresses the role of the body ego in reality testing and its importance in maintaining a sense of thought as a mental process inside the bodily and mental ego boundary and a sense of reality as outside the ego boundary. Phenomenologically, the cathected body ego leads to "a permanent evidential feeling of the outer world which originates in the fact that impressions from the outer world pass a bodily ego boundary charged with a particular quality of sensation and bodily ego feeling [p. 43]"; and the cathected mental "ego feeling enables the individual to distinguish between the ego as subject and the whole outer world, and also between the ego as object and all representations of object [1952, p. 212]."

Des Lauriers (1962), summarizing the theoretical positions of Freud and Federn, concludes that the self–object differentiation necessary for reality testing begins with an awareness of what lies within and what lies outside the body. Early infantile experiences of being held, touched, played with, and so forth help the infant to define and differentiate what stimulation comes from outside and what from inside. Along with Federn, Des Lauriers believes that schizophrenia is not a total withdrawal from the world, but a loss of the capacity to experience the self as real and separate from others because of a severe diminution of cathexis of body boundaries. The experiences of one's body and the differentiation of bodily sensations from external stimuli are important components in the development of representations of the self and of others, and of reality testing more generally. The persistence of bodily experiences as compared to the transitory quality of many other stimuli is one of the sources for distinguishing self from nonself and inside from outside. With the important role that bodily experiences play in the development of the differentiation of the self, it is not surprising that there has been considerable observation of the distorted bodily experiences of schizophrenic patients.

A number of clinical and theoretical statements (e.g., Arieti, 1961; Bruch, 1962; Schafer, 1960) have stressed the importance of bodily sensations of pleasure–pain and hunger–satiety as one of the necessary initial steps in the development of subject–object differentiation. Arieti (1961) has commented on the schizophrenic's fragmented sense of his body and his preoccupation with body parts rather than having an awareness of himself as an integrated being. Des Lauriers (1962) has also reported on the lack of body definition in schizophrenia and the importance of body experiences in the treatment of schizophrenic patients. Bruch (1962), Rosenfeld and Sprince (1963), Schafer (1960), and Thomas (1966) have stressed the importance of body image distortion in schizophrenia as well as the schizophrenic's inability to identify internal sensations and to differentiate them from external stimuli. Often the schizophrenic experiences his body as diffuse and insubstantial. The general instability in differentiating representations of objects and the self is expressed in bodily experiences as a lack of definition, integrity, and substance. It is also expressed in experiences of fusion and merging, a lack of a sense of volume, feelings of depersonalization and deanimation, and a preoccupation with physical decay and disintegration.

Fisher and Cleveland (1958) and B. Landis (1970) have studied body image as expressed in the Rorschach responses of primarily nonpsychotic (neurotic and psychosomatic) patients and normals. These investigators also analyzed Rorschach protocols of schizophrenic patients, and their findings have important implications for the role of boundary disturbances in the body image of schizophrenics. Fisher and Cleveland (1958), in their wide-ranging study of body image, note that many Rorschach responses contain references to surface attributes of animate and inanimate objects. These references seem to fall into two groups: those emphasizing definite structures, substance, and surface qualities and those emphasizing weakness, lack of substance, and penetrability. They labeled these two types of responses as "barrier" and "penetration." In their comparison among un-differentiated schizophrenic, paranoid, neurotic and normal subjects, they found that the more disturbed (schizophrenic and paranoid) patients had few barrier and a significantly greater number of penetration responses. In addition, many of the penetration responses in the two psychotic groups were highly atypical and contained frequent references to distorted and damaged bodies (e.g., "bloody, dripping nose," "a split womb," "a vaccination scar cut open to let out the poison," "a rotted body," "a circumcized penis," "a body torn open"). Reitman (1962) and Holtzman, Gorham, and Moran (1964) attempted to replicate the original Fisher and Cleveland study and found that it was primarily an increased number of penetration responses that differentiated psychotic from nonpsychotic samples. Cleveland (1960) found that schizophrenic patients who improved with medication and hospitalization had a significant decline in the number of penetration responses and a nonsignificant increase in the number of barrier responses. Cleveland interpreted these findings as indicating a dramatic firming up of body image boundaries in recovering schizophrenic patients. Fisher (1964, 1966) subsequently found that paranoid patients had significantly more barrier and significantly fewer penetration responses than nonparanoid schizophrenic patients.

Landis (1970) developed a system for scoring "permeable" and "impermeable" Rorschach responses similar to the penetration and barrier scores of Fisher and Cleveland. Landis found that normal subjects with high impermeability scores struggle to acquire greater control over impulses and environmental events and maintain greater interpersonal distance. Landis also found a marked decrease in impermeability and a significant increase in permeable responses in schizophrenics. But he, too, noted a sharp discontinuity in the type of permeable responses given by neurotic patients and those given by schizophrenic patients. These differences forced him to conceptualize permeability in schizophrenia as "fluidity." Like Fisher and Cleveland, Landis noted that the permeable (or penetration) responses of schizophrenics had a unique quality (e.g., "a very liquid kind of blood," "a person's eyes dissolving," "a jelly fish floating in either direction," and "nothing, I feel nothing so it must be nothing"). Landis concluded that these types of permeable responses indicate "radical boundary changes" that are qualitatively different from and incommensurate with boundary states in neurosis.

Research has suggested that the degree of articulation of bodily experiences is related to a more general capacity for boundary distinction and to the capacity for reality testing. There is also some evidence that heightened bodily experience facilitates the perception and representation of firm boundaries and increases the capacity for accurate reality testing. For example, Hozier (1959) studied spatial perception in schizophrenia based on Des Lauriers' conceptualization that disrupted reality testing involves a breakdown in the bodily self and therefore the loss of an adequate frame of reference from which to judge the reality of external events and one's own experiences. Twenty-five hospitalized women, diagnosed as schizophrenic for a period of 2–28 years, were matched on age, education, and intelligence with a control group of 25 women. The performance of the two groups was compared on a Figure Placement Task, a Doll Task, and the Draw-A-Person test. The Figure Placement Task involved placing human figures in an appropriate relationship to a structured background. Hozier found that the schizophrenic women placed the figures more in the foreground and clustered them more than did the control group. Hozier interpreted this finding as indicating that the schizophrenics showed underestimation of distance and a lack of differentiation among objects and between objects and the self. In the Doll Task, in which subjects were given the head of a rag doll and asked to attach the parts, and in the Draw-A-Person test, schizophrenic subjects showed more errors than did controls in terms of distorting size and misplacing and omitting essential body parts, which Hozier interpreted as reflecting disorganization and distortion of the bodily self.

A more recent study by Darby (1970) indicated that focused physical exercise (e.g., stretching, lifting weights, and stationary bicycle riding) and requests to report bodily sensations resulted in schizophrenics giving significantly more Rorschach responses that emphasized the firmness of boundaries of objects than they had given previously (Fisher & Cleveland's Barrier Score). These findings are consistent with earlier research (e.g., Fisher & Renik, 1966; Renik & Fisher, 1968) which demonstrated that definiteness of the representation of boundaries in normal subjects can also be increased by focusing attention on bodily experiences. While questions can be raised in these studies about the diagnostic criteria and composition of the schizophrenic groups, and other hypotheses could be used to account for the findings, the results are at least consistent with Des Lauriers' theoretical formulation that bodily distortion is an important aspect of the schizophrenic experience and that an awareness of the body is an important component of reality testing.

Another study (Reitman & Cleveland, 1964) comparing changes in body image following sensory reduction in schizophrenic and control groups is also relevant to these issues. Forty schizophrenic inpatients and 20 inpatients diagnosed as having anxiety reactions or character disorders were placed for 4 hr in a stimulus reduction situation—consisting of the patient lying on a hospital bed, wearing eye goggles and gloves in a bare chamber with two overhead lights and a white noise generator. A group of schizophrenic controls who had no stimulus deprivation experience was also included. Pre- and postmeasures were administered. Pretest scores indicated that schizophrenics were generally more expansive and inaccurate in their judgments and percepts of body image. Following the sensory reduction experience, schizophrenics showed an increase in somesthetic sensitivity and increased barrier and lower penetration scores on the Holtzman et al. (1961) inkblots, as compared to the nonpsychotic group. The authors interpreted their findings as indicating that sensory deprivation results in "both a breakdown in the nonpsychotic's body image organization as well as a redefinition or reintegration of body image by schizophrenic subjects [1964, p. 174]." Moreover, Reitman and Cleveland concluded that their "findings concerning body image changes in the schizophrenic group can best be understood if one regards sensory deprivation as an experience providing the schizophrenic patient with a uniform, nonthreatening pattern of stimuli which, so to speak, offers him a chance to pull himself together [p. 175]." While these intriguing results are open to alternative interpretations and raise many questions, they seem to indicate that isolation was an organizing experience for the schizophrenics. Perhaps the experience posed less threat of fusion in the absence of other people and less challenge in having to accommodate to variations in the external stimulus configuration, and it perhaps fostered increased cathexis of body boundaries by maintaining a consistent pressure on the body, through lying on the bed and wearing eye goggles and gloves.

The importance of deficiencies in the awareness of body sensations and experiences in schizophrenia is also consistent with recent observations of the unique deficit of proprioceptive and kinesthetic feedback in schizophrenia (Holzman, 1970; Rosenbaum, 1971). Proprioceptive feedback, more than any other sensory experience, requires a differentiated sense of bodily experience. As suggested by Hozier's data, the schizophrenic patient's difficulty in reality testing seems to be related to a lack of adequate subject–object differentiation, tendencies toward perceptual fusion, and a distorted sense of body. These factors seem to be interrelated in schizophrenia, and each contributes, in different ways, to difficulties in reality testing. Further research is needed to explore more fully the relationships between these various functions, not only in schizophrenia but in other psychological disorders, such as paranoia, and especially in normal developmental processes.

Object constancy

A disturbed sense of self, particularly in bodily terms, is only one aspect of the distortion of objects that results from impairment of the capacity to make and maintain boundary distinctions. Impairment of boundary distinction is expressed in disturbances in object constancy which can seriously interfere with reality testing. Object constancy has been considered as the capacity to maintain a libidinal attachment to an object, irrespective of frustration or gratification (e.g., Anna Freud, 1952), and as a stable level of mental representation (e.g., Piaget, 1954). While these two dimensions of the concept of the object and of object permanence are intertwined and develop simultaneously (Blatt, 1974), object constancy is used in this book to indicate a stable level of mental representation.

Searles (1965), in discussing the severe impairment of the capacity for differentiation in the schizophrenic, comments:

> It is difficult or impossible for him to differentiate between himself and the outer world; his ego-boundaries are unstable and incomplete. He often cannot distinguish between memories and present perceptions. Memories experienced with hallucinatory vividness and immediacy are sensed as perceptions of present events, and perceptions of present events may be experienced as memories from the past. . . . He may be unable to distinguish between emotions and somatic sensations. . . .
>
> He has difficulty in differentiating, perceptually, one person from another, so that he is prone to misidentify one person with another; part of this misidentifying often involves his experiencing transference phenomena not only at an unconscious level, as does the neurotic, but at a conscious level. He may *consciously* experience the therapist as being, for instance, his father or mother or brother [p. 319].

Piaget (1954) discusses the implications and consequences of the lack of self–object differentiation for reality testing in normal development prior to the attainment of the object concept:

> A world composed of permanent objects constitutes not only a spatial universe but also a world obeying the principle of causality in the form of relationships between things, and regulated in time, without continuous annihilations or resurrections. Hence it is a universe both stable and external, relatively distinct from the internal

world and one in which the subject places himself as one particular term among all the other terms. A universe without objects, on the other hand, is a world in which space does not constitute a solid environment but is limited to structuring the subject's very acts; it is a world of pictures each one of which can be known and analyzed but which disappear and reappear capriciously. From the point of view of causality it is a world in which the connections between things are masked by the relations between the action and its desired results; hence the subject's activity is conceived as being the primary and almost the sole motive power. As far as the boundaries between the self and the external world are concerned, a universe without objects is such that the self, lacking knowledge of itself, is absorbed in external pictures for want of knowing itself; moreover, these pictures center upon the self by failing to include it as a thing among other things, and thus fail to sustain interrelationships independent of the self [pp. 3–4].

Piaget suggests that without a stable sense of the self and an awareness of the independent and permanent existence of objects distinct from the self, reality, and persons in the reality, go through "continuous annihilations or resurrections." This type of experience was vividly expressed by a hebephrenic, nonintegrated patient of Searles (1965), who,

after many months of showing anxiety and antagonism in response to my moving about, or changing posture, finally let me know that when, for example, on a warm day I got up and shifted my chair round to the opposite side of her bed, to be closer to the open window, she now experienced the presence of two of me in the room, much as if, in watching a motion picture, one saw it not as one continuous motion, but as broken up into a series of 'stills'; in this patient's instance, moreover, the 'stills' remained on the scene, and accumulated. I now understood better why she had complained anxiously, in session after session earlier in her therapy, that there were 200 or 300 doctors in the room. She let me know also, on another occasion, that whenever I changed posture she misidentified me as some different person from her past [p. 307].

Searles' patient obviously had some sense of object constancy, for "the 'stills' remained on the scene and accumulated." Even Piaget's terms "resurrection" and "reappearance" seem to assume some sense of recognition of previously experienced "pictures"—already requiring some degree of object constancy—as well as perceptual articulation of the visual field, so that discrete, identifiable aspects emerge from the background. However, lack of stability of the object is reflected in Searles' patient's difficulty in maintaining a stable experience of her therapist when he changed his posture or location and she saw him from different vantage points, and in her tendency to misidentify him as figures from her past.

According to Piaget, there are several stages in the development of the concept of the object that lead to a grasp of the permanent existence of external objects, that is, to object constancy. Object constancy requires a basic differentiation between objects, including a differentiation between self and nonself. Initially, the infant has no concept of himself or of others; he is aware only of action sequences and sensations, and he does not differentiate objects from the action sequences. When an object disappears, the infant continues to stare at the place where the object was last seen. In a subsequent stage, the infant extrapolates beyond his immediate experience and seeks to maintain contact with objects by following and anticipating the movement of the object. He searches for a lost object rather than immediately giving up. But this search is still an extension of the action sequence rather than a concept of the object as a separate entity. When distracted from an object, the child can now relocate the original object and recognize and anticipate the whole object from a part property. But, according to Piaget, the emerging concept of the object at this stage is still primarily an extension of action sequences, rather than a concept of a permanent and separate object. The search for an object becomes more extensive in subsequent stages of development, and the child will search behind a screen for an object if he was reaching for, or was observing, the object when it was hidden. While the child's concept of the object is still dependent on the action sequence in this stage, the concept of the object is becoming increasingly independent of the action sequence, and he is able to infer visible, and later invisible, displacements. With the capacity to infer invisible displacements, the child becomes capable of representational and symbolic activity. Later on, the child begins to learn that objects have stable and consistent properties and that they exist as entities in their own right, separate and independent of the specific and immediate activity. He also comes to learn that the self is one object among many that have enduring properties and exist in their own right, independent of other objects (Flavell, 1963).

Thus, there are several levels in the development of the concept of the object that lead to the grasp of the permanent existence of objects. Object constancy depends upon the achievement of a basic capacity to differentiate between objects, including the self. Early stages of the concept of the object are established around particular action sequences, and it is likely that these sequences are drive-laden and that often the representation of objects is around their drive-reducing properties. As the representation of an object begins to occur independent of any particular drive-gratifying sequence, the child can begin to represent the object as an entity in its own right (Blatt, 1974; Fraiberg, 1969).

Pious' (1950) observations of an acute schizophrenic break in an obsessive–compulsive patient shortly after beginning analysis vividly communicate the disruption of object constancy in schizophrenia. Pious noted that the patient became increasingly disturbed during separations from the analyst and experienced a sense of panic when he was unable to maintain a mental image of the analyst. This image would be reconstituted with the analyst's return, and, as therapy progressed, the mental representation of the analyst became more stable.

The establishment of stable mental representations of objects (and of the self) is essential for thinking, concept formation, and a sense of time and causality. Only with object constancy can objects be represented as continuing through time, as having a past, a present, and especially a future. With object constancy, objects can have a permanent identity and existence even though they are not immediately present in the sensory field. But initially, object constancy requires a differentiation among objects and a differentiation of the object from specific and limited environmental contexts. This basic differentiation is required before the self and objects can begin to be represented as having stable and permanent attributes. In the more amorphous, nondifferentiated schizophrenic patient there may be only minimal capacity for object constancy, while the more fragmented, differentiated paranoid patient maintains a somewhat greater degree of involvement with more constant objects (Freeman et al., 1966), particularly around the representation of an object as part of a specific action pattern or drive-laden sequence.

Sense of time

According to Piaget (1969), a true and full sense of time is based on the coordination of motions of external objects or the coordination of an object and the self at different velocities. Piaget differentiates motion from simple displacements or changes in position. Motion involves a sense of velocity, and, while displacements can occur spatially, time appears only with a sense of velocity. Prior to understanding time as the ratio of distance covered to velocity, time can be experienced in spatial terms, so that temporal sequences can be confused with spatial order and temporal duration can be confused with the path traversed. The construction of a full sense of time occurs only with the correlation of velocities [p. 255].

For Piaget, the most elementary form of the sense of time develops at the sensorimotor level. When the infant cries, he has his first experience of duration (waiting); and when he tries to reach a distant object, he establishes a primitive order of succession between means and ends. Time at the sensorimotor level, however, is not an organized scheme; rather, succession or duration is correlated with spatial displacements. Prior to object constancy, the succession of events is related to motor responses and temporal series are established around these action patterns. In the initial stages of development, concepts of succession and duration are constructed around action patterns, and temporal constructs coincide with spatial constructs. Roth (1961), for example, in a study of the effects of unit transfer on psychotic patients, demonstrates how alterations in space can affect the sense of time. In normal development, the temporal concepts of sequence and duration, established initially, are followed by the development of appropriate signs and representations to signify the temporal characteristics of actions. With the acquisition of language, temporal notions are gradually extended to include the relative concepts of past, present, and future (Piaget, 1969).

A consistent pattern of gratification of intense needs by an external object enables the infant to sense some basic sequence of events, which initially may be perceived only as a sequence of before and after. Initially, time may not be experienced as having continuity and extent but simply as a basic two-step sequence. With further experiences of frustration and gratification, the child begins to establish a sense of anticipation in the expectation that needs will be satisfied. As object constancy begins to develop around the need-gratifying object, the memory of the object and of the gratifying experience leads to an appreciation of the past and later to a sense of continuity and causality. As full object constancy is established, and as the representation of the object becomes relatively free of specific action patterns or drive-laden sequences, the child can anticipate aspects of the future that are not simply expected repetitions of the past; the child can begin to consider the possibility of the object (and self) in novel and unique contexts. The awareness of relative velocity, which is essential for a true and full sense of time, requires a clear differentiation of self and object. It is this full development of object (and self) constancy, the mental representation independent of any specific context, which now permits the child to have a full sense of time and to extend psychologically into the future, developing goals and planning ways of achieving these goals.

Lack of dependable and predictable gratification following frustration, which interferes with subject–object differentiation and the establishment of self and object constancy, is disruptive to the development of a sense of time, including the awareness of sequence, duration, anticipation, causality, and continuity. As Erikson (1959) and Piaget (1969) have both pointed out, the beginning sense of time comes from the anticipation and expectation that needs will be satisfied. The infant's increasing ability to depend on and to predict his environment is an essential component of the emerging capacity for reality testing. In fact, Oberndorf (1941) suggested that the accuracy of time perception is directly proportional to the degree of reality contact. Even further, the more the infant has a sense of predictability and continuity, the more he can adapt his actions to the environment; and this sense of effective action further aids the development of the concept of a sequence between means and ends. It is only with the recognition of a separate object whose behavior is reasonably consistent and predictable that the infant can begin to experience time as a sequence. Werner (1948), in discussing various regressive changes in schizophrenia, comments that a loss of "temporal schema" is due to a "shrinking of the gap between object and subject [p. 188]."

It is not surprising that research findings consistently indicate temporal disorganization in schizophrenia. For example, Dobson (1954) and De La Garza and Worchel (1956) found that schizophrenics have significantly less temporal orientation. Schizophrenics also have an inconsistent (Orme, 1965) and less accurate (Rabin, 1957) sense of time. This distortion of time in schizophrenia is more severe when aggressive or sexual content is introduced into the situation (Pearl & Berg, 1963). Schizophrenics also seem to lack a sense of the past, or a historical context to their lives. Their experiences are less influenced by the past, they are unusually vulnerable to the characteristics of an immediate situation (Weinstein et al., 1958), and they frequently incorrectly report their current age as the age at which they became ill or were hospitalized (Dahl, 1958; Ehrentheil & Jenney, 1960; Lanzkron & Wolfson, 1958).

There are also several reports of an impaired sense of the future in schizophrenia (Stein & Craik, 1965; Wallace, 1956). Stein and Craik (1965) differentiated "motoric" from "ideational" schizophrenics and found that limited future-time perspective occurred primarily in the "motoric" schizophrenics. It seems reasonable to assume that the motoric–ideational distinction is closely related to the nonparanoid–paranoid distinction and that the findings of Stein and Craik suggest that the impairment of future-time perspective occurs primarily in nonparanoid schizophrenics. Orme (1966) also reports differences in the time sense of paranoid and nonparanoid schizophrenic patients. Time appears to move more rapidly for paranoid schizophrenics; that is, they give an interval greater than the objective time interval they are estimating, while nonparanoid patients seem to experience time as moving more slowly.

In general, the degree of temporal disorganization in schizophrenia appears, as Oberndorf (1941) suggests, to be related to the degree of reality contact and the accuracy of reality testing. Schizophrenics seem to have more difficulty appreciating the temporal dimensions of the present, less appreciation and understanding of the past, and less capacity to extend into the future. These difficulties seem more pronounced in nonparanoid schizophrenic patients. The development of temporal concepts is a function of subject–object differentiation (Werner, 1948) and of the capacity for object constancy. Difficulties in the process of subject–object differentiation result in disruptions in the development of the sense of time.

Perceptual articulation

One of the primary components of adequate reality testing is the capacity to differentiate and to perceive aspects of the environment accurately. Diffuse and unarticulated perceptual processes lead to inadequate differentiation and to reality distortion. Primary in articulated perception is the capacity to differentiate figure from ground (Witkin, 1965). Without this capacity, perception can be diffuse and unstable and there can be difficulty in maintaining separations among objects. There are suggestions that schizophrenics have difficulty perceiving in a focused and articulated manner, expressed in tendencies toward perceptual fusion and difficulty with perceptual constancy. The research on the tendency toward perceptual fusion (apparent movement, critical flicker fusion, and closure) and the research on perceptual constancy suggest that relative impairment of perceptual articulation in schizophrenia is related to difficulty in establishing adequate self–object differentiation.

Apparent movement

Though the literature is somewhat contradictory, there are several studies of apparent movement indicating that schizophrenics have lower thresholds for apparent movement (Saucer, 1958) and require a longer interval between flashing lights before they see them as separate (Saucer & Sweetbaum, 1958). This tendency toward perceptual fusion (a greater tendency to fuse stimuli and the requirement of a longer interval to perceive lights as separate) occurs primarily in nonparanoid schizophrenics. Chlorpromazine raised the threshold for apparent movement in nonparanoid schizophrenic patients to normal levels (Saucer, 1959). Acute and paranoid patients, on the other hand, seem to resist perceptual fusion more than do normals. There are reports, for example, that acute and paranoid patients have higher Critical Flicker Fusion (CFF) thresholds, and that this threshold decreases with chronicity to a point well below normal levels (e.g., Johannsen, Friedman, & Liccione, 1964; McDonough, 1960).

Perceptual closure

In several studies of perceptual closure, Snyder and his colleagues (Snyder, Rosenthal, & Taylor, 1961; Snyder, 1961) and Johannsen et al. (1964) found that paranoid patients were like normal subjects in their capacity to experience perceptual closure, while chronic schizophrenics experienced significantly less closure. This difficulty with perceptual closure is also supported by the findings that schizophrenic patients (particularly chronic patients) have difficulty recognizing the partial figures presented in the Street Gestalt Completion Test (Cohen, Senf, & Huston, 1956; Johannsen, Friedman, & Liccione, 1964). Because of their tendency toward perceptual fusion, schizophrenic patients might be expected to have greater than normal closure. But perceptual closure requires, at least in part, a capacity to articulate figure from ground and some capacity for object constancy, so that the object is recognized sufficiently for perceptual closure to occur (Goldstein & Scheerer, 1941, p. 15). A diminished capacity to articulate figure from ground, or impairment in object constancy, could account for the lower tendencies toward perceptual closure in chronic and undifferentiated schizophrenics. This diminished capacity to articulate figure from ground could also be one of the factors in the lower performance of chronic and undifferentiated schizophrenics on the Embedded Figures Test (e.g., Jannucci, 1965; Weckowicz, 1960; Witkin, 1965). The wish for closure in both zophrenia, however, is highlighted by Draguns' (1963) observations of the extensive premature guessing by chronic schizophrenic patients as they attempted, unsuccessfully, to articulate a blurred figure.

Perceptual constancy

A relative inability to establish adequate boundaries between figure and ground could also account for some of the findings on perceptual constancy in schizophrenia. As early as 1951, Bruner, primarily on theoretical grounds, commented that "withdrawal from object relations and an increasing concern for the self would lead to a breakdown in such phenomena as size and shape constancy [p. 142]." Though there are contradictory findings in the literature (e.g., Harway & Salzman, 1964; Jannucci, 1965; Leibowitz & Pishkin, 1961; Pishkin, Smith, & Leibowitz, 1962), there are a number of reports of both overconstancy (e.g., Raush, 1952; Reynolds, 1953; MacDorman et al., 1964; Sanders & Pacht, 1952; Perez, 1961) and underconstancy (e.g., Crookes, 1957; Hamilton, 1963; Weckowicz, 1957) in schizophrenia. There is some suggestion, however, that chronic and undifferentiated schizophrenics tend to be underconstant (e.g., Boardman et al., 1964; Lovinger, 1956); that is, in comparison with normals, they tend to underestimate the size of objects. This underconstancy is most pronounced when distance cues are minimal (Boardman et al., 1964; Lovinger, 1956). Paranoid and acute patients, on the other hand, tend to be overconstant (e.g., Hartman, 1962; Raush, 1952; Sanders & Pacht, 1952). Underestimation of the size of an object (underconstancy) could result from an impaired capacity to articulate the figure from its embedding context, whereas the overconstancy found in paranoid patients (e.g., Raush, 1952) suggests that the figure is vividly articulated from its ground. Weckowicz and his colleagues conducted some of the most extensive studies in this area (e.g., Weckowicz, 1957, 1964; Weckowicz, Sommer, & Hall, 1958; Weckowicz & Blewett, 1959; Weckowicz & Hall, 1960). They conclude, as does Hamilton (1963), that schizophrenics have impaired constancy and impaired depth perception. This tendency toward underconstancy has been found to correlate with an impaired capacity for abstract thought and an inability to break down gestalts, articulate figures, and maintain attention (Weckowicz & Blewett, 1959). Weckowicz and his colleagues conclude that schizophrenics live in a flattened world because they lack a sense of depth or three dimensionality. Without a stable sense of self, it is difficult to experience

one's relative distance from other objects. Johannsen et al. (1964) and Mc-
Ghie and Chapman (1961) confirm that there seems to be an increased
impairment of depth perception with chronicity. There are also clinical
reports of disturbances in depth perception. For example, one of Mahler's
patients, a 14-year-old psychotic girl with extensive difficulties in achieving
differentiation between herself and her mother, said, "I live in a world that
has a plane surface, flat like my reflection in the mirror . . . [Mahler, 1952,
p. 300]." Another patient, a severely disturbed, borderline young woman,
spontaneously reported an increased sense of depth while looking at an art
book and while walking, immediately following a weekend when, for the
first time, she discussed with her mother a lifelong fear that her mother
would "take her over."

Thus, some of the research on perception and some clinical reports suggest that chronic and nonparanoid schizophrenics have greater difficulty in
separating stimuli and articulating figure from ground, resulting in distortions of perceptual constancy and depth perception. However, in paranoid
patients, these capacities are not only unimpaired, but are often reported to
be greater than those usually observed in normal subjects.

Size estimation

In contrast to the overconstancy of paranoid patients in the studies of
size and distance constancy, paranoid and acute schizophrenic patients significantly underestimate the size of a hand-held stimulus in studies of size
estimation (Davis, Cromwell, & Held, 1967; Harris, 1957; J. Silverman,
1964; Webb, Davis, & Cromwell, 1966). J. Silverman (1964) suggested that
acute and paranoid patients underestimate hand-held stimuli in size estimation experiments, because of their extensive scanning of those stimuli. Similarly, the paranoid patient's extensive scanning of the perceptual field and
fuller articulation of figure from ground in constancy experiments increase
awareness of textural and other distance cues and lead to overconstancy. In
size and distance constancy experiments, it is the chronic and nonparanoid
patient's lack of articulation of figure from ground that results in underconstancy. This interpretation is consistent with general experimental evidence
(e.g. Gibson, 1950; Osgood, 1953), which indicates that a reduction in the
availability of textural and other distance cues results in underconstancy.
When there is a reduction in the availability of distance cues in constancy
experiments with schizophrenic patients, underconstancy is particularly
marked in chronic and nonparanoid patients (Harway & Salzman, 1964;
Lovinger, 1956; Raush, 1952). Thus, chronic and nonparanoid patients
seem to experience objects that are close as much larger, and objects at a

distance as much smaller, than do normal subjects and paranoid schizophrenic patients. It would be of interest in subsequent research to consider
the relationship of these findings on the perceptual experience with close
and distant objects to the schizophrenic patient's experience of a "need–
fear dilemma," in which intimacy and closeness stimulate fears of merging
with a symbiotic partner, while separation and distance result in fears of
abandonment and annihilation.

Field dependence–independence

Witkin's (1965) work on field dependence–independence defines two basic cognitive–perceptual styles. Analytic and articulated versus global and
diffuse cognitive–perceptual styles are defined by the capacity to keep an
object separate from its surrounding field. The field independent person
experiences the object as discrete from the field or background, while the
field dependent person's perception is dominated by the field—the object is
not differentiated from the field. These cognitive styles have been found to
be associated with degree of articulation of body concept, sense of separate
identity, and specific defensive constellations in normal subjects. While
schizophrenics as a total group range widely on measures of field dependence–independence, ambulatory schizophrenics with well-developed defensive structures have articulated (field independent) cognitive styles, as
do paranoids. Also, psychotic patients who hallucinate are more likely to be
field dependent than delusional patients, who tend to be field independent
(Witkin, 1965). This finding is consistent with the hypothesis that hallucinations represent an inability to discriminate thoughts from perceptual experience, while delusions can be seen as attempts to maintain separate identity
and ego integrity. Paranoid delusions involve an excessive emphasis on part
properties. The splitting of objects, the heightened perceptual articulation,
and the conceptual fragmentation of paranoid patients may indicate exaggerated attempts to preserve boundaries and to maintain a sense of separateness. Freeman et al. (1966) have noted that patients with well-organized
delusions (paranoid pathology) have fewer cognitive and perceptual impairments and a greater capacity for interpersonal relationships than nonparanoid patients.

Summary

The differences in the perceptual processes of paranoid and nonparanoid
schizophrenic patients seem to occur primarily when the stimuli have interpersonal or affective dimensions (Pishkin et al., 1962; Raush, 1956; White-

man, 1954; Zahn, 1959) and when the stimulus cues are minimal. When stimulus conditions provide maximal cues, the differences between acute and chronic schizophrenics and normals tend to be minimal (Leibowitz & Pishkin, 1961; Lovinger, 1956; Raush, 1952; Rosenbaum et al., 1965). Maximal stimulus conditions probably highlight figure–ground differentiation and aid the more chronic and undifferentiated patients in perceiving and articulating the stimulus. It is interesting to note in this regard that Pishkin et al. (1962) found that chronic schizophrenics tend to seek greater illumination than normals in perceptual experiments.

Thus, schizophrenic disturbances in reality testing seem to be partly a function of "global" undifferentiated perception in which the separateness and uniqueness of objects and stimuli are not maintained. There is a tendency toward perceptual fusion and a difficulty in articulating figure from ground.

Attention

There is a great deal of recent evidence which indicates that schizophrenics as a group show difficulties in establishing and maintaining focused attention and a task set (e.g., Chapman & McGhie, 1962). These difficulties have been interpreted as reflecting a lack of inhibition of irrelevant stimuli, a breakdown in stimulus or countercathectic barriers, or a faulty filter mechanism, leading to distractibility, passive assimilation of stimuli, diffuse and global experiencing, and inability to pursue a task consistently. There is also evidence (e.g., J. Silverman, 1966) of systematic differences in styles of attending between various subgroups of schizophrenics, particularly along paranoid–nonparanoid and reactive–process (Kantor & Herron, 1966) dimensions.

The ability to focus attention is a fundamental ego function necessary for reality testing. Normally, attention is freely mobile and flexible, yet capable of being directed toward the most salient aspects of both internal and external perceptual experience to promote adaptation. It is active, purposely scanning the environment for relevant information, not captive and passively drawn as in a state of dreaming or preoccupation with hallucinatory experience. Stimuli may be registered but not necessarily drawn into awareness (Klein, 1959) until they become relevant to the individual's adaptation. Schizophrenics often have problems with actively scanning the internal and external environment, articulating a stimulus field into its more and less relevant aspects, selecting and focusing on one aspect of a situation, and actively sustaining goal-directed attention to a task. They consistently show difficulty in excluding irrelevant stimuli from awareness and in discriminating between internal and external stimuli so as to enable them to maintain focus on the task at hand. Clinical examples may serve to illustrate how these problems in selective focusing can be integrated with a developmental formulation of boundary difficulties.

Both the loosening of associations in schizophrenia described by E. Bleuler (1911) and the overinclusion described by Cameron (1944) can be seen as reflections of problems in maintaining the boundaries of goal-directed thought and attention to a particular task set. E. Bleuler quotes excerpts from a schizophrenic's letter to his mother that vividly illustrate these points:

> Dear Mother: Today I feel better than yesterday. Actually I don't feel like writing. Still I like to write to you. . . . I would have been very glad yesterday, on Sunday, if you and Louise and I would have been allowed to go to the park together. . . . I am writing on paper. The pen I use for it is from a factory called Perry and Co. The factory is in England. I am assuming that. After the name Perry Co. the city of London is scratched in; but not the city. The city of London is in England. That I know from school. There I have always liked geography. My last teacher of it was Professor August A. That is a man with black eyes. I like black eyes, too. There are blue and grey eyes too and yet others. I have heard it said that snakes have green eyes. All people have eyes. There are those who are blind. . . . [Bleuler, 1951, pp. 589–590].

This letter clearly shows intrusions of irrelevant details from the immediate external stimulus situation, such as the description of the pen, and an inability to exclude internal preoccupations such as his associations about "eyes." The word following the first use of "eyes" is "I," possibly a clang association, which can also be seen as an irrelevant association to the sound quality of the word rather than to its meaning. There is obvious difficulty in maintaining the goal of writing a letter to his mother, since one association leads to another, with a loss of the initial task set. The inability to empathize with the reader of his letter is striking too, a point that will be elaborated in Chapter 3.

The overinclusion observed by Cameron (1944) in the performance of schizophrenic subjects on the Hanfmann–Kasanin sorting tests, defined as "inability to maintain the boundaries of the problem and to restrict their operations within its limits [p. 56]," appears to be an expression of problems in cognitive focusing. Thus, for example, on the Object Sorting test, schizophrenic patients may show loss of the task boundaries by including the examiner's red blotter, on which the objects for sorting are placed, in a grouping of red objects or say that they cannot make a grouping with a ball because no baseball bat or catcher's mitt is included among the test objects. In addition, Cameron noted an "interpenetration of themes" or intrusion of personal preoccupations into the task, which also seems to reflect difficulties in cognitive focusing and maintaining the boundaries of the task. When there are difficulties in focusing attention and maintaining the task set, the patient is not only responsive to external stimuli; he is also responsive to internal stimuli (e.g., memories and bodily sensations). There is a breakdown of a hypothetical "filter mechanism," which results in a flooding by stimuli, leading to severe distractions, loosening of associations, and an inability to perceive accurately and think logically (e.g., Chapman & McGhie, 1962; Lang & Buss, 1965; Livingston & Blum, 1968; McGhie & Chapman, 1961; McGhie, Chapman, & Lawson, 1965; Maher, 1966; Payne, 1961; Venables, 1964). Loose associations, distractibility, confusion, and disturbances in language are, in part, a function of the overwhelming bombardment of stimuli created by an inability to separate relevant from irrelevant input. This inability to distinguish relevant from irrelevant stimuli can be considered as a filter deficit. But it can also be considered as a function of failure to establish adequate boundaries between different events, stimuli, and objects—a deficit in the concept of the object and in the capacity to establish object constancy. There is a relative lack of the internal representations and schemata that provide a stable framework for determining what is salient and relevant.

The importance of the schizophrenic's deficit in maintaining focused attention is indicated by research findings (e.g., Rappaport et al., 1966; Livingston & Blum, 1968; Trunnell, 1965; Shakow, 1962) suggesting that schizophrenics are aware of appropriate cues but have primary difficulty in attending to them and keeping them in focus. The attention deficit is greatest when there is a variety of stimuli to select from and is least when there are few irrelevant stimuli, when the stimuli are congruent—such as in modality and temporality—and when the stimuli are intense and unequivocal (Lang & Buss, 1965). Studies (e.g., Lehmann, 1967) indicate that tranquilizers improve the ability for selective attention. Disturbances in attention seem to be markedly different in paranoid and nonparanoid patients. The disruption of the filter mechanism is most pronounced in nonparanoid patients who have difficulty in responding selectively to stimuli and separating relevant from irrelevant stimuli (Chapman & McGhie, 1962; Lang & Buss, 1965; Payne, 1961; J. Silverman, 1964). In contrast to the severe distractibility of the nonparanoid patient, the paranoid patient has an exaggerated capacity for focused attention and a tendency to relate irrelevant stimuli to a single basic and central theme. This highly organized, overly focused functioning may be a mechanism that defends against a more disoriented and distracted state.

J. Silverman (1966) also finds different types of attention disturbance in subgroups of schizophrenic patients along the dimensions of paranoid and nonparanoid, reactive and process, acute and chronic. He divides attention

processes into (1) scanning—the degree to which stimuli are sampled from
the environment—and (2) field articulation—the degree to which salient
stimuli are discriminated from irrelevant stimuli. In a summary of his own
and other investigators' research on attention and cognitive style, Silverman
concludes that extreme forms of scanning and field articulation characterize different schizophrenic subgroups. Extensive scanning and heightened
field articulation are likely to occur in paranoid patients, who rely heavily
on defensive projection, whereas minimal scanning and field articulation
are typical in the catatonic, hebephrenic, and simple subtypes. Furthermore, undifferentiated field articulation, with blurred, uncertain perception, is characteristic of process schizophrenics with poor premorbid
histories, while reactive schizophrenics with good premorbid histories show
more highly differentiated field articulation. Similarly, Freeman et al.
(1966) report findings that paranoid schizophrenics differ from hebephrenic
schizophrenics in their performance on tasks with a distraction, such as a
visual tracking task with a buzzing noise as an irrelevant sensory input. On
some tasks, paranoids attend as well as normals and differ from hebephren-
ics in this respect. Consistent with Witkin's report that delusional psychotics are more field independent than are those who experience
hallucinations, Freeman et al. find that the presence of systematized delusional thinking is negatively related to distractibility. In summary, Freeman
et al. state:

> The hypothesis is advanced here that in the schizophrenias and allied conditions
> attentive disturbances fall into two extreme forms. In the one case purposive atten-
> tion fails because the individual is unable to insulate awareness from perceptual
> stimulation. Percepts on different levels of organizational complexity interfere with
> the attention mechanism and thus distract him from his current undertaking. In the
> second group are the patients who cannot concentrate upon a particular stimulus
> because attention has become fixed to other mental contents [p. 81].

Thus, they postulate that the type of attention disturbance associated with
a hebephrenic disorder reflects passive assimilation of stimuli, with a disintegration of the barriers against being overwhelmed by internal and external stimuli. If there are attention disturbances in the paranoid subtype, it
is because these patients are preoccupied with their own, internal mental
contents, on which their attention is fixated.

The work of Singer and Wynne (1965a,b) indicates that patients with
more "amorphous" or more "fragmented" forms of thought disorder come
from families with different styles of attending and communicating. Utilizing data primarily from individually administered projective tests and family therapy-sessions (Morris & Wynne, 1965), these investigators have
defined amorphous and fragmented transactional styles of attending and

communicating, both in individuals and in the family as a whole. Amorphous forms of attending are loosely organized, with attention drifting off before any point or meaning has been achieved, perception is blurred and uncertain, and communications are vague and indefinite, with marked imprecision of terms and referents. Fragmented forms of attending are relatively more differentiated; but there is a serious failure in integrating aspects of experience, so that abrupt, disruptive shifts in attention and chaotic disruptions of thought processes occur. Subsequent studies in which manifestations of transactional attention disturbances on individual test protocols were scored, show that parents of schizophrenics reveal a higher frequency of such disturbances than do parents of normal control subjects on the Object Sorting test (Wild et al., 1965) and than do parents of neurotic and normal offspring on the Rorschach (Singer & Wynne, 1966).

J. Silverman (1966), Freeman et al. (1966), and Singer and Wynne (1965a, b) suggest that their findings can be interpreted as indicating lower and higher developmental levels of sensory, perceptual, and conceptual differentiation. It seems fairly well established that nonparanoid, hebephrenic, process, and hallucinatory schizophrenics have more undifferentiated, global styles of attending and that paranoid, acute, and delusional patients tend to have more articulated, even at times excessively selective, attention styles. As Freeman et al. (1966) point out, delusional patients also differ on a continuum according to the rigidity and fixity or openness to change of their delusional systems. As discussed earlier, perceptual discrimination of complex stimulus fields evolves developmentally. Initially, there is little differentiation between self and nonself, and there is a relatively passive assimilation of incoming sensory experiences without selection and inhibition. Experiences of the self and environment are vague, global, and diffuse, becoming progressively more articulated. Wynne and Singer's work suggests that parental styles of communicating may foster vague, global, amorphous, unclear perceptions and modes of attending, leading to minimal field articulation, or more articulated, fragmented modes with momentary fixation on details. Of course, these observations raise the question as to whether early dispositions toward either extreme of attention style result in a propensity toward certain types of schizophrenia, or whether schizophrenia represents a failure of development beyond these earlier levels, or some complex mixture of these two possibilities.

Symbolic Processes

Introduction

In this section we shall review some of the literature on symbolic processes in schizophrenia including concept formation, language, and thinking. Symbolic processes require the capacity to establish a mental representation of an object and the capacity to distinguish this representation from the object itself. As discussed by Piaget (1954) and Wolff (1967), the first representations are internalized action patterns that can be rearranged in thought without action. There is a sequence in the development of representations and symbolic processes that progresses from sensorimotor action to imagery to symbolic thought to socialized language. The infant gradually learns to distinguish his own actions from the object acted upon, what is inside the self from what is outside the self, and his actions from the physical, spatial, and causal attributes of the object, which comes to be seen as existing independently of the self. Freud's model of thought as initially developing from frustration and delay of gratification leading to a hallucination of the desired object (i.e., the breast) appears untenable, since such hallucinatory imagery would already require a differentiation of objects in the environment and some capacity for memory and for representational thought. As Wolff and Piaget state, thought seems to be an internalized derivative of action and motor schemas, not a substitute for them. Wolff (1967), in a discussion of the acquisition of language in which he attempts to integrate psychoanalytic theory with the conceptualizations of Piaget, considers object constancy as a prerequisite for the development of representational thought. Bettelheim (1967), in a discussion of autistic children, also examines the relationship of representational thought to the development of a consistent and distinct sense of self and of the environment. He stresses that an awareness of the self as subject, or a consistent representation of the self which exists independent of its own activity in time and space, and an awareness of objects external to, and independent of, the self are important in the development of representational thought. Like Piaget (1954) and Werner and Kaplan (1963), Wolff (1967) and Bettelheim (1967) emphasize the importance of object constancy in the development of representational thought and symbolic processes.

Concept formation

Symbolic thought, a necessary aspect of concept formation and language, seems to be contingent upon the development of stable representations of the self and of objects. It is not surprising that the schizophrenic's difficulty in subject–object differentiation should also be expressed in impairments of concept formation and language. There is fairly consistent evidence suggesting that schizophrenics have difficulty with various levels of abstraction. Werner (1948) and Searles (1965) have noted the schizophrenic's basic problem in maintaining a differentiation between concrete and metaphorical thinking, and Federn (1952) has stressed the schizophrenic's relative lack of discrimination between the object and its representation. A great deal of research has been devoted to studying concept formation in schizophrenia. Goldstein (1944) presented early findings concerning the schizophrenic's impairment in abstract ability, and Benjamin (1944) also found that schizophrenics were more literal and concrete in interpreting proverbs. Cameron (1944, 1951), on the other hand, found that the performance of schizophrenics on sorting tasks was best characterized as overinclusive, with an inappropriate broadening of conceptual categories, as when objects are sorted together because they are all "part of the universe." Cameron considered overinclusion as an expression of conceptual disorganization. Payne and his colleagues (e.g., Payne, 1961) have systematically studied this phenomenon. Initially Epstein (1953) and later Payne, on the basis of extensive studies, concluded that overinclusive thinking occurs primarily in schizophrenics. Payne et al. (1959) found a very high positive correlation between overinclusive thinking and a measure of perceptual overinclusion, which suggested to them that overinclusiveness is an expression of a more fundamental disturbance in the "filter mechanism" involved in attention (Payne, 1966). This disturbance in the capacity to attend to relevant and screen out irrelevant stimuli makes selective perception difficult, if not impossible. However, later research by Payne and his colleagues (Payne et al., 1970) failed to substantiate their earlier finding of an interrelationship between overinclusive thinking and perceptual overinclusion. This led them to question their earlier formulation that overinclusive thinking, so frequently observed in schizophrenia, can be attributed to a defect in a hypothetical filter mechanism. While an attention defect in the ability to screen out irrelevant perceptions and ideas "can be demonstrated very dramatically in some schizophrenics, it cannot be the basis of overinclusive thinking [Payne et al., 1970, p. 192]."

Payne and his colleagues (e.g., Payne & Caird, 1967) also attempted to demonstrate that overinclusive thinking and high distractibility occur primarily in paranoid patients. However, no significant differences were found between paranoid and nonparanoid schizophrenics. McGhie and his colleagues found that paranoid patients are the least distractible of many clinical groups (McGhie, 1970). Thus, the role of the hypothetical filter defect as a basic issue in schizophrenia and its relationship to the various subtypes of schizophrenia remain unclarified.

Chapman and his colleagues are also among those who have studied the schizophrenic's overinclusive category system, in which objects, for example, are seen as related because they share a common physical property even though they lack any conceptual similarity (e.g., Chapman & Chapman, 1959; Gottesman & Chapman, 1960). They found that with reduced external structure and definition, schizophrenics tend to be responsive to the most prominent aspect of meaning, whether or not appropriate to the task or concept (Chapman, Chapman, & Miller, 1964). This tendency to respond primarily on the basis of predominant meaning can give thinking either a concrete or an overly abstract quality and can interfere with the ability to differentiate the important from the trivial, so that the thinking appears irrelevant and loose.

Cameron described overinclusive thinking as the patients' "remarkable inability to maintain the boundaries of the problem and to restrict their operations within its limits [1944, p. 56]." This inability to maintain the definition of a task is similar to Shakow's (1950) observations that schizophrenics are unable to maintain a major task set or a "readiness to respond" and to Chapman's findings that schizophrenics are unable to establish and maintain an image of the total context of a problem or situation. These observations of overinclusive thinking and an inability to maintain a task set are not inconsistent with the formulation of a faulty filter mechanism in attention. However, they are also consistent with an alternative formulation of developmental disturbances in the capacity to establish and maintain stable representations.

In another approach to the study of the cognitive aspects of schizophrenia, Jortner found that a Rorschach scale, designed to measure the lack of boundaries "between different levels or realms of abstraction, the fusion and confusion of the concrete and the abstract or of the animate and the inanimate [1966, p. 559]," differentiated 25 schizophrenic from 24 nonschizophrenic patients and correlated positively with interview ratings of "disturbances in thought processes" and "poor reality testing." Zucker (1958) also found that 30 hospitalized paranoid schizophrenics, as compared to 30 ambulatory outpatient paranoid schizophrenics, showed more instances of "fusion of different cognitive realms" on the Rorschach. Singer and Wynne (1965a), using projective techniques, observed that families of schizophrenics demonstrate erratic, inappropriate distance and closeness, both in concept formation and interpersonal relationships, fluctuating unpredictably from intrusive intimacy to remoteness and from concrete literalness to global generalities. Wild et al. (1965) also noted "shifts of contexts of reference," when subjects "shift fluidly from one frame of reference to another, as from concrete to abstract or from affective to physical aspects of the stimuli [p. 472]" in the performance of parents of schizophrenic patients on the Object Sorting test.

In summarizing the literature on concept formation in schizophrenia, Weiner (1966) concludes that overabstraction is the most distinctive feature of schizophrenics on concept formation tasks, differentiating them from both organics and normals, whereas overconcreteness discriminates them only from normals. Also, the schizophrenic is likely to show extremely variable functioning, ranging from appropriate levels of abstraction to the overly abstract and overly concrete, often within the same response. The responses of two schizophrenic patients to the Similarities subtest of the

Wechsler Adult Intelligence Scale illustrate these fluctuations. While a young female patient was able to say that a table and a chair are alike because they are both "furniture," she overgeneralized in saying that air and water are "both environment" and was overly concrete in her response to orange and banana, saying, "Orange is sweet, banana has more texture, but still sweet. I like bananas and fruit." An 18-year-old male patient shows a progression from a concrete to an appropriate to an overgeneralized level of abstraction when he says that an eye and an ear are alike because "both are on your face, one of your senses, part of the sea of information."

While these problems with concept formation can be interpreted as overly abstract (overinclusive) and concrete (underinclusive) functioning, they can also be interpreted as reflecting difficulties in maintaining consistent images and representations of objects. In order to find the most meaningful similarity between objects, stable mental images of the objects are required, as well as an ability to discriminate between their more and less salient characteristics. If there is an impairment in the representational process, with limited distinction between objects and difficulty in establishing stable mental representations of objects and in maintaining a distinction between objects and their representations or verbal signifiers, then disordered concept formation will occur. Several studies (Blatt, 1952, 1959; Harrington & Ehrmann, 1954; Rabin, King, & Ehrmann, 1955) have demonstrated that schizophrenics have significantly more difficulty with a recall type of vocabulary test, in which they are required to define words, than with a recognition type of vocabulary test, in which they have to select the correct response (a definition or an illustrative picture) from several alternatives. This relative difficulty with recall increases with estimates of chronicity (Blatt, 1959). While there may be several explanations for these findings, they are consistent with the formulation that one of the primary problems in schizophrenia is an impaired capacity to evoke and maintain a stable mental representation. Schizophrenic patients can do reasonably well and, in fact, approximate normal functioning on tasks that provide direct perceptual support and do not make extensive demands for representational processes.

Concept formation, as well as articulated perception and focused attention, require some sense of distinction among objects (including the self). Classification and categorization also require separate and stable internal images of objects, so that they can be identified in different contexts and from different perceptual stances. Misrecognition and difficulty in identifying objects, such as occurs with schizophrenics and their parents in the Object Sorting test (e.g., a bell is called a "cigarette lighter" or a "tool"), reflect a lack of consistent, stable mental representations of objects and difficulty in articulating their most important features. Concept formation involves a constant process of checking perceptions of objects against their stable mental representations, so that one can identify the objects and relate them to prior experiences while still maintaining a differentiation between the external object and the past experience. Otherwise, a bell is likely to be seen as a cigarette lighter when the perceiver needs a light. The lack of stable mental representations based on salient features of objects leads to a disruption of the capacity to maintain adequate differentiation, and objects become equivalent because of some inessential feature (e.g., a knife with a rounded end is sorted with a cigar because both are "round" objects). Identifying objects, subsuming them under differing conceptual domains, and establishing specific verbal signifiers for them all require the advanced developmental capacity to separate the symbol from the object signified. As Lidz (1968) points out, adequate concept formation and language are important in organizing experience, and the schizophrenic patient's impairment of these symbolic processes compounds his already limited capacities for differentiation and integration.

The lack of stable mental representations of objects, which disrupts conceptual functioning, also affects the capacity to establish a concept of the self as separate from other people and objects in the environment. A basic lack of differentiation of the self from external objects or of self representations from object representations results in the inappropriate closeness and distance observed in the interpersonal relationships of schizophrenic patients, in the characteristic lack of discrimination between the self and other human, animate, and inanimate objects, and in experiences of depersonalization such as being mechanical or machine-like. Often in schizophrenic patients, there is a confusion between the external realm of inanimate objects and the self, so that human attributes may be applied to inanimate objects and vice versa.

These points are illustrated in the response of a hospitalized, articulate, 19-year-old college student to Card IX of the Rorschach. He immediately begins, "This picture has some of the sharpness and clarity of the others, but the green is blurred," a comment suggesting some concern with perceptual articulation. He continues, "over here—a fire—electric fire—brilliant, incisive, destructive, and without heat—an explosion in which something is created, in which the clouds create something and make shapes." When he speaks of an "explosion" and of the clouds "making shapes," he seems to experience a sense of passivity and of being inundated by stimuli, feeling that the blot determines his percepts rather than his having active control over them. He goes on to say:

> The first shape is a boxer, a mechanical boxer. These are the eyes, but nobody knows what he sees, his eyes are inward as well as outward, and he hates everything

he sees. He's rather strong. This green area here is his mind. No, the whole thing is mind divided into three parts somehow mixed together. One part has to do with jealousy, the green, poison, another has to do with eyes which are also here in the green and white. The green looks outward and the white looks inward. The figure is also like a child, very confused, very unhappy, and the mind is attacking this child constantly, bringing fire on it and poisonous gas. The child wants to escape, but he's caught by his neck . . . The child is split in two. The juxtaposition of the child and boxer is very apparent. One is on top of the other, they are the two central figures, but the child is inside the boxer's mind.

A great many aspects of this complex response could be elaborated, but only a few that are relevant to our discussion will be considered. His confusion around what is inside and outside himself seems apparent in his statement that the boxer's eyes are "inward as well as outward," paralleling his confusion between what is on the blot and what is inside his own mind—a confusion between reality and fantasy. Consistently, his somewhat unsuccessful struggle to keep his percepts separate is evident in his comment that the child is "inside the boxer's mind," a comment showing a contaminatory trend, since the concepts of boxer and child tend to fuse. Thus, he seems to have difficulty both in keeping his own fantasies separate from the reality of the blot and in keeping external percepts separate from one another. Although he struggles to keep them distinct, he seems unable to maintain discrete, consistent, stable percepts. The "mechanical boxer" is a blend of animate with inanimate content, suggesting experiences of estrangement and depersonalization. While he seems to have a tendency to exhibit his loose thinking with some enjoyment, his chaotic experience of himself and the world comes through in his topsy-turvy feeling of being passively bombarded by internal and external stimuli that become confused with one another. He also seems to be threatened by fears of annihilation, as when he says that the "mind is attacking this child" with "fire" and "poisonous gas." He does attempt, however, to maintain the boundaries between inside and outside and between separate percepts through the use of paranoid mechanisms, emphasis on intense and vivid experiences, and aggression. The struggle between the child and the boxer could also reflect aspects of his attempts to manage his disturbing experiences and to achieve some differentiation in his confused world. The themes of boxer and child suggest that aggression may serve as an attempt to maintain a sense of separateness. Bettelheim (1967) and Roth & Blatt (1961) have stressed the importance of aggression with accompanying self-awareness and sense of effective action as an important step in the development of a sense of self. Despite the indications of psychopathology in this response, the active struggle, the use of paranoid mechanisms, and the complexity of the response, all indicate a considerable degree of intactness.

There is a great deal of clinical and empirical evidence to support the well-known finding that paranoid schizophrenics as a group show less impairment of intellectual functioning than do other schizophrenic subtypes. Weiner summarizes Shakow's (1962, 1963) findings as follows:

> The paranoid type of schizophrenic . . . is an alert, vigilant person highly sensitive to personal reference, whose intellectual functioning is relatively preserved and who concentrates his energies on protecting his personality against the inroads of his environment. He governs his experience rigidly, imposing accurate limits on what he perceives and cautious strictures on how he responds. The hebephrenic type of schizophrenic, in contrast, is quite disturbed intellectually, venturesome and inaccurate rather than circumspect in his dealings with his environment, relatively defenseless in the face of external affront, and unresponsive to personal reference [1966, p. 304].

Paranoid patients consistently seem to show less conceptual deficit than nonparanoid patients. As suggested by the research on cognitive focusing and J. Silverman's differentiation between maximal and minimal scanning and field articulation, the paranoid patient would be apt to organize a maximum input of information into tight and narrow conceptual categories, while the nonparanoid would be more likely to organize a minimal input of information into vague, broader conceptual categories. Paranoid patients seem to function on a higher developmental level than nonparanoid patients in the area of concept formation, perhaps because of having attained or retained a greater degree of boundary differentiation and consequently a greater capacity for stable object representation.

Language

According to Piaget, the early stages of sensorimotor development involve the establishment of schemata, the internalizations of specific action patterns in which initially there is little differentiation between subject, object, and the action sequence. In subsequent development, the child begins to differentiate the object within the specific action patterns, and it is only with this progressive differentiation that the child develops symbols for the object and for the action. Initially, the action sequences are internalized as thought, and later the child evokes these thoughts in anticipation of the object. Piaget (1954), Werner and Kaplan (1963), and Wolff (1967) consider this anticipation and contemplation of the object essential to the development of symbolic functions. The establishment of the concept of the object eventually enables the child to develop stable and consistent mental representations of the object, even when the object is no longer present in the immediate sensory field. According to Piaget and Werner and Kaplan, thinking proceeds from the internalization of sensorimotor action patterns, to imagery, to symbolic thought, to language (Wolff, 1967). The capacities to establish distinctions between self and nonself, between one's actions and the object acted upon, among representations of various objects, and between objects and their representations are essential steps in the development of the concept of the object, object constancy, and symbolic thought.

Brown (1973), based partly on the observations of Lois Bloom (1970), describes a sequence of language development that proceeds from initially establishing nominal terms for objects immediately present in the sensory field (e.g., *mama, dada*), to references to the recurrence of objects (e.g., *more*), to references to the nonexistence of an object (e.g., *all gone*), to references to noticing an object (e.g., *hi*). With expressions of noticing, such as *hi,* the child seems to be beginning to develop object constancy and this is followed by the use of symbolic expressions for objects and the "vocative" use of names for persons, animals, or things, including the self (e.g., *mama look*).

— The first stages of nomination and recurrence indicate the child's capacity to recognize and anticipate objects and actions. While these initial stages suggest that the child has begun to establish a concept of the object, it is only later that the child develops an enduring and stable mental representation of the object, which persists even when the object is absent from the immediate perceptual field. Brown (1973), in summarizing these observations, states:

> The first sentences express the construction of reality which is the terminal achievement of sensori-motor intelligence. What has been acquired on the plane of motor intelligence (the permanence of form and substance of immediate objects) and the structure of immediate space and times does not need to be formed all over again on the plane of representation. Representation starts with just those meanings that are most available to it, propositions about action schemas involving agents and objects, assertions of nonexistence, recurrence, location, and so on. But representation carries intelligence beyond the sensori-motor. Representation is a new level of operation which quickly moves to meanings that go beyond immediate space and practical action [p.200].

Evidence suggests that in some ways the language disturbances in schizophrenia are similar to functioning at earlier sensorimotor levels. Schizophrenic language disturbances often involve a relative inability to maintain distinctions between the action patterns directed toward the objects, the symbols used for objects, and the actual objects. The schizophrenic's inability to maintain the separation between perceptions and personal meanings, and between mental representations and objects, results in loose associations (Bleuler, 1950) and disorganized language and thinking. Lidz (1968; Lidz et al., 1958) points out that the mother's inability to establish boundaries between herself and her child often limits the utility of verbal communications as a means of solving problems. Lidz (1968) speculates that the failure of schizophrenic patients and their parents to establish boundaries between self and nonself may disrupt the capacity to form discrete and useful concepts and categories.

Werner and Kaplan (1963) attribute the primitiveness of language in schizophrenics to a lack of basic differentiations:

> The distinction between self and nonself (other persons and things), the differentiation between a world of independent objects and one's attitudes and expectations concerning such objects, the distinction between the meanings one feels and seeks to convey and the semantic values of conventional words, the polarity between symbolic vehicles and objects—distinctions all gradually attained during the course of ontogenesis—appear to break down, to varying degrees, in schizophrenic states [p. 254].

In schizophrenia, objects lack definition, contour, constancy, and stability. Werner and Kaplan discuss the loss of a distinction between symbolic vehicles and their object referents. Objects that are perceived, dreamed, remembered, wished, imagined, thought, and so forth all tend to lose their distinctive "substance" and take on a more or less imagery-like character [pp. 257–258]. This lack of distinctive "substance" of objects and of thoughts fosters extensive alteration of linguistic forms. There is not only a loss of the distinction between objects and their symbolic referents, but also "an underlying collapse in distance between the inner and external forms of symbolic vehicles [p. 259]," so that word forms (e.g., sounds, letters, and syllables) begin to carry meaning in their own right. Words become equivalent to things, concrete actions begin to have ulterior and profound meaning, and abstract meanings easily become images [p. 261]. There is a confusion between the actual object, its mental representation, and its verbal signifier. As summarized by Werner and Kaplan "the patient's handling of language as a concrete realistic substance fused with imagery, action, objects, etc., and often treated as interchangeable with them, reflects the decreased distance between the addressor and his symbolic vehicles in schizophrenia [p. 263]." In schizophrenia, words do not represent and refer to stable objects and specific actions, but rather to "states of affairs that are fusions of affective–impulsive–sensory–motor–perceptual impressions [p. 265]." Words designate referents that lack contour and stability, interfering with the formation of true lexical units and syntactic relations and permitting an infusion of idiosyncratic themes and sudden alterations, mergings, and transformations [p. 265].

Grand, Freedman, and Steingart (1973) compared aspects of language in "isolated" and "belligerent" chronic schizophrenic patients. They compared these two groups on the Stroop Color–Word test, linguistic complexity, sentence construction, and the integration of speech with hand gestures. Higher levels of integration of speech with motor activity (hand movements) were previously found to occur in "object focused" speech and to be related to more complex linguistic constructions. Isolated, as compared to belligerent, chronic schizophrenic patients performed significantly less well on simple linguistic encoding, utilized significantly more simple language constructions, and had significantly less integration of speech with hand gestures. Generally they showed a greater "deficit in the capacity to utilize verbally encoded thought to represent their experience [p. 424]." Earlier, Steingart and Freedman (1972) compared language usage and construction in different clinical states and observed a relationship between the degree of complexity in syntax and the level of self–object discrimination. They found the most complex form of syntax in a paranoid patient and the simplest form in a schizophrenic patient, while the complexity of syntax of a depressed patient was in between these two levels. Thus, language construction seems to be more integrated and complex in belligerent and paranoid schizophrenic patients than in isolated schizophrenic patients.

Studies of speech patterns of schizophrenics indicate that often there is a lack of essential connectives and conjunctions, and phrases and concepts are put in arbitrary juxtaposition. Speech is often vague and idiosyncratic with frequent discontinuity, disruption, and blocking (Cameron and Magaret, 1951). Cameron also noted a phenomenon he labeled "interpenetration" in schizophrenic speech, in which ideas from an earlier part of the speech inappropriately reappear later in the speech. Cameron compared this interpenetration in speech to the schizophrenic's inability to maintain the boundaries of a problem, which results in overinclusive thinking. In addition, Cameron (1944), analyzing the performance of 25 schizophrenics on a logical problem consisting of 15 incomplete sentences, called attention to the "asyndetic thinking" of schizophrenics and the relative lack of causal links in their thinking. "In place of well-knit sequences, which the situations demanded, the best our schizophrenics were able to do was to throw in a cluster of more or less related elements." Thus, one patient completed the sentence, "I get warm when I run because . . ." with "quickness, blood, heart of deer, length, Driven power, motorized cylinder, strength [p. 53]."

Cameron interprets this response as indicating an inability to screen out and eliminate irrelevant elements. More recently, McGhie (1970) concluded that the speech disturbances of schizophrenics are not a function of an inability to understand individual words. Rather, the difficulties are a function of "an inability to perceive the words in meaningful relationship to each other as part of an organized pattern [p. 12]." Schizophrenic patients seem to be "unable to utilize the transitional bonds between words which normally facilitate our perception of the passage as an organized whole [p. 13]." Maher (1975) reports that semantic disturbances ("associational fluidity") in the language usage of schizophrenic patients are more likely to occur at transitional points such as at a comma or at the end of a sentence.

This impaired ability to utilize causal links and transitional bonds, which distorts and limits the establishment of any meaning, is similar to the observations of Von Domarus (1944) and Arieti (1955), who compared the thinking of schizophrenics to culturally and ontogenetically more primitive forms of thinking in which the primary defect occurs in the connective link between premise and conclusion. Like the tendency toward overinclusive thinking, this difficulty in establishing the appropriate connectives in thinking and language can be considered as another expression of the difficulty in keeping ideas, concepts, and experiences separate, rather than as a primitive form of logic. These disruptions of the causal links in thinking and language tend to occur more often when patients are confronted with personal, rather than impersonal, and emotionally charged, rather than neutral, materials (Williams, 1964). Whiteman (1954) also found significantly greater "thought decrement" in schizophrenics when the patients were dealing with social rather than with formal concepts. Likewise, Bannister and Salmon (1966) found significantly greater thought disorder (defined as a lack of stability in utilizing constructs) in schizophrenics when constructs were applied to people rather than to inanimate objects.

The observations by Von Domarus (1944) of paralogical or predicate thinking, in which there is a deficit in reasoning about causal relationships, has recently been elaborated by Weiner (1966) who points out that in such thinking identity is established, not on a conceptual level, but on the basis of three types of predicate—quality, spatial contiguity, and temporal contiguity. Holt's examples of autistic logic on the Rorschach serve as excellent examples of predicate thinking. Thus, in the response "Everything's so small it must be the insectual kind of thing," the quality of smallness shared by insects and the blot area seems to have led this subject to identify the blot area with insects. The predicate of spatial contiguity leading to identity is illustrated by position responses on the Rorschach such as "The North Pole, because it was at the top [Holt, 1963, pp. 30–31]."

According to Piaget, early stages of sensorimotor development are characterized by a mixture of efficacy, or a sense that one's own efforts are responsible for external events, and phenomenalism, or temporal (not spatial) contiguity, in which the simultaneous occurrence of two events is interpreted as meaning that one caused the other. Then, as the capacities for representational thought, objectification, and spatialization increase, the child begins to be able to differentiate cause from effect, an achievement that is dependent on the development of the object concept. Flavell's description of aspects of sensorimotor and preoperational thought is similar in some respects to descriptions of schizophrenic predicate thinking, in which identity or causality is assumed on the basis of common qualities or of contiguity in space or time.

> Piaget uses the term *transductive* for the types of reasoning by which the preoperational child links various preconcepts. . . . Neither true induction nor true deduction, this kind of reasoning proceeds from particular to particular. Centering on one salient element of an event, the child proceeds irreversibly to draw as conclusion from it some other, perceptually compelling happening. . . . There are other characteristics of transductive reasoning which may be mentioned very briefly. First, the child tends to make associative "and-connections" rather than true implicative and causal relations between the successive terms in a reasoning chain; that is, he tends simply to *juxtapose,* as Piaget calls it, elements rather than connect them through appeals to logical necessity or physical causality. . . . Parts and class members are not related to their respective wholes and classes by the specific relations of inclusion, unilateral implication, etc.; for the young child, the two terms just "go together." Similarly, the child's reasoning is *syncretic;* a multitude of diverse things are inchoately but intimately co-related within a global, all-encompassing schema. . . . Since almost anything can be "causally" related (by juxtaposition, of course, rather than true causality) to almost anything else within the syncretic whole, the child tends, when pressed to do so, to find a reason for anything [Flavell, 1963, pp. 160–161].

Though the causal reasoning of the young child is different in important respects from the thinking of the schizophrenic, there are phenomenological similarities between them that may foster understanding of schizophrenic thinking. Piaget's descriptions of transductive thinking, in which elements are related because of juxtaposition, and his descriptions of reasoning that is syncretic, global, and undifferentiated can be helpful in differentiating levels and types of disturbances in thinking. Schizophrenics appear to lack a clear differentiation of boundaries, particularly between self and nonself, which is essential for the objectification of reality, for the development of the concept of the object, for the capacity for representational thought, and for the understanding of causality. This difficulty in understanding causality and the interrelationships among objects and events is clearly expressed in the schizophrenic's linguistic difficulties in using transitional bonds and perceiving meaningful relationships among words.

In schizophrenia, the relative lack of definition and stability of objects is expressed linguistically in a reduction of adequate qualification and specification. Schizophrenics have significantly less description in their written (Lorenz & Cobb, 1954; Mann, 1944) and spoken (Fairbanks, 1944) language and significantly less specification per structural unit of speech than normals (Slepian, 1959). This reduction in description and specification is greater in process, as compared to reactive, schizophrenics (Maher, McKean, & McLaughlin, 1966). Schizophrenics also use fewer different words than normals and again, this is most marked in process schizophrenics (Maher et al., 1966). Werner and Kaplan (1963), based on an unpublished study by Slepian (1959), discuss the degree to which schizophrenics and normals qualify primary nouns either by modification (e.g., *a black car*) or by specification of a context (Chapman et al., 1964; Maher, 1972; Salzinger et al., 1970) or a function. They, like Vygotsky, consider qualification (either by modification or by specification) to involve a "process of differentiation and articulation" that is characteristic of "higher levels of symbolic articulation." Slepian found that normals use significantly more specification per structural unit of speech than do schizophrenics and that the degree of specification in schizophrenics is significantly less influenced by stimulus conditions or conditions of communication than it is in normals.

In terms of the relative lack of nouns and qualifiers, schizophrenic language is similar to inner speech. According to Vygotsky (1962), inner speech is a function in its own right in which thoughts are connected with words but in a "dynamic, shifting, unstable" way, "fluttering between word and thought. . . . Inner speech is to a large extent thinking in pure meanings [p. 149]." Initially in development, internal and external speech are closely related, as when a single word expresses an entire "dim, amorphous," undifferentiated experience. As thoughts become differentiated, they can be expressed in increasingly complex communicative external speech. Inner speech, in contrast, is more like an "inarticulate inner experience" which serves an orienting and organizing function that becomes increasingly independent of external speech. In inner speech the "sense of a word" takes preponderance over meaning. Vygotsky (1962) considers meaning to be the stable characteristic of a word while the sense of a word depends on the context. In inner speech, sense predominates over meaning, sentence over word, and context over sentence. This often leads to word combinations; several words may merge into one word and the "new word not only expresses a rather complex idea but designates all the separate elements contained in that idea [p. 147]." Another basic semantic peculiarity of inner speech is the combination and unification of meaning. There is an "influx" of meaning such that "the senses of different words flow into one another" so that earlier meanings "are contained in, and modify, the later ones [p. 147]." "In inner speech, the phenomenon reaches its peak. A single word is so saturated with the sense that many words would be required to explain it in external speech [p. 148]." According to Vygotsky, the transition from inner to external speech is not achieved by merely vocalizing silent speech. "It is a complex, dynamic process involving the transformation of the predicative, idiomatic structure of inner speech into syntactically articulated speech intelligible to others [p. 148]."

In contrast to external speech, "inner speech appears disconnected and incomplete"; subjects, objects, and their modifiers are omitted and only the predicate is preserved. The lack of qualifiers and nouns in inner speech makes transductive and predicative thinking the basic syntactic form of inner speech. Pure predication occurs and is effective as a communication in external speech only when the thoughts of two people coincide. If two people are thinking about the same thing, then the simplified syntax, condensation, and greatly reduced number of words of predicative speech is effective. Vygotsky (1962), citing Tolstoy, concludes that communication by abbreviated speech is common between two people who live in very close psychological contact. People in very close contact apprehend one another's complicated meanings in the fewest words [pp. 139–142]. It is impressive that Tolstoy, and later Vygotsky, commented that external speech similar to inner speech is effective as a communication only between two people living in very close psychological contact. As discussed by Werner and Kaplan (1963), there is greater use of symbolic vehicles that are more "idiomatic and idiosyncratic" when there is little distinction between addressor and addressee. With increased differentiation of self from others, symbolic vehicles specify referents in a more socially conventional manner and there is greater distinction "between speech for the self and speech for others [p. 328]."

The similarity between normal inner speech and schizophrenic language (i.e., predicative thinking, combination and fusion of words, and the unification of meaning used for communication in close interpersonal relationships) raises interesting questions about the possible relationship between inner speech and external speech in schizophrenia and about the schizophrenic's relative capacity to maintain a distinction between these two levels (Werner & Kaplan, 1963, p. 318). Without adequate differentiation of the boundaries between self and others, and between inside and outside, schizophrenic patients have difficulty appreciating differences in perspective. Patients with serious boundary problems may assume that their thoughts and feelings are not only similar to those of other people but are, in fact, identical and always shared.

Thinking and thought disorder

In this section we shall focus our discussion on the concept of primary process thinking and how a classification of the various types and levels of primary process thought provides insight into the levels of organization and types of disruptions that occur in psychotic states. As Holt and Havel (1960) have pointed out, primary process thinking has both content and formal dimensions. The content aspects of primary process thinking are the presence of drive representations, and the formal aspects are the mechanisms originally delineated by Freud (1900) in his discussion of dream work condensation, displacement, and symbolization. The formal features of primary process thinking can be considered as related to the development of the concept of the object and, therefore, as having particular relevance for understanding schizophrenic thinking such as the loosening of associations described by E. Bleuler (1911).

Starting from Freud's (1900) delineation of condensation, displacement, and symbolization as mechanisms of dream work, Gill (1967), Holt (1967), and Wolff (1967) have called attention to the psychic structures that are required for specific mechanisms or types of distortions to occur. They point out that various primary process mechanisms tend to predominate at early stages of development and that these early forms of thought provide the groundwork for later stages in the development of thought. For example, "magical thinking," in which thoughts or actions are seen as causing or stopping external events (as in a compulsion), is similar to thinking in the various stages of sensorimotor development. At this level, when a child's movement is followed by an independent event, he often behaves as if his action caused the event. As Holt (1967) notes, when magical thinking comes about through regression in adults, it occurs in a more organized, structured personality setting, so that it obviously differs in important ways from the thinking of the infant. Yet, considerable understanding may be gained by considering various levels of formal primary process thinking from a developmental model.

According to Holt (1967) and Gill (1967), condensation, or fusion, requiring some notion of similarity, can be seen as the developmental groundwork for synthetic functioning, a secondary process activity; and displacement, requiring some awareness of the difference between one mental content and another before investment can be shifted from one to the other, can be viewed as a precursor of differentiation. Condensation, displacement, and symbolization all assume a degree of differentiation, and they can be considered as part of a developmental process, rather than simply as primitive mechanisms or as disruptions of the organization of adult thought. Primary process modes of thought appear to undergo a complex development, just as secondary process thinking does, constantly being modified through experience with the environment in conjunction with evolving cognitive structures. One important aspect in the development from primary process to secondary process thought is the degree of boundary differentiation. Various types of thinking disturbances can be distinguished by the degree to which they require a separation of self from nonself, of action from object, and of object from its mental representation. Holt (1967), for example, suggests that "simple" schizophrenics and those patients and their families whom Wynne and Singer (1963b) describe as amorphous function at a most undifferentiated level. They seem to live in a "mist," similar to patients Searles (1965, p. 311) describes as nondifferentiated—their perception is diffuse and unarticulated and for them events are disconnected, causal relationships are lacking, meanings are blurred, and there is no order or intelligibility. Consistently, Wynne and Singer found that amorphous patients tend to have poor premorbid histories, seeming to indicate failure of developmental progress, rather than loss of previously attained achievements. In contrast, patients with flagrant and blatant thought disorder and a wide range of primary process thinking seem more similar to Wynne and Singer's fragmented group, who are apt to show higher levels of premorbid functioning. The thinking of these fragmented patients seems to show a higher level of developmental attainment than does that of the more amorphous group. Of course, many patients fall between these extremes of vagueness and flagrant thought disorder, and Wynne and Singer refer to a "mixed" group. There seems to be a continuum along the amorphous–fragmented and nondifferentiated–nonintegrated dimensions.

As indicators of thinking disturbances, various types of formal primary process thinking can also be seen as ranging in degree from more to less serious, and within each type more and less serious manifestations can be distinguished. The range of primary process thinking can be viewed as reflecting forms of thought characteristic of earlier and later developmental levels. Although all of the formal manifestations of primary process thinking on the Rorschach show varying degrees of illogic and reality distortion, they can be divided into at least three basic types that have been defined by Rapaport et al. (1946) and further refined by Holt (1963):

1. Arbitrary or unlikely combinations of separate percepts, in which the percepts are placed in an unrealistic relationship because they are contiguous in space or time, as in the fabulized combination;
2. Unrealistic elaborations around at least partially accurate percepts, as in the fabulation or confabulation, reflecting a loss of the distinction between internal experience and external reality;
3. Fusion or partial fusion of percepts given to the same area of the blot, as in the contamination response, reflecting a loss of the boundary between separate images.

Each of these basic groupings can, in turn, be differentiated into more and less serious subtypes involving greater and lesser loss of the distinction between self and external reality, between the external percept or object and its internal mental representation, and between the mental representations of different external objects.

Arbitrary, unlikely, and impossible combinations reflect unrealistic reasoning about the relationship between two percepts simply because the two percepts are contiguous in space or time (Holt & Havel, 1960). An example of an arbitrary combination given to Card III of the Rorschach is: "Two monkeys wearing suits and there are the tails of the suit. They both have crewcuts and large noses—they're standing on top of a woman's torso." The unlikely combination is evident both in the monkeys wearing suits and having crewcuts and in standing on a woman's torso.

Unrealistic elaborations of Rorschach responses range along a continuum from fabulations to confabulations. Fabulations involve relatively mild attribution of internal motivations and feeling states to external perceptions, as in the response: "An Arab with a fiery temper, a red beard, and a drippy nose." Confabulations are more extensive, unrealistic elaborations of responses in terms of internal reactions, such as a response given to Card V: "Rabbit's ears and this rabbit has pouchy cheeks. . . . But this rabbit's probably dead and his spirit's rising up. . . . But there's nowhere to go, so he'll rise until he has no direction, so he'll suffocate to death." Such responses seem to reflect some lack of the capacity to differentiate between internal states and external percepts. Mild fabulations often occur in normal subjects, while confabulations seem to reflect a greater loss of the distinction between what is inside and what is outside the self, between thoughts and reality.

Mild self-references, such as relating percepts to the subject's own experience, can be distinguished from extreme forms of self-reference, which seem to reflect a greater loss of the boundary between self and objects than do arbitrary combinations or confabulations. On Card VIII of the Rorschach, a patient responded: "Reminds me of a wolf, a crazy wolf, not vicious, just loony. I'm not sure whether he's making fun of me or I'm making fun of him. . ." The projective, fabulated qualities of this response are clear when he attributes to the wolf his own fears of being "crazy" and "vicious." But the instability of the projection, resulting in fluidity of the boundary between himself and the wolf, is most apparent in his lack of certainty about whether the wolf is making fun of him or he of the wolf. Rorschach responses like "my family" seem to involve an extreme loss of distinction between objects and their representations and between internal representations and external perceptions.

Holt and Havel (1960) distinguish several types of responses involving image fusion or condensation, where the boundaries between separate images are not maintained and the images fuse. They place "composition" responses in a "borderline category" between arbitrary combination and contamination in terms of degree of boundary loss. An example of a composition is a rabbit with "bat's wings." Comparing compositions with arbitrary combinations, Holt states:

In both types of responses, reality is violated in that they bring together what does not belong together in literal reality. The difference, however, is that when this combination results in something with an organic unity or an unbroken boundary, it is considered a Composition, and when the incongruous elements are merely brought into juxtaposition, it is an Arbitrary Combination. Theoretically, it requires more violation of the integrity or object-constancy of an image to invade its natural boundaries with a foreign element that is grafted on, than merely to bring them into an unusual or even bizarre arrangement, which still respects the identities of the separate images [1963, p. 21].

Contamination responses appear to reflect the most extreme loss of boundaries between representations. In the contamination response, percepts given to the same area of the blot merge or partially merge, so that images or ideas become fused. For example, in the response "batterfly," the percepts of "bat" and "butterfly" are fused. Neologisms also often reflect the fusion of two ideas as in Rapaport's example of "ambisextrous." As already discussed, Holt (1967) suggests that amorphous patients function at an undifferentiated level with vague and diffuse forms of thought. The forms of primary process thinking that require more complex structures appear in more differentiated patients, who may show the whole gamut of flagrant thought disorder. These patients may be functioning at a higher developmental level, with a greater capacity for accurate perception, selective attention, and object constancy. Contamination responses, probably more than most other types of primary process thinking, reflect an extreme loss of boundary differentiation and less stable levels of object representation. Rorschach (1942) stated that contaminations were found only among schizophrenics, and Rapaport et al. (1946) also present findings which indicate that contamination responses are almost exclusively limited to schizophrenic patients. But even for contaminatory thinking to occur, there must be some degree of discrimination among the separate components of experience before they can become fused. The most global, amorphous patients may present percepts that are more vague and less articulated than those occurring in obvious contaminatory thinking, where two clearly distinguishable percepts are mingled with one another. Thus, a 17-year-old, hospitalized, schizophrenic high-school student, showing serious disturbances in perception and ego functions, yet sufficiently organized to function in the Bright Normal range of intelligence, gave the following contaminatory response to Card V of the Rorschach: "Looks like an asexually reproducing squid. What does a squid look like anyway?" When asked what he meant by "asexually reproducing," he replied, "One was going one way, one was going the other way, and they came from the same origin." His response to what made it look like a squid was simply "the ink." The vague, formless quality of his response is obvious, as it is in his response to Card VI, "Visual impressions I get when I listen to music." His difficulty in specifying even the relatively formless percept "squid" is apparent in his remark "What does a squid look like anyway?" as if he were having difficulty checking his percept against a mental image of "squid" with its various characteristics. The contamination occurred in his apparent mingling of the ink on the inkblot with squid, a creature that produces ink. His thinking seems to have proceeded as follows: The blot has ink on it, the squid produces ink, therefore, the blot looks like a squid. It is as if he equated the ink on the blot with the ink-producing squid, losing the differentiation between the blot and the percept "squid." There does not appear to be a loss of boundaries between two independent perceptions or mental representations but a more basic lack of distinction between the percept and its context, the inkblot. This contamination response may be compared with that of the child and boxer, cited earlier, where the percepts were obviously much more complex and articulated and where the struggle was more one of keeping independent mental images separate, rather than of losing the boundaries between the percept and its context.

As previously stated, contamination responses are often considered to occur almost exclusively in schizophrenic patients. Our experience and evidence cited by Weiner (1966); Quinlan, Harrow, Tucker, and Carlson (1972); Quinlan and Harrow, (1974); and others, however, indicate that contaminatory thinking is certainly not found in all patients considered to be schizophrenic, and occasionally it can be found in people not considered to be schizophrenic. For example, Jortner (1966), utilizing the Holtzman Inkblot Technique, compared the performance of 25 schizophrenic inpatients with that of 24 hospitalized nonschizophrenics on nine scales designed to measure cognitive aspects of schizophrenia, including the contamination response. While Jortner found that a significant number of schizophrenic patients gave contamination responses, he also found that three nonschizophrenic subjects also did so. However, it is difficult to compare studies in this area because of the differing definitions of contaminatory responses as well as the lack of a definition of schizophrenia and of specification of the subtypes of patients included in the various studies. There is a great need for studies investigating precisely defined types of primary process thinking in carefully defined groups of patients to obtain further clarification of these issues.

Zucker's (1958) study of "Ego Structure in Paranoid Schizophrenia" is a noteworthy step in this direction. She tested the following hypothesis: "As revealed on projective tests, the hospitalized schizophrenic has more fluid ego boundaries; the ambulatory schizophrenic patient, on the other hand, has more stable ego boundaries making him a better prognostic and therapeutic risk [p. 14]." She compared the performance of 30 male and female paranoid schizophrenics, hospitalized for 5 years or less, with that of 30 outpatients, also diagnosed as paranoid schizophrenic, on various measures of boundary fluidity derived from the Rorschach, Mosaic, and Figure Drawing tests. These included:

1. contaminations;
2. fluid contours, including
   (a) concepts with fluid subject matter, like jellyfish on the Rorschach or broken contours in figure drawings and
   (b) fusion of different cognitive realms;
3. "extension of the ego field into other fields," defined as Rorschach self-references (similar to Holt's definition discussed earlier);
4. disturbed body image and other impairments of ego boundaries on the Mosaic and Figure Drawing tests, as when a patient drew a figure with the brain outside the person.

Zucker's results show that 100% of the hospitalized group had some indications of boundary disturbance, as compared with 33% of the ambulatory group. Only thirteen contamination responses occurred in the entire sample, and they were limited to the hospitalized group. Concepts with fluid subject matter were also restricted to the hospitalized group. The other measures interpreted as indicating boundary disturbances also occurred with significantly greater frequency in the hospitalized group. Zucker concludes that although some boundary fluidity appeared in the ambulatory group, the hospitalized group showed much more severe boundary problems. Furthermore, the ambulatory patients generally demonstrated a more active and turbulent picture with greater anxiety and conflict as well as more arbitrary and autistic thinking. Zucker states: "A performance that shows complex boundary problems in more than one area against a flat and undynamic background is prognostically unfavorable. If the loss of ego boundaries is embedded in a rich and colorful setting, even though of a schizophrenic nature, it seems to be less damaging to the integrity of the ego [p. 92]." Although some questions can be raised about the effects of hospitalization on Zucker's hospitalized group and the lack of matching of the samples on age and education, her results can be interpreted as consistent with the hypothesis that global, undifferentiated schizophrenics with severe boundary problems function at a lower level than do ambulatory schizophrenic patients who have more stable boundaries.

More recently, Blatt and Ritzler (1974) conceptualized types of thought disorder on the Rorschach as reflecting different levels of boundary disturbance and tested whether this conceptual model provided further understanding and discrimination of levels of psychopathology, particularly within the psychotic range. They distinguished the three basic types of formal primary process thinking that have been described previously [p. 56] in terms of degree of boundary disturbance:

1. The boundary between separate percepts is maintained, but the separate percepts are placed in an arbitrary, unrealistic relationship because they are contiguous in space or time, as in the *fabulized combination* (FC) response (e.g., to Card VIII: "Prairie dogs standing on a butterfly").

2. There is a loss of the distinction between internal experience and external reality manifested in extensive unrealistic elaborations around at least partially accurate percepts, as in the *confabulation* (CF) response (e.g., to the lower detail of Card IX: "Looks like twins on the bottom. It looks spiritual or something like the beginning of the world. The division line in the middle is the difference between them, heaven or earth or something").

3. There is a loss of the boundary between separate images or concepts, expressed in a fusion or partial fusion of percepts given to the same area of the blot, as in the *contamination* (CT) response (e.g., to the lower detail of Card X: "Rabbit hand," in which the separate images of rabbit and hand are fused).

Three groups of 10 patients each were selected whose Rorschach protocols manifested one of the three types of thought disorder (contamination, confabulation, and fabulized combination) and none of the other two types of thought disturbance. In addition to the "pure" contamination (CT), confabulation (CF), and fabulized combination (FC) groups, two additional groups of patients were selected whose Rorschach protocols manifested both contamination and confabulation responses (CT–CF) or both confabulation and fabulized combination responses (CF–FC). Thus, 50 patients were selected, 10 in each of 5 thought–disordered groups (CT, CT–CF, CF, CF–FC, and FC). In addition, a sixth group of patients was selected whose Rorschach protocols manifested at least one response indicating ideational, integrative efforts (combination responses) that were comparable to the integrative efforts of the five thought-disordered groups, but the Rorschach protocols showed none of the types of thought disorder represented in the other groups. The relationships between the levels of thought disorder and other aspects of the clinical record were investigated.

In selecting patients for the various groups, Blatt and Ritzler found that the types of thought disorder at the extreme ends of the continuum (CT and FC) rarely co-occurred in the same Rorschach record. Patients usually exhibited only one type of thought disorder; if there was more than one type of thought disorder, such types occurred in clusters of either CT–CF or CF–FC. Occasionally, a protocol showed all three types of thought disturbance (CT, CF, and FC), but it was most unusual for a record to show responses from only the two extreme ends of the continuum of boundary articulation (CT and FC). The lack of co-occurrence of CT and FC responses without the presence of CF responses was interpreted as offering some support for the validity of a thought disorder continuum based on degrees of disruption of boundary articulation. Further support for types of thought disorder indicating degrees of disruption of boundaries was also suggested by an analysis of the primary diagnostic formulation in the patient's clinical record; patients with more disrupted boundary articulation (CT and CF) were usually considered to be psychotic, while patients with somewhat better boundary articulation (FC and Comb) were generally considered to be in the neurotic or character disorder range.

There were no significant relationships between types of thought disorder and age, educational level, or the various measures of cognitive efficiency assessed on the Babcock test. There were, however, highly significant differences between the six groups on many of the subtests of the Wechsler Intelligence test, on many variables derived from the Object Sorting test and the Rorschach, and on clinical reports obtained from nurses and from hospital records. On the Object Sorting test, patients with more serious types of thought disorder had significantly greater disruption in concept formation. Their sorts and verbalizations were less adequate, less conceptual, and more likely to be characterized as idiosyncratic and disturbed. The range of conceptual span was significantly more narrow (underinclusive) in the patients with less intact and less stable boundary articulation (CT and CF). Excluding the extreme group (CT), there was a significant positive relationship between severity of boundary disturbance and looseness of conceptual span (overinclusiveness). The CT group was primarily comprised of chronic patients who may have lacked the vitality to become involved in a concept formation task. Their excessive narrowness without accompanying looseness supports Payne's observations (1961, 1966) that chronic patients are unlikely to have overinclusive thinking; rather, overinclusive thinking is comparatively more likely to occur in acute patients with confabulatory types of thought disorder.

Comparison of the six groups on aspects of the Rorschach protocols not previously considered shows that patients with types of thought disorder that indicate less intact boundary articulation think in less appropriate and realistic ways and have less cognitive and affective control. However, these Rorschach findings may be confounded to some extent, since the criteria for evaluating boundary disturbances were also based on Rorschach responses.

An analysis of nurses' reports showed that nurses tended to comment relatively more often on aspects of the interpersonal involvement of those patients with more intact boundaries. The incidence of disruptive behavior (reports of aggressive and sexual behavior and of use of alcohol and drugs) was also significantly greater among them, a finding consistent with observations that aggression is one form of maintaining boundary differentiation (Jacobson, 1964; Roth & Blatt, 1961) and with formulations (Bettelheim, 1967; Mahler, 1968) that locomotion, action, and negativism can be ways of achieving individuation and separation. A review of the discharge summaries indicated that, while patients with less articulated boundaries had only a 50–50 chance of being considered improved at discharge, patients with more articulated boundaries (FC and Comb) were almost invariably discharged as improved.

The tendency toward relatively greater interpersonal involvement of the patients with types of thought disorder that indicate more intact boundary differentiation is consistent with findings obtained from a detailed examination of the human responses on the Rorschach. Patients with less intact boundary differentiation had significantly more disrupted representations of human figures on the Rorschach. In addition, they gave a significantly greater number of Rorschach responses that were human–inanimate blends. This finding offers some support for the hypothesis (Mahler, 1968; Rosenfeld & Sprince, 1963, 1965; Searles, 1960, 1965; Thomas, 1966) that failure in basic individuation and separation is accompanied by difficulty in maintaining the distinction between human, animate, and inanimate realms. Werner (1948) also discussed human–animal and human–inanimate blends in psychotic imagery, and he considered them to be condensations of multiple meaning in a single object, or composite gestalts of various characteristics derived from different objects.

The findings of Blatt and Ritzler that the relative degree of disturbance in the ability to establish and represent boundaries relates to the degree of disruption in psychosis is given further support by the recent findings of Brenneis (1971), who applied the conceptualization of types of thought disorder based on the degree of boundary articulation to the study of the manifest content of the dreams of 50 male psychiatric inpatients, 25 of whom were considered to be schizophrenic. Clinical judgment and analysis of numerous dimensions of these dreams, such as the "relative accessibility of primitive content and blatant failures of defense," were relatively unsuccessful in differentiating the dreams of schizophrenic from those of nonschizophrenic patients. However, an analysis based on thought disorder distinctions significantly differentiated ($p < .001$) the dreams of schizophrenic from those of nonschizophrenic patients. Schizophrenics had significantly more expressions of all three types of boundary disturbance in the manifest content of their dreams (fabulized combinations, confabulations, and contaminations), but the difference between the two groups of patients was most significant in relation to contaminations. While contaminations occurred infrequently in the manifest content of dreams, when they did

occur, they were almost invariably in the dreams of a patient considered to
be schizophrenic.

The findings of Blatt and Ritzler (1974) and Brenneis (1971) indicate that
the conceptualization of degrees of impairment of boundary articulation
has important implications for understanding levels of psychosis. The research and clinical data suggest that these various levels of boundary articulation, as measured by types of thought disorder, are related to the relative
intactness of a variety of ego functions, to the capacity for reality testing, to
the quality of object relations, and to the nature of object representations.
Poorly articulated boundaries occur primarily in more disturbed, chronic
patients who have poor or impoverished object relationships, impaired ego
functions, and a lifelong history of estrangement, isolation, and generally
poor adjustment. Thought disorder involving more adequately articulated
boundary distinctions occurs primarily in patients with more acute psychological disorders. Patients with greater boundary articulation seem to be
more actively involved in interpersonal relationships, but these interactions
are often characterized by intensity, hostility, and acting out. These patients
seem to be more acute, more fragmented, and more responsive to therapy.

In a series of studies, L. H. Silverman (1970) attempted to test the relationships between interpersonal experiences of merging and amount of pathological thought. He found that a less intense merging stimulus
(presented subliminally) reduced pathological thinking in more differentiated schizophrenic patients, while a more intense merging stimulus increased
pathological thinking in less differentiated patients. Silverman concluded
that schizophrenic patients need to maintain a partial fusion with the mother, but that intense experiences of merging are disruptive to less differentiated patients. Silverman speculated that thought disorder may be a
manifestation of as well as a defense against merging. While questions can
be raised about Silverman's measure of degree of differentiation (by means
of the degree of difference between the subject's checklist descriptions of
his mother and himself) and his assumption that the subliminal stimuli
provoked experiences of merging, his findings support the hypothesis of
a relationship between thought disorder and experiences of merging. Subsequent research should be directed toward establishing criteria and measures
for levels of interpersonal merging and fusion, so that the relationships
between levels of merging in the cognitive, perceptual, and interpersonal
realms can be studied.

Summary

In this chapter on cognitive and perceptual processes we have seen how
the various disturbances in schizophrenia can be considered, at least in

part, as expressions of the impairment of early developmental processes and specifically as impairment of the capacity to experience, perceive, and represent boundaries. As suggested by psychoanalytic theory (e.g., Mahler, 1968; Jacobson, 1964), cognitive developmental psychology (e.g., Piaget & Werner), and developmental research (Kagan, 1971), boundary differentiation is one of the most fundamental steps in development. We have examined the role of boundary differentiation in the development of self–object differentiation and in the development of a number of ego functions. We conceptualized the capacity to articulate boundaries as a developmental continuum that ranges from differentiation among perceptions and experiences (including the distinction of self–nonself), to the capacity to distinguish between an external event and an internal experience, to the capacity for developing mental representations and verbal signifiers for objects and for maintaining distinctions between the actual objects and their various representations and signifiers. In reviewing the theoretical, clinical, and research literature on different aspects of schizophrenia, such as reality testing, attention, concept formation, language, and thinking and thought disorder, we considered how disturbances of these various functions in schizophrenia could be understood as expressions of an impairment in the capacity to articulate and maintain boundaries between objects or between objects and their mental representations and verbal signifiers.

Early developmental disturbances in experiencing, perceiving, and representing boundaries may be expressed in and influence many functions at later developmental stages. The multifaceted cognitive and perceptual dysfunctions in schizophrenia can be viewed as expressions of difficulty in maintaining boundaries between independent events, between self and others, and between inside and outside. Inadequate boundaries interfere with reality testing; hallucinations and delusions are dramatic illustrations of this impairment of the boundary distinction between self and others and between inside and outside. Difficulties in boundary articulation are also expressed in perceptual processes. Chronic and undifferentiated schizophrenic patients have difficulty in articulating figure from ground, they have a greater tendency toward perceptual fusion, and they have difficulty maintaining perceptual constancy; global and undifferentiated perception reflects the difficulty of this type of patient in establishing and maintaining boundaries. Paranoid and acute schizophrenic patients, on the other hand, appear to have greater than normal field articulation, less tendency toward perceptual fusion, and overconstancy, in which they overestimate the size of objects.

There are consistent reports that schizophrenic patients also have difficulty in maintaining attention. While schizophrenic patients are aware of appropriate cues, they often have difficulty keeping them in focus. Well articulated and stable perceptions are necessary to distinguish more from less relevant dimensions of an object or a situation. Without stable perceptions and stable object representations, there can be intrusions of irrelevant stimuli from the environment and from personal preoccupations. Lack of stable representations not only results in diffuse and global attention, distractibility, and loose associations; it also interferes with concept formation and symbolic thought. Concept formation requires the capacity to evaluate the salient characteristics of an object and the capacity to maintain a constant representation of an object so that it can be compared with other objects in order to identify similarities and differences. Without such stable representations, concept formation becomes disordered and there is interpenetration of ideas and themes. However, paranoid and acute patients, in contrast to more chronic and amorphous patients, and even normals, often have highly focused attention and excessively rigid and articulated concepts.

Language disturbances in schizophrenia also can be seen as reflecting an inability to maintain boundary distinctions between objects, between objects and actions toward the objects, and between objects and their symbolic referents. The language of schizophrenics suggests a loss of these differentiations; words in schizophrenic speech often do not refer to stable objects and specific actions, but to "fusions of affective–impulsive–sensory–motor–perceptual impressions." Words often lack stability, and, as with attention and concept formation, this instability permits the intrusion of idiosyncratic themes and the sudden alteration, merging, and transformation of themes. The relative impairment of object articulation in schizophrenia is indicated by the finding that chronic schizophrenic patients have significantly less specification in their speech than do normals. With this relatively poor object articulation, objects are more often defined by limited and direct perceptual features or by the drive or action contexts in which they occur rather than by any intrinsic property, quality, or concept (Blatt, 1974).

Types of thought disorder on the Rorschach can also be evaluated in terms of the degree to which boundaries are maintained between independent percepts and between internal experience and external perception. Arbitrary relationships between independent percepts (fabulized combinations) and unrealistic elaboration (drive-infused confabulations) in which there is a loss of the distinction between inside and outside have a greater degree of boundary differentiation than thinking in which there is a loss of differentiation between self and external percept (as in self-references and contaminatory thinking), where there is a loss of the boundary between percepts. Research findings indicate that thought-disordered patients with relatively greater impairment of boundary articulation (as demonstrated by contaminatory responses) are considered to be relatively more seriously disturbed. They have greater cognitive impairment, are less able to establish meaningful interpersonal relations, and have a less favorable outcome in psychotherapy.

Many of the recent attempts to distinguish between types of schizophrenic patients (e.g., process–reactive, nonparanoid–paranoid, chronic–acute, amorphous–fragmented, nondifferentiated–nonintegrated) have explicitly or implicitly included the capacity for boundary articulation as one of the criteria for differentiating levels of schizophrenia. Patients in the process, nonparanoid, chronic, amorphous, and nondifferentiated subgroups seem to have less capacity for boundary articulation than do the other subgroups. They often have difficulty in distinguishing figure from ground and relevant from irrelevant stimuli; and their concept formation and language are characterized by an interpenetration of themes. Objects are often perceived and represented as merged and fused. Paranoid or fragmented patients, on the other hand, seem to be struggling actively to maintain boundary differentiations. These patients frequently have a heightened capacity for articulating figure from ground, excessive cognitive control, and an exaggerated capacity for focused attention. The exaggerated cognitive control, heightened perceptual articulation, and hyperalertness of paranoid patients, as well as their guardedness, suspiciousness, and interpersonal distance, may serve partly to maintain boundary differentiations and to ward off feelings of merging, dissolution, and annihilation.

The recent differentiation of subtypes of schizophrenic patients has contributed extensively to research in schizophrenia. Formulation of the early development of the concept of the object and of the capacity for boundary differentiation may also provide a way of evaluating the level and extent of the schizophrenic disturbance and how it can be differentiated from other types of psychosis. Consideration of the impairment of the early development of the concept of the object may contribute to a fuller understanding of various types of psychopathology through the integration of observations and concepts of psychopathology with the formulations and findings of normal developmental processes.

In our review of cognitive–perceptual processes in schizophrenia, we have considered a number of functions separately, but our review suggests that disturbances in these various functions are interrelated and can be understood, in part, as expressions of basic and early problems in the development of the concept of the object and object constancy. In subsequent research on psychosis, it may not be sufficient to specify disturbances in a variety of separate functions; rather, it seems necessary to study the interrelationships among disturbances in a wide range of functions in various types of psychopathology. Equally important, it is necessary to understand how these functions evolve during normal development and how various types of disruptions occur and are organized in the various distorted modes of adaptation we define as types of psychopathology.

3 / Sense of Self and Interpersonal Relationships

Introduction

In Chapter 2, we have attempted to show how normal cognitive development can be seen as involving an ever-increasing series of boundary distinctions between inside and outside, between self and nonself, and between inanimate, animate, and human objects. These most elementary distinctions are followed by the attainment of the object concept and the capacity to differentiate objects from their representations, as well as the representations from one another, leading to the development of symbolic thought. Our major goal has been to point out how further conceptual clarity can result from viewing the greater and lesser degrees of cognitive disturbance found in the various subgroups of schizophrenics as similar in some ways to developmentally earlier levels of functioning, before such boundary distinctions are firmly established. The parallel and interrelated development of cognitive and interpersonal capacities has been stressed, as has the importance of the child's interaction with the human environment in fostering or hindering such development.

While such a point of view assumes that it is artificial to separate development of sense of self and capacity for interpersonal relationships from cognitive development, in this chapter we shall be concerned primarily with the former issues. In the following sections, we shall examine the hypothesis that schizophrenic disturbances in sense of self and human object relationships can also be seen in part as manifestations of a difficulty in establishing and maintaining clear-cut distinctions between self and others, related to early developmental problems with attainment of the object concept. Throughout, we have stressed the interdependence of cognitive and interpersonal development; and a capacity for stable representation of self and others seems to depend on attainment of the object concept. The ever-increasing development of the sense of self as an independent entity and the experience of other people as existing apart from the self seem even more interdependent, for as Schafer (1968) points out, the self is initially defined in relationship to important human objects, and other human objects are defined in relation to the self.

Sense of Self

In *Aspects of Internalization,* Schafer (1968) discusses the ambiguities associated with the use of the term "self" in the psychoanalytic literature:

> Sometimes, self seems to refer to the aggregate of the more general or schematic self representations; sometimes, it seems to refer to an assumed (but never empirically demonstrated) synthesis or internal consistency of all self representations; sometimes, self refers to the sense of personal continuity or 'identity'; and sometimes, it seems to be synonymous with organism, personality, something unspecified that lies behind all subjective experience, or another regulatory system that is superordinate, coordinate, or subordinate to id, ego, and superego [p. 27].

There is the self as it appears to an objective observer, as well as the experienced, or subjective, self. Here, we shall be concerned primarily with aspects of the latter, particularly the sense of sameness and continuity over time (constancy of the self), which seems to depend on a capacity for stable representations of the self, as well as of other human objects (human object constancy).

In addition to a stable set of more or less integrated self representations (constancy), self-awareness, or what Federn (1952) calls "ego feeling" or "self-experience," is another crucial aspect of the subjective self. According to Federn, phenomenologically, the ego

> includes the subjective psychic experience of [its] functions with a characteristic sensation. This self-experience is a permanent, though never equal, entity, which is not an abstraction but a reality. It is an entity which stands in relation to the continuity of the person in respect to time, space, and causality. It can be recognized objectively and is constantly felt and perceived subjectively. We possess, in other words, an enduring feeling and knowledge that our ego is continuous and persistent, despite interruptions by sleep or unconsciousness, because we feel that processes within us, even though they may be interrupted by forgetting or unconsciousness, have a persistent origin within us, and that our body and psyche belong permanently to our ego [1952, p. 61].

Schafer (1968) discusses the subject's perception of his own mentation as "reflective self representation." This term "refers to the implicit or explicit notation accompanying realistic thought that it is thought (e.g., memory, perception, anticipation, etc.) and not concrete reality [1968, p. 109]." Without such reflective self representations (e.g., "I think," "I know"), thoughts are experienced as concrete realities, so that for example, a memory is experienced as a present occurrence, as happens with some schizophrenics. Thus, reflective self representation is a crucial component of reality testing, in terms of taking distance from one's own thinking and distinguishing thoughts from reality.

Viewed in somewhat schematic and oversimplified fashion, self and object constancy, self-awareness, and empathy all seem to require fundamental boundary distinctions between self and other, as well as the attainment of the object concept, a prerequisite for the establishment of stable and consistent mental representations of self and others. Furthermore, self-awareness and empathy appear to depend on later developmental steps, involving capacities to distinguish between the self and representations of the self and to go beyond an egocentric stance and see one's own subjective point of view as only one among many possibilities.

As many authors (Bettelheim, 1967; Jacobson, 1964; Mahler, 1968) have pointed out, a mature sense of self with constancy and a capacity for self-observation and empathy depends on a long series of developmental achievements. Schizophrenic difficulties in establishing and maintaining a stable sense of self, self-awareness, and empathy can be seen ranging on a continuum from greater to lesser manifestations of boundary problems in distinguishing inside from outside, self from nonself, the representation from the actual object, representations of self from representations of others, and the signifier from the object (e.g., "I" from its referent).

Constancy of the self

Object constancy is required for a sense of self as having continuity through time and a past and a future. It is also required for a sense of other human beings and nonhuman animate and inanimate objects as having independent, permanent identities when they are not immediately present in the sensory field. If there is no differentiated, stable concept of the self or of significant others (as in the very young child before the concept of the object has been attained) when people are not immediately present to the senses, they cease to exist.

Bettelheim (1967) notes many parallels between his observations of the behavior and experiences of autistic children and Piaget's delineation of the six stages of sensorimotor development. He stresses the importance of interaction with significant figures, particularly the mother, in fostering or hindering maturational progress from one stage to the next, including the evolution of the sense of self. "For it is the emotional experience, we surmise, that in the normal infant supports the intellectual development Piaget investigated so admirably (p. 445)." He emphasizes how the child's self-initiated, spontaneous activity and experience of mutual give and take can be encouraged or hampered by the external response.[1] The frustration of needs, followed by their alleviation, is one of the first experiences leading to a differentiation of boundaries between self and outside (Jacobson, 1964; Mahler, 1968). Thus, as discussed in Chapter 2, it is postulated that sequences of frustration–gratification, depending on the relief of needs by an outside agent, lead to a sense of anticipation, continuity, and the development of a sense of time. The repeated reappearance of the disappearing mother can be seen as contributing to the development of human object constancy and individuation of the self. Such predictability of gratification is seen as helping the infant to discriminate his own internal experience into pleasurable and unpleasurable at the simplest level, and then to a recognition that his own reactions to various internal needs are met by different environmental responses. Thus, various experiences of discomfort such as hunger, if they call forth environmental action suitable to relieve the need, help the child to differentiate between types of discomfort and the different signals necessary to indicate various kinds of distress. Furthermore, as Schafer (1968, p. 76) points out, once an image of the absent object begins to be established, the repeated appearance of the object provides the infant with experience enabling him to distinguish the actual object from its image. This capacity for differentiating the mental image from the actual object is a crucial step in the development of reality testing and concept formation.

The distorted sense of self of schizophrenics is often expressed in bodily experiences. As discussed in Chapter 2, there have been numerous observations of a fragmented and distorted sense of body and a preoccupation with body parts in schizophrenics (Arieti, 1961; Bruch, 1962; Des Lauriers, 1962). The schizophrenic's inability to identify internal sensations (and bodily urges) and to differentiate them from external stimulation (Bruch, 1962; Schafer, 1960) interferes with the development of an awareness of the self. The absence of consistent pleasure–pain sequences in the mother–child relationship can contribute to an impairment in the awareness of bodily sensations (Bruch, 1962), an inability to differentiate the mother as an object separate from the self, and experiences of being helpless and externally controlled and of not being active and effective.

We have seen how, in Piaget's view, a grasp of the permanent existence of external objects distinct from the self followed by a capacity for their stable internal representations seems to be required for the occurrence of thinking and of concept formation. Likewise, the object concept is a prerequisite for the development of a distinct sense of self with permanence and continuity despite external change. Without the object concept, there can be no sense of stability or separation of the self from other people and the environmental context. Such was the case with one of Searles' nondifferentiated patients who "felt herself to be coterminous with the bed in which she lay [1965, p. 312]," or the 6-year-old psychotic boy, Stanley, described by Mahler and Elkisch (1953) who at times "seemed to be a quasi-part of the environment, a 'particle' of the surroundings, in a state of cohesion with it and undifferentiated from it [p. 255]."

Mahler and Elkisch point out how this child, with both symbiotic and autistic characteristics, was fused with and undifferentiated from his mother, so that, for example, he confused himself, his mother, and the picture of a crying baby in a book. Cognitively, Stanley lacked the capacity for selective perception and recall and his ability to abstract was faulty, apparently because of a lack of clear differentiation between the actual object and its representation; he had no sense of the causal connection between events, and he could not differentiate past from present or perception from a diffuse affective and motoric response. At times, Stanley appeared to have some sense of object constancy (recognition) in that similar verbal or pictorial stimuli would elicit the same diffuse response. However, when he appeared "cohesive with his environment," he seemed totally unable to differentiate inside from outside, and there was a complete loss of the constancy of self and of external objects. Consistent with Bettelheim's (1967) stress on the infant's experience of his own activity as a crucial initial aspect of self-differentiation and with Piaget's view that sensorimotor achievements leading to the object concept are linked with actions relating to external objects, Mahler and Elkisch see Stanley as seeking a sense of himself in action in order to avoid an experience of extinction.

> According to our observation, it was in this state of semi-stupor that he would, all of a sudden, touch the arm of the mother substitute and with this excitation, at first slight, the child would "switch himself on," as it seemed, into an intense and diffuse affective state. . . . It seemed as though the patient *very deliberately* sought such a sweeping excitation, via the trigger stimulus, as if to defend himself against his apathetic state, as if to ward off the danger of symbiotic fusion through which his entity and identity would become dissolved in the matrix of the environment. It appeared as if the child had switched himself into excited crying or catatonic-like motor paroxysms as well, to gain momentum, as it were, like an engine, to counteract symbiotic dissolution of the boundaries of his "self" [1953, p. 255].

While Stanley's excited behavior can be interpreted in other ways, he seems to show parallel boundary disturbances in cognitive functioning, sense of self, and self–other discrimination.

Self–awareness

Self-awareness, or what Federn calls the "unique paradox" of the ego which is "subject and object in one [1952, p. 216]," and what Schafer (1968) refers to as "reflective self representation," appears to require the concept of the self as object, as well as a later capacity for symbolic representation of the self. Thus, a capacity for self representation seems necessary for taking distance from and contemplating the self as distinct from its immediate activities and experiences, and for maintaining the concept of self as distinct not only from concepts of other people but also from inanimate objects. It can be postulated that the sense of self develops in stages similar to those involved in cognitive development. The earliest sense of self can be seen as involving self–other discrimination, or a capacity to distinguish the self from other human or inanimate objects when they are physically present. Only after the attainment of the object concept, with the concomitant capacity for representational thought, is a stable sense of self, with continuity in past and future, possible. Rather than being defined only in terms of separation from the momentary environmental context, self is experienced, then, as having a permanent existence apart from environmental changes and fluctuations and internal states of frustration; and needs are not experienced in such all-or-none fashion, since continuity no longer depends on immediate gratification. The simultaneous development of permanent representations of other human objects, along with the capacity to differentiate representations of self from those of others, also tends to free the young child from the immediate environmental context. A capacity for self-observation and a sense of "I" and "me" seems to require the further cognitive capability of distinguishing the signifier from significate, or symbolic thought, since it seems to call for a differentiation between the mental image of the self and the verbal signifier used for it. Thus, mature use of the terms "I" and "me" seems to involve a capacity for distinguishing the mental image of the self from the symbolic label of the self.

Piaget considers imitation, where accommodation to the external environment is more important than assimilation to pre-existing schemata, to be an important step in the development of the symbolic function. According to Flavell:

> Now the central point of Piaget's argument is that accommodation-as-imitation is the function which supplies the infant with his first signifiers, signifiers capable of internally representing for him the absent significate. What happens, he believes, is that with the growth and refinement of the capacity to imitate the child is eventually able to make internal imitations as well as external, visible ones. He is able to evoke in thought, as opposed to actually carrying out in reality, imitations made in the past. This internal imitation takes the form of an image, broadly defined, and this image constitutes the first signifier (the significate being here the action, object, or word of which the image is a reduced and schematic replicate). . . . Once the capacity to evoke image-signifiers is established, the child can of course use them as anticipative outlines of future actions [1963, pp. 152–153].

Interaction with the environment, particularly the human environment, is crucial for this stage of imitation, which begins to emerge as a pattern that can be clearly identified in stage six of sensorimotor development (18–24 months). The object concept is required for the child to imitate an absent model, followed by a capacity to represent actions and make "internal imitations" of his own actions and those of external human, animate, or inanimate objects. These capabilities lay the groundwork for testing out and experimenting with action internally before trying it in reality, the precursor of the ability to plan and foresee the consequences of action.

Some of the examples of schizophrenic behavior which follow (Chapter 4) suggest that at times some patients function at levels similar in some ways to phases of normal development, before capacities for stable self representations (constancy), reflective self-awareness (viewing the self representations as objects), and symbolic representations of the self ("I" and "me") have been established. It should be stressed that everyone functions at different levels of self-awareness, depending on the internal and external situation. For example, as Schafer (1968) points out, normal daydreaming involves the temporary and intermittent suspension of self representation, for momentarily the daydream can be experienced as concrete reality. While different subtypes of schizophrenics vary in their overall level of functioning, and many show a wide range in levels of self-awareness (fluctuating quickly from higher to lower levels), their capacity for self-awareness is, in general, tenuous and precarious. They are susceptible to involuntary lapses and losses, when they are unable to take distance from and observe themselves.

The imitative behavior of some schizophrenic patients, such as echolalia, is well known, as are more subtle manifestations. For example, gestures or habits of the therapist of which he may not be aware become strikingly apparent to him when they are reproduced by a schizophrenic patient in what seems like an exaggerated or caricatured fashion. This type of behavior would seem to represent imitation of external, visible objects, not internal imitations modeled after representations of the absent object. The shifting, fluid identity of some schizophrenics, who seem to take on the characteristics of the person they are with and imitate his traits or what they perceive to be that person's view of them, can also be seen as reflecting a lack of any consistent sense of separate identity. Such imitative behavior appears to require some degree of object constancy in terms of maintaining the consistency of the imitated model, particularly if the model is absent. However, it also seems to involve lack of consistent self representations as differentiated from representations of other people, and lack of a sufficient distinction between actions of the self and the representations of those actions—as if they could not be tried out in thought and judged as consistent or inconsistent with a view of the self before being directly imitated.

Freeman et al. (1966) present an interview with a 36-year-old schizo-

phrenic woman hospitalized for 14 years, who shows severe parallel disturbances in cognitive functioning and interpersonal relationships. Serious
cognitive impairments of attention, speech, thinking, and perceptual discrimination were accompanied by an inability to discriminate herself from
other people in the past and present or to maintain stable representations of
herself or other people, as her use of pronouns shows. In a portion of the
interview, this woman said:

> "I am going to bash you to pulp say. . . That girl doesn't like you say. . . Get them
> off the chairs father please. . . Can she go out father please?. . . She's a bad girl say
> . . . Nan Gordon say. . . She would hit you say. . . Livid say. . . (She continued
> walking up and down). . . (She talked about someone named Blanche in a way
> impossible to follow). . . I don't like this office say. . . (she went to go out). I once
> hit you for playing at offices. . . Your mother say. . . Get out of this say. . . The
> child say. . . She's always been running away say. . . She's a naughty miss say. . .
> Smith was a pain in the bloody arse say. Your mother say. . . shall we go today say?
> . . . Away home say." She was silent for quite a time and remained sitting on the
> chair. At this point she slapped herself on the head. *Patient:* "I hit you for that say
> . . . I hit you just now say. . . You were needing hit say. . . I had to hit her. She's
> a bad girl say" [p. 91].

While she starts out referring to herself as "I", saying, "I am going to bash
you to pulp," she quickly begins referring to herself in the third person,
"She's a bad girl," and her confusion between herself, her mother, the interviewer, and her father are apparent. Some of her phrases in the third person
seem like echoes of what she perceives to be her mother's statements toward
her, as when she says, "She's a naughty miss." Then, when she slaps herself,
she seems to confuse herself with her mother completely; her anger at her
mother is indistinguishable from her mother's anger at her, so that hitting
herself is equivalent to hitting her mother. Her pacing, followed by sitting
and then slapping herself, can also be seen as attempts to preserve some
sense of separation from the interviewer through activity, similar to 6-year-
old Stanley. The fluctuations in her capacity for self-observation are also
striking.

Empathy

The most fundamental sense of self as having continuity and stability
over a period of time seems to require a boundary between inside and
outside, between self and nonself. Furthermore, the much more advanced
capacity for self-awareness seems to depend on a boundary distinction between the self and representations of the self. A consistent and accurate use
of pronouns appears to require an ability for symbolic thought, with separation between signifier and significate. According to Piaget, the even more
mature ability to view one's own thought processes as objects of thought

occurs only after the preoperational subperiod; the preoperational child's egocentrism and tendency to center on only one striking feature of an object result in his inability to take the role of another or to see his own point of view as only one among many possible points of view. In Flavell's words:

> One of Piaget's firmest beliefs, repeated over and over in scores of publications . . . is that thought becomes aware of itself, able to justify itself, and in general able to adhere to logical–social norms of noncontradiction, coherence, etc., and that all these things and more can emerge only from repeated interpersonal interactions (and especially those involving arguments and disagreements) in which the child is actually forced again and again to take cognizance of the role of the other. It is social interaction which gives the ultimate *coup de grace* to childish egocentrism [1963, pp. 156–157].

Like self-awareness, a capacity for empathy seems to depend on all the preceding developmental achievements. The previously quoted 36-year-old female patient was obviously unable to maintain a separate sense of self while taking another person's point of view. She shifted fluidly from being her mother to being herself.

Schafer (1959) discusses "generative empathy," occurring in the context of a high level of adult psychic organization, in the therapist's or analyst's response to his patient. He states that both cognitive and affective aspects are equally important in the empathic process, which involves regulated regression, including increased permeability of ego boundaries. The mechanisms of empathy include building up an internal image of the patient's world:

> The building up of this image of the patient is based on a series of partial introjections, emotional reactions, and revival of memories concerning oneself and the object; this is followed by (or alternates with) re-externalizations or projections onto the patient and by reality testing to check the validity of the image thus far developed. The hypercathected internal image is thereby increasingly enriched, focused, hierarchically organized, and stabilized. It becomes a substructure within the analyst's ego, which means it does not need to be re-created anew on each occasion of stimulation but remains steadily available. It may be said, therefore, that an identification with the patient gradually takes place. Optimally, however, this identification remains segregated within the ego as an object of actual or potential contemplation. It does not to any great extent unconsciously merge into the analyst's own ego and superego [1959, p. 357].

In generative empathy, the empathizer's ego boundaries emerge intact and the patient's separateness and individuality are recognized and protected. Generative empathy "is unlike the actor's narcissistic appropriation of the characteristics of others; it is also unlike the schizophrenic's confusion as to where he leaves off and the other person begins [p. 353]."

Interpersonal Relationships

In this section on interpersonal relationships in schizophrenia, we shall endeavor to show how schizophrenic problems with human relationships can also be seen as manifestations of degrees of difficulty in maintaining boundary distinctions between self and other people, among other people, and between representations of self and representations of others. Thus, the fused and symbiotic forms of relationships that numerous writers (e.g., Hill, 1955; Lidz & Lidz, 1952; Mahler, 1968; Reichard & Tillman, 1950; Searles, 1965) have described as characteristic of schizophrenics may be viewed as reflecting a relative lack of self–other differentiation, comparable in some ways to developmentally earlier types of relatedness before constancy of inanimate objects, the self, or other people has been firmly established.

Here, we shall be concerned primarily with five major topics. The first is a brief presentation of the relationship between Piaget's description of the normal development of inanimate object permanence and psychoanalytic formulations of the normal and atypical development of human object ties—a subject that has been thoroughly discussed by several authors (e.g., Ainsworth, 1967; Décarie, 1965). This first topic begins with the review of a study by Bell (1968) that provides some empirical evidence of a parallel normal development of inanimate and human object permanence, or constancy. Then, briefly presented, are psychoanalytically oriented views of normal and abnormal development which suggest that schizophrenic disturbances with interpersonal relationships can be seen as being at least in part manifestations of earlier and later developmental difficulties with self–other boundary discriminations. The second topic deals with various aspects of schizophrenics' apparent difficulties in maintaining boundaries between themselves and other people, and it includes an attempt to spell out the manifestations of such fusion and symbiosis. We try to convey the experience of the persons involved in a symbiotic relationship, particularly the dilemma around intimacy, called the "need–fear dilemma" by Burnham, Gladstone, and Gibson (1969), where both closeness and separation result in devastating experiences of dissolution and annihilation of the self, as well as of the symbiotic partner. Some ideas about how differing degrees of disturbance in human relationships appear to coincide with different levels of cognitive difficulty in the various subgroups of schizophrenia are also presented at this point, especially the view that paranoid schizophrenia can be seen as a defensive effort to defend the self against dissolution and boundary loss. The third topic deals with specific interpersonal behaviors of some schizophrenics—flight reactions, assaultiveness toward significant figures, homosexuality in men and promiscuity in women—to see whether further understanding results from viewing them as reflecting in part attempts to compensate for serious boundary problems.

In contrast to the first three topics, which are discussed primarily from the point of view of the individual patient, topics four and five deal with the total family constellation of schizophrenics. Thus, topic four concerns blurring of generation boundaries (Lidz et al., 1965) in families of schizophrenics, in which there is a loss of distinction between who is the parent and who the child. This seems to reflect problems with differentiation in both the schizophrenic offspring and his parents. Finally, some theoretical formulations, clinical observations, and findings from family studies are presented, further suggesting that parental lack of differentiation may be relevant to both the etiology and maintenance of the schizophrenic's inability to discriminate himself from his parents, and his tendency to merge and fuse with them.

The relationship between person and object permanence

In his introduction to Décarie's *Intelligence and Affectivity in Early Childhood,* Piaget writes: "The affective dynamics and cognitive structuring represent two inseparable aspects of all behavior regardless of whether relationships to people or to things are involved [1965, p. xiii]." Thus, Piaget has been primarily concerned with describing the development of the inanimate object concept, or object permanence. More psychoanalytically oriented theorists (e.g., Jacobson, 1964; Mahler, 1968) have been interested in the development of human object relationships, or person permanence, and how emotional experience supports intellectual development. But Piaget also recognizes the parallel development of object and person permanence. Recently, Bettelheim (1967) has discussed the relationship between the development of object and person permanence in regard to infantile autism, and Décarie (1965) has made a comprehensive comparison of Piaget's delineation of the phases of development of the concept of the inanimate object with psychoanalytic views of the stages of development of interpersonal object relationships. A significant developmental study by Bell (1968, 1970) on "The Relationship of Infant-Mother Attachment to the Development of the Concept of Object-Permanence" (both inanimate and human) will be reviewed in some detail, since it provides empirical evidence in support of the hypothesis that person and object permanence develop in parallel fashion.

Bell (1968) and others postulate that the mounting body of evidence supporting the conclusion that "the beginnings of object-permanence occur in the third quarter of the first year, at the same time that specific attachments emerge, suggests that the fundamental change in cognitive structures implicit in the search for hidden objects makes attachments possible [p. 4]." Attachments to human objects cannot be formed before there is some sense of a distinction between self and other and of constancy of both self and other. According to Bell, Piaget suggested that the concept of persons as permanent objects develops in parallel fashion with inanimate object constancy, but in advance of the latter because the mother is usually the most interesting and important "object" in the infant's environment. Bell's (1968, 1970) empirical results suggest that mother permanence develops in advance of object permanence. Bell's sample consisted of 33 male and female children of middle-class parents, aged 8½ to 11½ months, who were given parallel tests of both object and person permanence utilizing Décarie's (1965) objectal scale as a basic guideline for person permanence and Piagetian hide-and-seek tasks to measure inanimate object permanence. To place Bell's study in context, Piaget's view of the development of the object concept will be reviewed briefly.

Piaget identifies six stages in the development of the object concept. At first, the infant has no conception of himself or other objects existing independently. He is aware only of actions and sensations, unable to differentiate objects from the act of assimilating them. In the third sensorimotor stage, or about 3 months, the infant goes beyond his immediate perception to try to recapture or sustain sensorimotor relationships with objects. Thus, he will anticipate future positions of moving objects, such as looking after a dropped object, he will anticipate the whole object from seeing only a part, he will free his perception to see an object, and he will abandon an object he has been active with and then relocate the original object. However, he is unable to search for an object hidden under a screen, so that an object out of sight completely disappears. In the fourth stage, about 8–10 months, the child will initially search actively for a hidden object only if he has been in the process of reaching for the object at the moment it was hidden. Later in this stage, the object becomes more free from motor activity, and the child will find objects that he has seen being completely hidden behind a screen. However, he cannot follow visible displacements. Thus, if the object is hidden at A, found there, and then the child watches the object being hidden at B, he will look for it at A. The baby seems unable to separate the object from its context and to coordinate the motor sequence by which the object was previously found with his latest perception of it. In Stage 5 (12–18 months), the child is capable of visible displacements and will look for a hidden object at the place where it was last seen, but he cannot find the object if he has not observed it on its way to the hiding place. By Stage 6, about 18 months, the child is capable of invisible displacements, indicating a capacity for representational adaptations. The object exists in its own right when the subject is neither perceiving nor acting on it, and, similarly, there is a recognition that the self is an object among others in a common spatial field.

In Bell's object permanence test, toys were used with felt pads for screens, and in the person permanence tests, the mother or sometimes the experimenter hid behind doors, a specially constructed mobile screen, or a blanket. Thus, to provide an illustration of an item designed to test whether or not a baby had reached stage four, defined as the capacity to find an object that he has seen being hidden, the item was considered passed if the baby removed the screen from the toy and picked it up or removed a blanket from the mother and greeted her.

Subjects were tested four times between 8 ½ and 11 ½ months, and 17 of the subjects were tested again at about 14 months. For each subject, a discrepancy score between person and object permanence was obtained. The babies were classified into three groups: (1) those who showed significantly higher scores on person than object permanence on at least one testing; (2) those who showed the reverse pattern on at least one testing; and (3) those who showed no significant differences. Twenty-three of the 33 babies fell into the first group, consistently showing higher scores on person than on object permanence until scale ceiling was reached for both persons and objects; seven babies belonged to the second group, showing higher scores on object than on person permanence. Of the three babies in the third group, with no discrepancies, two showed higher scores on object permanence by the fourth testing and one never showed any discrepancy. Thus, the subjects could be divided into two main groups, the larger group of 23 babies developing person permanence before object permanence. These findings are consistent with the hypothesis that the development of person permanence is parallel with that of object permanence, but begins earlier.

To investigate the relationship of the quality of infant–mother attachment to the development of object and person permanence, the same sample of babies was again divided into three groups on the basis of ratings of their reunion behavior following brief separations from their mothers, when they were alone with a stranger. Group B babies showed comparatively greater attempts to gain contact and interaction with the mother following brief separations and used her as a secure base from which to explore before the separations. In this group, 23 of the 24 babies showed higher person than object permanence. The 5 infants in Group A tended to ignore their mothers or to go or look away following separation, and they were likely to turn to inanimate objects in their environment for solace. All of these Group A babies showed a more advanced level of object permanence than of person permanence by the fourth testing. The four Group C babies, who showed highly ambivalent behavior in the reunion situation, also showed a more advanced level of object than of person permanence by the fourth testing at about 14 months. Thus, all but 1 of the 24 babies who seemed to show the most positive attachment to their mothers developed person before object permanence. Furthermore, the babies with higher person permanence developed person permanence earlier than the babies with higher object permanence developed either person or object permanence. In summarizing her findings, Bell states that they "suggest that babies who consistently have significantly higher scores on person-permanence are, because of their experience with persons at the higher levels, facilitated in the development of the permanence of inanimate objects [1968, p. 48]."

There is considerable research evidence from the study of normal developmental processes indicating that there are significant relationships between cognitive development and the nature and quality of the interpersonal relationship between mother and child. As summarized by Clarke-Stewart (1973), the mother's attitudes toward child rearing and her capacities to enjoy the experience have important effects upon the child's development (e.g., Davids, 1968; Escalona, 1953; Heinstein, 1963; Lakin, 1957; Lewis, 1954; Milner, 1951; Spitz, 1951; Stern, Caldwell, Hersher, Lipton, & Richmond, 1969). Gentle, firm, and close physical contact (e.g., Ainsworth, Bell, Blehar, & Main, 1971; Lewis & Goldberg, 1969; Provence & Lipton, 1962; Yarrow, 1963), distinctive and frequent auditory stimulation (e.g., Goldberg & Lewis, 1969; Gordon, 1969; Kagan, 1971), and a high degree of eye contact all have a positive effect on the infant's early development of cognitive, linguistic, social, and motor capacities and his attachment and responsiveness to his mother. Clarke-Stewart (1973) also concluded that research findings indicate that a mother's prompt and appropriate response to her infant's signals facilitates the infant's adjustment and development and his awareness that his behavior has consequences and that his actions can influence his environment (Ainsworth et al., 1971; Lewis & Goldberg, 1969; Ramey et al., 1972). The trust and security developed in the interaction with the mother serve as the basis for the child's subsequent exploration of the environment and the quality of his interpersonal interactions. In a study of the transaction between mothers and their infants, Clarke-Stewart (1973) found that the mother's positive attitudes and competence in child care were significantly related to the development of the child's cognitive, linguistic, and social capacities and to the quality of the infant's attachment to the mother. The amount and type of stimulation provided by the mother correlated with the infant's general cognitive development as well as with the infant's development of specific skills. There was a significant parallel between the modes of stimulation provided by the mother and the infant's development. Also, the more the child responded to the mother, the more affectionate, stimulating, and responsive the mother became. Clarke-Stewart's findings highlight the transactional nature of the mother–child relationship and indicate that cognitive development is significantly related to the quality of the maternal caring relationship.

The results of these studies suggest that early disturbances in the trans-actional mother–child relationship can have a significant disruptive effect on cognitive development, particularly on the development of the concept of the object. Such conclusions, based on the study of developmental processes in normal infants, are consistent with formulations based on clinical observations (e.g., Bettelheim, 1967; Bruch, 1962), and they indicate the need for further longitudinal studies to investigate the relationships of disturbances in the mother–infant relationship, particularly around issues of separation and individuation, to the child's future cognitive and interpersonal development.

Jacobson (1964), Mahler (1968), and others have postulated that a symbiotic phase is part of normal development; and Jacobson stresses the importance of experiences and fantasies of merging as the foundation on which all future object relationships and identifications are based. Comparable to Piaget's observations of the fourth stage of sensorimotor development at about 8–10 months, when the child will actively search for a concealed object after he has seen it hidden, Mahler states that at 6–8 months the normal infant begins to be able to distinguish familiar figures from strangers, a prerequisite for reacting to the disappearance of familiar people. According to Jacobson (1964), from about 3 months until the age of 2 years, corresponding approximately to Piaget's third to sixth sensorimotor stages, the child undergoes alternating experiences of complete reunion and fusion when held close, fed, or gratified in other ways, followed by a greater sense of separation with increases in frustration, accompanied by longing and anticipation of gratification as the constancy of the mother as a separate person becomes more firmly established. Furthermore, according to Jacobson (1964), only after the child is able to differentiate the various part aspects of his mother and others and to integrate the parts into a coherent whole including both the "good" and the "bad" mother is he capable of identification in a mature fashion. In mature identification, the child is capable of selecting aspects of significant figures to model himself after, rather than becoming completely like them.

According to Mahler (1952) a basic criterion for distinguishing autistic from symbiotic child psychoses is that in the former the mother is not perceived as a separate person representing the outside world and distinguished from inanimate objects. But in the symbiotic child, there is some awareness of the difference between self and mother, so that intense, diffuse separation reactions occur. In Mahler's words: "Whereas in primary autism there is a deanimated frozen wall between the subject and the human object, in symbiotic psychosis, on the other hand, there is fusion, melting, and lack of differentiation between the self and the nonself [1963, p. 309]." In the symbiotic child, boundaries between representations of self and of mother are blurred, but there is at least some degree of object permanence.

Otherwise, there could be no longing for fusion or reaction to separation. Both Mahler and Searles (1965) postulate that while a symbiotic relationship between the infant and the maternal figure is necessary for healthy development, with schizophrenic patients the symbiotic relationship never became sufficiently established or was established and not resolved in a normal way. Scarles and others relate this problem to the mother's own difficulties with ego boundaries and with differentiating her own needs from those of her child, a topic that will be developed more fully below.

Symbiosis

We shall first attempt to define symbiotic relatedness as it pertains to schizophrenia, involving loss of the boundary distinctions between self and other, between representations of self and representations of other, and between the symbols standing for self and other, as in confusing the pronouns "I" and "you" (Rosenfeld & Sprince, 1963; Thomas, 1966). Then, the dilemma around intimacy of both partners in a symbiotic relationship will be explored, where closeness and separation are experienced in varying degrees by both partners as threats to the basic integrity of the self. We shall try to relate this experiential dilemma to difficulties with establishing and maintaining object and person permanence, placing it in a more theoretical context of developmental psychology. We shall go on to examine problems with self–other discrimination, which also seem to be associated with difficulties in distinguishing people outside the self from each other and representations of one from those of another, so that a nurse may be confused with the patient's mother, for example. Finally, projection and paranoia in schizophrenia will be discussed as representing more or less successful attempts to cope with and stave off threats of boundary loss, involving dissolution of the self. As discussed in Chapter 2 in relation to cognitive functioning, paranoids are apt to function at the opposite extreme from nonparanoid patients on dimensions such as field dependence–independence and size constancy. From an interpersonal point of view, paranoia can be seen as an exaggerated position, with excessive barriers erected to protect the self against merging with other people.

Mahler defines symbiosis as follows:

> From the second month on, dim awareness of the need-satisfying object marks the beginning of the phase of normal symbiosis, in which the infant behaves and functions as though he and his mother were an omnipotent system—a dual unity within one common boundary. . . .
> The essential feature of symbiosis is hallucinatory or delusional, somatopsychic omnipotent fusion with the representation of the mother and, in particular, the delusion of a common boundary of the two actually and physically separate individ-

uals. This is the mechanism to which the ego regresses in cases of the most severe
disturbance of individuation and psychotic disorganization, which I have described
as "symbiotic child psychosis" [1968, pp. 8–9].

She considers symbiosis to be a normal stage during the first 18 months of
life. While there is an increasing differentiation between the need-gratifying
object and the self, there is also a tendency to merge with the object and
maintain an intense tie to it. But, she hypothesizes, if the symbiotic phase is
never fully reached or never resolved in a normal way, serious psychopathology is likely to result, and many authors (e.g., Hill, 1955; Lidz & Lidz,
1952; Reichard & Tillman, 1950) have described the symbiotic relatedness
between the schizophrenic patient and his mother.

However, the concept of symbiosis has been used in other ways. Thus,
Pollock (1964) extends the concept to cover the whole range of development as a constantly evolving continuum. Similarly, Stierlin (1959) uses
the term very broadly, even including aspects of husband–wife and boss–
worker relationships. But this more extensive use of the concept seems to
confuse phenomena at different levels of development. In this book we
shall adopt Mahler's more restricted definition of symbiosis, which refers to
a psychological relationship in which there is an experience of fusion and a
failure to distinguish boundaries between representations of the self and
representations of another person. However, we agree that symbiotic relationships do range along a continuum; and even within the confines of
serious lack of differentiation between self and other, varying degrees of
boundary loss can be delineated. Thus, we shall present clinical evidence,
consistent with the findings on cognitive processes presented in Chapter 2,
that the interpersonal difficulties of process, amorphous, nondifferentiated
and nonparanoid schizophrenics can be seen as more similar to developmentally earlier levels of relationships, as compared with those of acute,
fragmented, nonintegrated, and paranoid schizophrenics. The former
groups seem to show less self–other differentiation than the latter, even
though they all manifest some evidence of symbiosis in their relationships,
along with mechanisms to defend against it.

Another definitional distinction should be made in regard to the concept
of symbiosis. As in the section on thinking, where adaptive, constructive
uses of primary process thinking were implied, fusion experiences can also
be viewed as serving an adaptive function (Rose, 1971), as in empathy,
intercourse, and creativity (Schafer, 1958), "peak experiences" of awe (Maslow, 1959), religious conversion (Allison, 1967), and mystical experiences of
mingling with the absolute. In addition, more and more attention has been
paid recently to the adaptive aspects of brief psychotic experiences, which
may result in increased personality integration and development (Allison,

1967). However, as with primary process thinking, reversibility, duration, degree of control, adaptability to the current situation, and long-term goal-directedness seem to be important criteria by which to distinguish more from less adaptive regression to less differentiated modes of interpersonal functioning. Therefore, in addition to distinguishing symbiosis from less serious and developmentally more mature problems with "dependency" and "identity," these further criteria must be used in judging whether the occurrence of symbiotic object ties is maladaptively "schizophrenic" or not.

We shall now attempt to delineate the various manifestations of schizophrenic symbiotic relatedness from the point of view of both subject and observer.

The dilemma around intimacy

Searles gives a poignant and succinct description of the experience of both partners in a symbiotic relationship:

> In such a relatedness, each person finds himself oscillating helplessly between a position of intense "closeness" to the other person, and an utterly contrasting position of total psychological divorce from that person, the latter position being experienced as a sense of having completely *lost* the deeply cherished relatedness of a moment before. It may well be that, for the adult schizophrenic patient, the prospect of death is intolerably reminiscent of such experiences of loss—and, of course, of similar experiences in the present with parent – figures—of bleak, death-like interruptions in his sense of contact with this other person who is felt to be necessary to his very survival [1965, p. 498].

This moving account of schizophrenic relatedness seems more comprehensible when placed within the framework of the concepts of symbiosis and lack of development of object and person permanence in Piaget's sense. It can be compared to Jacobson's and Mahler's description of the normal child in the symbiotic phase undergoing alternating experiences of complete reunion and fusion when gratified, followed by a greater sense of separation with increases in frustration, accompanied by longing and anticipation of gratification through fusion with the absent object. Piaget's observations seem to show that before the object concept has been firmly achieved, the object is lost, or partially lost, when it is not immediately apparent to the senses. If object and person permanence are unstable to varying degrees in schizophrenics, then spatial separation can involve greater and lesser experiences of total loss, or death, of the symbiotic partner.

On the one hand, the schizophrenic yearns for a state of complete union, usually with the mother or mother substitute, sometimes with the father or later displacements from parental relationships. But such union and intimacy involve the drastic danger of complete loss of self, analogous to death or annihilation, through becoming one with the other person. At the same time, there seems to be a fear that the symbiotic partner also will be destroyed through fusion, so that closeness brings the simultaneous or alternating existential threat of being lost or losing, of being engulfed or engulfing, of being devoured or devouring, often with a lack of distinction between the more passive and active positions. It is as if closeness involved both surrender of the precarious sense of self to be passively absorbed, and absorption of the other person. Often, these concerns are expressed literally in terms of the threat of being eaten and eating (Rosenfeld & Sprince, 1963, 1965; Thomas, 1966).

Burnham, Gladstone, and Gibson describe the schizophrenic's dilemma around object relationships in similar terms, calling it the "need–fear dilemma." According to these authors, difficulties in the early relationships of schizophrenics interfere with the development of both differentiation and integration.

> Interference with differentiation results in a lack of separateness and relative autonomy or the capacity for self-regulation. Interference with integration causes inability to assimilate major areas of experience into a reality construct, and inability to articulate subsystems of personality into a coherent and harmonious whole. . . .
> These deficiencies contribute, in turn, to what we have termed the need–fear dilemma of the schizophrenic person. He has both an inordinate need and an inordinate fear of objects. His lack of separateness and self-regulatory structure renders him dependent upon external structure and extraordinarily susceptible to the influence of objects . . . Furthermore, inordinate need generates fear by raising the threat of loss or unavailability of the object [1969, pp. 31–32].

Burnham, Gladstone, and Gibson (1969) point out how the schizophrenic's lack of autonomy and internal structure make him tremendously dependent on others to provide external organization and how others can also destroy him through either abandonment or engulfment leading to collapse of the self, citing many clinical examples of these phenomena. They also relate the need–fear dilemma to object constancy and separation anxiety. Thus, it is consistent that schizophrenia occurs most frequently in adolescence when societal and cultural forces emphasize independence and separation, bringing the dilemma of symbiotic fusion to the foreground.

This dilemma can be seen in a 28-year-old schizophrenic man, who sought outpatient treatment, complaining of "anxiety. . . . some sort of identity problem" and preoccupation with fears of "losing myself in the family. . . . I was whatever other people wanted me to be." In talking about how his married sister, who was also schizophrenic, visited their mother every day, he said:

> They can't separate. . . . They lean on each other. . . . People in the family don't know their bounds. No one is himself, sister is mother, I realize it, I have to prevent myself from being swallowed up.

In a subsequent session, he told his therapist:

> I felt bad last night. It was tense in the house with my mother. I have to get away from her. She's there, lording it over everyone, controlling everyone. I felt my identity leaving me, going into her, I need her. I'm not a mama's boy.

His need for his mother seemed to be associated with a fear of being swallowed up. On the other hand, this patient feared that separation would lead to his becoming nothing, as well as "hurt the family, leave a wound. . . . If there were no people around, my mother wouldn't exist." Thus he also feared that both he and his mother would no longer exist without each other. Closeness to people outside the family also led to fears of annihilation and self-destruction, as when he described his experiences with male friends he was close to: "I become frightened, panicky when I feel I'm becoming A. He got inside of me, destroyed something"; and again, "I was lying in bed, I felt I was him, his body, his face."

Because the symbiotic relationship is simultaneously desired and feared, it is fraught with extreme conflict and intense ambivalence. Often the mother is alternately seen as comforting and supportive and as cold and ungiving, as powerful and protecting and as engulfing and intrusive, as nurturant and bountiful and as poisonous and venomous. Thus, the relationship with the mother is experienced as necessary to the very survival of the self and as completely destructive of the self. Furthermore, if no clear differentiation from parental figures has occurred and the self is experienced as part of the very substance of the parent, then separation involves not only loss of self but also draining the essential being of the symbiotic partner; it is like being "ripped and torn apart. . . only half of a self."

Inability to differentiate people

Just as lack of full establishment of the object concept leads to difficulty in discriminating self from inanimate objects and various kinds of inanimate objects from each other, lack of person permanence is accompanied both by an inability to discriminate self from others and by an inability to distinguish other people as separate individuals. Representations of other people tend to be fused one with another, so that, for example, there is no clear differentiation between mother, father, sister, brother, friend. An 18-year-old schizophrenic outpatient demonstrates an inability to keep people separate in his story to the TAT card, Picasso's "La Vie," depicting a nude couple together with an older woman holding a baby:

The gentleman in the picture and the lady with the child are son and daughter or husband and wife. The other girl is the mistress, new wife, or sister. The mother is the girl's sister—looks too young—or servant or daughter.

When asked about whose child it is, he says it is "the child of the person with the clothes on, it's the only way you can distinguish them." His confusion in differentiating close family members from each other and close from more distant attachments seems obvious here.

Inability to empathize with and discriminate among people contributes to the schizophrenic's difficulties in establishing relationships outside of his family of origin. Since all people are likely to be experienced as parental or other significant figures, the schizophrenic has little flexibility to relate in ways that are different from those he has learned to use within his immediate family. Thus, in addition to many other factors, such as the general isolation from the community of schizophrenic families, which tends to cut the members off from new contacts (Lidz et al., 1965), schizophrenics are apt to have extreme difficulty in forming extrafamilial relationships because of problems with clearly discriminating peers, teachers, and others from family members.

Moreover, in attempting to break away from their families, schizophrenics are apt to feel "stuck," unable to move toward new relationships or to relinquish old ones. In the words of a 25-year-old schizophrenic man, who had told two preceding TAT stories about a son who "proclaimed his independence from his mother" and "had to go his way" in leaving his father: "He was suspended in time between two cultures almost—he can't quite make it to the new one, and has cut himself off from the past." When asked for the outcome of the story, he said, "Slow, painful death, I guess." Consistent with the lack of a sense of continuity of the self back into the past and forward into the future, the schizophrenic struggling with separation seems to experience a loss of his very existence in the process, feeling hopeless and dead.

Projection and paranoia

In working with nonparanoid schizophrenic patients, therapists are likely to encounter phenomena that seem like "projections," an interpretation which can be questioned. A patient may assume that the therapist has read his mind or "understood" him, without having uttered a word about his thoughts and feelings. The patient also may assume that he is fully aware of the therapist's reactions to him, without the therapist's having shared them. Because of difficulty in distinguishing their own from others' thoughts and feelings, schizophrenics are likely to assume a unity, mutual comprehension, or communion of minds, perhaps reflecting their experience with their parents, which will be elaborated in a later section. If there is a problem with differentiation and awareness of the complex differences and similarities between self and others, the schizophrenic is therefore likely to attribute his own experience to the therapist and to assume that the latter functions similarly, attributing his experience to the patient. An impasse can result if this situation is not clarified in therapy by fostering an open expression of both the patient's and the therapist's thoughts and feelings, continually pointing out the similarities and differences.

Furthermore, the apparent "projections" of schizophrenics, or imputations of thoughts and feelings to others, do not seem to reflect a stable position in which unacceptable aspects of the self are consistently disowned and attributed to outside influences or people, as in the more paranoid patient. Rather, there is a confusion about the locus of internal experience, which may shift from one moment to the next, because the patient is unsure whether his neediness, aggression, love, or hate reside within himself or in the person he is with. A consistent paranoid position seems to require some degree of firmness of boundaries, so that unacceptable parts of the self can be persistently attributed to outside agencies which, for example, constantly threaten the self with sexual temptation, hostility, or moral judgments. But schizophrenics with serious boundary problems are more likely to show a fluid shift, or what sometimes appears to be almost an osmotic flow, between their experiences and those of others. Often, this marked vacillation seems to be associated with a shift from a more active (experiencing own feelings and impulses) to a more passive position (attributing them to external sources).

For instance, the 18-year-old outpatient, whose difficulty with differentiating people has been cited above, told the following TAT story to a card which is an impressionistic line drawing (see Rapaport et al., 1946) usually seen as two old men in aggressive interaction. After saying that the two characters "don't look like they're real people," he stated that they are "superimposed on each other. . . . Maybe it's a nightmare or perhaps a hermit." Here, the tendency for the figures to become merged, his difficulty with distinguishing fantasy from reality, and his attempts to gain distance from his story by calling it a nightmare or the character a hermit are apparent. He proceeded, stating, "they are in a position ready for any unexpected assault, looks like they're ready to attack something." His last comment, which shows a sudden switch from a passive to a more active position— they are prepared for an "unexpected assault" to they are "ready to attack something"—seems to exemplify a fluid change from attributing hostility to outside sources to locating it in the central characters of his story. Such examples could be multiplied to illustrate the problems many schizophrenics have with distinguishing their thoughts and feelings from those of other people. These problems result in an alternating and inconsistent shift from activity to passivity and from assuming to externalizing responsibility for internal experience, and they reflect serious difficulties in maintaining boundaries between the self and others.

There is evidence supporting the conclusion that paranoid pathology and well-organized delusional systems are more likely to be found in differentiated persons with greater field articulation, less cognitive impairment, and greater capacity for object constancy (Freeman et al., 1966; Witkin, 1965). Witkin suggests that articulated delusions and the projection of distinct ideas onto distinct objects are attempts to preserve the self and maintain separate identity and ego integrity, requiring a personality structure with some degree of differentiation in developmental terms. Freeman et al. (1966), however, point out that within the paranoid subgroup, patients differ in regard to how rigid and tight their boundaries are. Some paranoid patients are more flexible and open to assimilating new experiences and forming new relationships than are others.

While a consistent paranoid stance seems to require more differentiation between self and others than is found in other types of schizophrenia, extreme forms of paranoid traits can also be seen as desperate attempts to fortify the boundaries of the self in order to ward off experiences of dissolution and loss of self-integrity. Excessive constriction, guardedness, suspiciousness, need for protection, and reluctance to become committed to anyone or anything serve to keep the paranoid person at a safe, uninvolved distance from other people. Furthermore, the paranoid schizophrenic's view of other people as dangerous, threatening, and with hostile intent may not only involve the imputation of his own anger to others. Since closeness brings the threat of merging, the anger and suspicion may also serve a crucial differentiating function, perhaps comparable to the defiance and stubbornness of the young child, fostering individuation in normal development.

The test protocols of a hospitalized, 24-year-old female college graduate provide vivid illustrations of these points. The tests show an extremely guarded, cautious, paranoid schizophrenic person, manifesting excessive constriction, suspicion, blocking, and an array of primarily projective maneuvers to avoid revealing herself and becoming involved with the test stimuli or examiner. Problems of differentiating what is inside from what is outside herself are suggested in many different ways, and she seems to be struggling to maintain firm boundaries between her thoughts and external reality, between herself and other people. Thus, when asked to draw a picture of a family, she first drew an irregular, vaguely circular external boundary, then proceeded to draw a rectangle and circle merging with one another inside the boundary, labeling them "pater" and "mater," and finished by making three scribbled circles, separated from one another but attached by lines to pater and mater, which she labeled "son," "daughter," and "grandchild." In commenting on her drawing, she stated that she herself was not there (in the drawing): "She exists, she is outside." This statement seems to reveal her experiences of isolation and to represent an attempt to preserve her individual integrity by distance.

Similarly, her insistence that the TAT cards were "only pictures and pictures don't have thoughts and feelings—they are inanimate objects" and her lack of capacity to identify with the characters and tell a story appear to indicate how threatened she was with losing distance from the depicted people and from her fantasies about them. She seemed to be afraid that if she told stories about the people on the cards, they might become real, and she would be unable to separate her experience from theirs. Her alienated and alienating hostility can be seen as another necessary attempt to maintain distance; and such responses also appear to reflect her fear of being trapped and of making any commitment to her thoughts or perceptions.

Much more clinical evidence could be adduced consistent with the hypothesis that paranoid schizophrenia represents an extremely defensive posture, serving to preserve and solidify boundaries between self and others. However, studies are needed to investigate whether or not such clinically derived hypotheses receive empirical support.

Special forms of interpersonal behavior

Some deviant forms of behavior found in schizophrenics can also be considered as defensive attempts to deal with problems of closeness and distance and to stave off fusion and merging.

Flight

Many schizophrenic patients fear being enveloped and engulfed if any degree of intimacy develops. Therefore, in the treatment of hospitalized schizophrenics, moves toward closeness in the therapeutic relationship or toward involvement and immersion in the hospital milieu may lead to drastic flight reactions. The patient may retreat into severe withdrawal, literally flee spatially by leaving the hospital, or engage in assaultive behavior, which can also be seen as an attempt to gain separation. Closeness and distance may actually be experienced by the patient in spatial terms, as in an example given by Lidz: "A patient's feelings that I was withdrawn in some sessions and oppressively intrusive in others depended upon inadvertent changes of two or three inches in the customary placement of her chair (1969, p. 244)."

Assault

Roth and Blatt (1961), in citing cases of adolescents who had assaulted maternal figures, discuss this behavior as a primitive means of achieving differentiation. In these adolescents, there seemed to be a preoccupation with alternating fusion with, and differentiation from the mother in terms of spatial rather than temporal parameters. Thus, assault can be viewed as a simultaneous effort to fuse spatially and to gain distance through aggressive action.

Homosexuality and promiscuity

Fuller comprehension of homosexuality in male patients and promiscuity in female patients seems to result from viewing these behaviors within the context of boundary difficulties. First, as will be discussed further in a later section, if one or both parents has serious problems with differentiation, the parent(s) is likely to have a confused sexual identity. Furthermore, if the parents constantly undercut one another and turn to the child instead of the spouse for gratification, parental age and sex roles are confused, and the child lacks differentiated role models of male and female behavior and characteristics. The basic problem that many schizophrenics have with discriminating themselves from other people makes the concept of "sexual identity" seem at too high a developmental level to be applied to them. It would seem that a distinct sense of self and awareness of the differences between male and female are required before sexual identification can occur. Of course, schizophrenics have attained some sense of being male or female, but preoccupations with and fears of actually changing into the opposite sex are not uncommon. There cannot be a stable sense of sexual identity without a stable sense of self.

Homosexual preoccupations and relationships are often found in male patients and can be viewed as attempts to establish closeness with an object dissimilar to the mother. Often, in fact, the first relationships that are initiated outside the family as the patient begins to improve are homosexual ones, which because they are more distant from the mother–child symbiosis, may be fraught with less danger of complete merging and loss of self than are heterosexual relationships. Fears of being engulfed and swallowed up during intercourse are common. Similarly, promiscuity in the female patient may represent an attempt to separate from the mother by engaging in heterosexual contacts that are more distant from the mother–child ties than are relationships with women. Furthermore, in both men and women, these relationships often seem to be primarily attempts to gain maternal care from the homo- or heterosexual partner, containing many elements that seem like repetitions of the relationship with the mother or with the actual or longed-for mothering aspects of the father. For example, the 28-year-old male schizophrenic patient cited earlier, who felt that he had to get away from his controlling mother because he experienced "my identity leaving me, going into her," described a relationship with an older male friend, B, who had the same name as his father:

> I submitted myself to him. . . . I exposed myself to him. I trusted him with my emotional life. He put me on. . . . My father's name is B. . . . I never had a father. I hugged B, but I did it when I was crazy, not responsible. . . . I saw my father in B. . . . When he was sick he came under my mother's wing. . . . I did the same with B. . . . It scares me to act as if I'm someone else. I want my own identity. . . . I take on B's personality. . . . I imagine my head looking like B's.

Here his tendency to fuse himself with B and B with his father and his mother are apparent. He sees his father in B and also appears to experience closeness with B as submitting to and coming "under my mother's wing." Confusion of wife with mother and husband with father are also common occurrences in married schizophrenic patients.

Blurring of generation boundaries

Turning now to a discussion of the family constellation of schizophrenics, both Lidz et al. (1965) and Wynne et al. (1958) refer to a "blurring of boundaries" in families of schizophrenics, using the term in somewhat different ways (Mishler & Waxler, 1966). According to Wynne et al. (1958), schizophrenics' families are characterized by collective defensive styles of pseudo-mutuality or pseudo-hostility, whereby they maintain some sense of togetherness without having to confront the basic meaninglessness of their relationships. Thus, in the pseudo-mutual family, there is "a predominant absorption in fitting together, at the expense of the differentiation of the identities of the persons in the relation [p. 207]"; in pseudo-hostile families, there is a situation of chronic conflict, which constitutes the major mode of interrelating and reacting to one another. In both pseudo-mutual and pseudo-hostile families, "Distinctions are not made between the person and his role. This 'blurring' of boundaries between individual and role results in the family's being experienced by the developing child as all-encompassing of the self; there is no identity separate from one's role within the family (Mishler & Waxler, 1966, p. 390)." According to the Wynne group, the schizophrenic's family environment interferes with his development of a stable ego identity.

Lidz et al. (1965) stress the importance of blurring of generation boundaries in terms of gender-linked sex and age role distortions in the families of schizophrenics. For both male and female patients, the same-sexed parent does not provide an adequate identity model. Because the parents do not provide gratification for one another, the opposite-sexed parent depends on the patient to satisfy his own needs. The Lidz group finds two main types of disturbed marital relationships in the families of schizophrenic patients, schismatic and skewed, the former being more often associated with female and the latter with male patients. In the schismatic marriage, there is chronic strife, discord, and mistrust, with constant threats of separation, each spouse undermining the other in the eyes of the child and turning to the child for loyalty, support, and satisfaction. The skewed marriage is a situation in which the spouse with more serious psychopathology dominates and the more passive partner goes along with him or her. While the Wynne group places more emphasis on familial styles of communicating and interacting, and the Lidz group stresses individual parental psychopathology and the dynamics of intrafamilial relationships leading to role reversal and lack of adequate role models for the children, both stress blurring of boundaries as a core problem in the families of schizophrenics.

Lidz et al. present a case study of the Nebb family, consisting of an older son and two identical male twins, one of whom was hospitalized with a diagnosis of schizophrenia. This family vividly illustrates distorted sex and age role relationships and a skewed marital situation, where the mother turned to the twins for gratification of her own needs, which she was unable to separate from theirs:

> The twins belonged exclusively to the mother, and the family was consequently divided into two groups: the father and oldest son, comprising the outgroup, were supposed to adjust to the primary purpose of raising the extraordinary twins to live out their full capacities. . . .
> The twins were raised as a unit. They were dressed identically until nine or ten, and they were practically indistinguishable in appearance. Often they were not differentiated by the parents, and both were punished or praised for the deeds of one. Further, Mrs. Nebb had trouble differentiating their needs from her own. . . . Often, when she was ill and received medicine, she also gave it to the twins. At one time, the boys could not keep awake in school, and learned that Mrs. N had been placing the sedative she had received for herself in their breakfast food. They were both bowel trained starting at three months. . . . Later, indeed until late adolescence, mother would give both twins enemas together, often because one was angry with her, which meant to her they were constipated. . . .
> Mrs. Nebb not only systematically abjured setting controls and limits herself, but, in addition, undermined her husband's sporadic efforts at discipline. . . . Even when the boys were in college she encouraged them to disregard their father and even her own authority. She would try to get her way in the home by having hysterical "fits" and spells of uncontrolled crying. When Philip (the nonhospitalized twin) was in college he took it upon himself to stop her outbursts by taking her over his knee and spanking her [Lidz et al., 1965, pp. 209–212].

In discussing similar erratic and disruptive shifts in both cognitive and interpersonal distancing found in the families of schizophrenics, Singer and Wynne (1965a) also relate inappropriate emotional distancing to boundary problems:

> Thus, parents of amorphous schizophrenics tend to have fixedly close sets toward most events and objects, yet mix into their communication obtuse, overly abstract, distant terms, thus conveying both inappropriate closeness and distance, but less dramatically and actively than do the parents of fragmented schizophrenics. These parents fail to step back sufficiently in either interpersonal or cognitive acts, yet in communicating use disjunctively distant terms. Their schizophrenic offspring usually have unclear ideas of their own identities, seem verbally vague and unable to differentiate the self from others, to distinguish one experience from another, etc.. . . .
>
> We hypothesize that the capacity for appropriate emotional distancing appears to be a necessary condition for developing stable differentiation of self and nonself (that is, the establishment of "ego" boundaries) and for developing, at the same time, stable object relations, in the psychoanalytic sense. Parental responses replete with inappropriate and unpredictable shifts between aloofness and intrusive closeness very likely make for confused expectations in a child. Further, parents who behave in those ways serve as odd and fragmented models for identification [pp. 196–197].

Both of these formulations consider lack of differentiation as a total family problem rather than as a difficulty limited to the schizophrenic family member.

The role of the family in the etiology and maintenance of boundary disturbances

The role of the family in the etiology and maintenance of boundary disturbances in schizophrenia has been discussed from at least four points of view:

1. lack of differentiation in individual family members, particularly the mother;
2. problems in paired family relationships, such as mother–child symbiosis, or the influence of schismatic or skewed marital disharmony on the schizophrenic offspring's premorbid development;
3. the interaction of the total family group seen as an aggregate of individuals;
4. the interaction of the total family group seen as a social system.

The fourth point of view considers "interactional configurations" (Lennard & Bernstein, 1969) or "transactional styles" (Singer & Wynne, 1965a and b) of the family as a whole. Thus, when a parent consistently loses the focus of a task in an interaction setting, this behavior can be seen from the third point of view as a reflection of his individual attention disturbance, exacerbated or lessened in the family grouping; or, from the fourth point of view, it can be considered for its impact on the family process, serving to further or hinder communication and problem-solving, taking the responses it elicits into account. Despite the complexities of such an approach, all aspects must be considered to gain a comprehensive view of the family's role in contributing to boundary disturbances.

Etiology

The important role of the mother and other caregivers in helping the child to differentiate himself from other human, animate, and inanimate objects, and to distinguish his own bodily sensations and experiences from each other and from those of other people has been discussed above. As Bruch (1962) states, the infant needs repeated confirmation and reinforcement of his own sensations by appropriate environmental response to develop a sense of self-awareness and effectiveness. "The larger the area of appropriate responses to the various expressions of a child's needs and impulses, the more differentiated will the child become in identifying his bodily experiences, and other sensations, thoughts, and feelings as arising within him, and as distinct from the human or nonhuman environment [p. 20]." Otherwise, the child is apt to feel helpless and controlled by external forces, since he lives by responding to stimuli from other people without being aware of or relying on his own inner processes and to lack a sense of autonomy.

Searles (1965) emphasizes the mother's own difficulties with *her* mother, the grandmother, in the etiology of her symbiotic relationship with her child. In discussing "Positive Feelings in the Relationship between the Schizophrenic and his Mother," he calls attention to three prominent features: her fear of her positive feelings, her low self-esteem, and, especially, "*a transference to this child, on the mother's part, of feelings and attitudes originally operative in a symbiotic relationship which obtained between herself as a small child and her own mother* [p. 225, italics his]." According to Searles, the mother has learned that the expression of love is dangerous, for it led to withdrawal and anxiety in *her* mother, and in some respects, she reenacts with her offspring her own symbiotic relationship with the grandmother. Thus, the mother's experience of an inconsistent and capricious maternal relationship, in which caring was suddenly replaced by rejection, renders her unable to accept her own child's love. Put somewhat more generally, if the mother is herself undifferentiated, she is unable to separate her own needs from her infant's and incapable of recognizing him as a separate person. For such a precariously integrated and undifferentiated mother, the normal period of symbiotic relatedness would tend to exacerbate her anxiety and increase her threat of boundary loss, so that she is unable to develop or resolve such symbiotic relatedness (Mahler, 1968; Searles, 1965).

Furthermore, Searles (1965) postulates that the mother's perception of her child includes "projections" of her own personality of which she is unaware, as well as perceptions of figures from her own childhood, so that she is unable to respond to the child as an individual in his own right. "Such a development is unconsciously sensed, I believe, by the mother—and eventually by the child also—as tantamount to mutual annihilation [p. 226]." On the basis of his experience with schizophrenics and their families, Searles further postulates that the father tends to be infantile, reacting to both his wife and his child as mother figures, intervening between mother and child to have both for himself.

The literature contains many examples of parents of schizophrenics who treat the patient in a stereotyped manner that bears little resemblance to his actual personality. For example, Laing and Esterson (1964) describe how the parents require complete conformity of their schizophrenic offspring; and as soon as the child fails to "echo" the parents' mold, they consider him "mad" and "bad" so that any disagreement or even initiative toward separation on his part is seen as a reflection of his "illness." Laing and Esterson also cite examples of how the parents' own problems with differentiation prevent them from viewing the child as an authentic, separate person. For instance, one schizophrenic daughter, who was named after the mother's younger sister, who had committed suicide at 19, became schizophrenic at 20. Thus, it can be hypothesized that parents with their own serious boundary problems cannot sufficiently distinguish themselves from their children or their children from other significant figures in their lives to deal with their offspring as separate individuals.

The "imperviousness" of the schizophrenic's mother and her lack of "confirmation" of her child's experience has been documented repeatedly by clinical observations (e.g., Lidz et al., 1965). Laing (1962) extends the concept of lack of confirmation to the whole family of the schizophrenic, rather than limiting it to the relationship between the patient and his mother. According to Laing (1962):

> In those families of schizophrenics that have been studied in detail, a consistent finding appears to be that there is minimal genuine confirmation of the parents by each other and of the child by each parent, separately or together, but there may not be obvious disconfirmation. One finds, rather, interactions marked by pseudo-confirmation, by acts which masquerade as confirming actions but are counterfeit. These may be pretences to confirm the child's being—acts that go through the

motions of confirmation in the absence of genuine confirmation: or pseudo-confirmation may take the form of actively and genuinely confirming some fictional child which the child is taken to be, without the authentic self of the child ever receiving recognition [pp. 90-91].

The work of Mishler and Waxler (1966, 1968) lends some empirical support to such clinically based observations in that degree of "acknowledgment," defined as responsiveness to and recognition of other family members' statements, was a reliably scorable category of behavior that distinguished families of normals from families of schizophrenics in a revealed differences situation. Control families show more acknowledgment than do families of patients with either good or poor premorbid developmental histories (Phillips, 1953), the latter being lowest on acknowledgment. Lennard, Beaulieu, and Embrey (1965) compared the interaction of 10 families of 9- to 14-year-old boys who had been diagnosed as schizophrenic, borderline, or psychotic, to 8 families of normal sons, in a situation where parents and child discussed three topics, such as the best occupation for the son. These investigators found that in the families with seriously disturbed offspring, the rate of the child's attempts to intrude into a parental dyad and the rate of parental responsiveness to these attempts was lower than in the control families. These results are consistent with those of Mishler and Waxler (1968), who also found higher rates of interruptions in the family interaction of controls than in that of families with a schizophrenic offspring. These findings suggest that there is less support for the child's independent, self-initiated activity in the families of schizophrenics.

Intensive, clinical study of the families of schizophrenics leads a number of investigators to interpret their observations of individual family members, pairs of family members, and the style of interaction of the family as a whole as reflecting serious problems with differentiation that have etiological importance. Thus, numerous authors postulate an early disturbance in the normal symbiotic phase of development or failure to resolve it , as at least an important predisposing factor in the background of the child who becomes schizophrenic. Such problems with mother–child symbiosis can be seen as partly reflecting the mother's own difficulties with differentiation and precarious self–other boundaries. However, as will be discussed further in Chapter 5, the transactional nature of the mother–child relationship must be taken into account. Infants with unfortunate biological and psychological predispositions at birth, due to genetic or other factors, may be particularly difficult to care for and respond to. The role of the father is also important. Lidz et al. (1965) have been prominent in stressing the father's role and the quality of the marital relationship in fostering or counteracting problems in families of schizophrenics. Thus, if there is a schismatic or skewed parental relationship, in which the parents provide little gratification for one another, or an extremely infantile father who competes with his child for maternal attention, the mother may be more likely to become engaged in a symbiotic relationship with her infant than if she can turn to her husband for support and satisfaction.

Wynne and Singer (1963 a, b) and Singer and Wynne (1965 a, b) emphasize persistent disturbances in overall family structure and styles of communication as important in the etiology of schizophrenia, relating them to the disorders in thinking and interpersonal relationships found in schizophrenic patients. Wynne and Singer (1963 a) state:

> Characteristically, in the families of the young schizophrenics, the degree of disturbance in family transactions is greater and qualitatively different from that found in the contributions of any individual family member. . . . Although the *isolated* statements of individuals may even appear "normal," nevertheless, viewed from beginning to end, the over-all transactional disorder in a family's communication sequences may be comparable stylistically to that found in the vagueness or fragmentation of a severely impaired schizophrenic. That is, the form or structure of these family-wide transactions is comparable to that of individual schizophrenic thought disorder [p. 194].

As discussed in Chapter 2, more amorphous and more fragmented styles of transactional communication disorder involve difficulties with establishing, maintaining, and sharing foci of attention. Viewing individual projective testing of patients' parents as a transaction between tester and subject, in which the parent interprets reality to the tester in a similar style as he would to his child, criteria have been developed for scoring transactional thought disorder from individual test protocols. Studies using these criteria provide some empirical evidence consistent with the view that the presence of transactional thought disorder in both parents is more likely to be associated with having a schizophrenic offspring than the presence of such thought disorder in one parent. Thus, Wild et al. (1965) found that the sum of both parents' transactional thought disorder scores from the Object Sorting test differentiated the parents of schizophrenics from the parents of normal children better than did the scores of individual parents. Singer (1967) and Wynne (1967) reports similar findings from a study in which 118 Rorschach protocols of parents of schizophrenics, neurotics, and normals were scored according to a manual based on transactional communication difficulties and problems with sharing foci of attention. Over 32% of the parents of nonschizophrenics (neurotics and normals) had scores above a cutting point, defined by the lowest score of any parent of the 19 schizophrenics. However, only 15% of the pairs of parents of nonschizophrenics had scores higher than the lowest score of any schizophrenic parent pair. These findings suggest that a less disturbed parent may offset or counteract the influence of the other.

Thus, there is evidence that scores developed to operationalize difficulties in sharing foci of attention differentiate the individual Rorschach and Object Sorting test protocols of parents of schizophrenics from those of neurotics and normals. There is also evidence that Wynne and Singer's criteria discriminate the interactional process of families of schizophrenics from that of neurotic and normal families. Behrens et al. (1968) found that composite scores from the Relation Rorschach (Loveland, 1967), in which parents (or a parent surrogate) were given the Rorschach together and asked to agree on responses, differentiated 17 lower-class black and 11 lower-class white families of schizophrenics from 11 black control families. The scores were based on global ratings of exposition (defined as clarity of statement), grasp (defined as demonstration of understanding of previous discussion), and relationship (defined as degree of cooperation from collaborative to disruptive). Based on interviews with the whole family present, ratings were made of general attentiveness and ability to share and maintain a focus of attention on a particular topic. These ratings also yielded significant differences between each schizophrenic group and the control group. There were no significant differences between the black and white schizophrenic families on these dimensions. Morris and Wynne (1965) applied criteria for evaluating problems with sharing foci of attention to excerpts from tape recordings of 12 family therapy sessions and were able to predict accurately which parents had schizophrenic and which parents had neurotic offspring.

In Chapter 2, we attempted to link such cognitive difficulties in selective attention and cognitive focusing to boundary problems and inadequate development of the object concept in the patient. If at least one parent has similar serious boundary problems, with associated difficulties in cognitive focusing, the family interaction may show greater or lesser cognitive disturbance than the parent(s) does individually, depending on such factors as the degree of boundary problems in the other spouse, the quality of the marital relationship, and the relative covert or overt dominance or passivity of the more disorganized spouse.

Maintenance

In their presentation and discussion of various investigators' views of the maintenance of disturbed interaction patterns in the families of schizophrenics, Mishler and Waxler (1966) point out the basic issues of survival that are hypothesized to account for the persistence of distorted styles of communicating and relating. From the point of view of the individual family member and the family as a whole, there is an intense, even desperate, need to maintain disturbed interaction patterns, so as to preserve the equilibrium of the family (homeostasis). Bateson (1959), Searles (1965), and Wynne et al. (1958), despite their many differences, seem to reach this conclusion based on their observations of schizophrenics' families. Thus, in summarizing the position of Bateson et al. (1956) on the maintenance of the double bind, Mishler and Waxler (1966) state:

> In families, stable coalitions are necessary for successful problem-solving and successful problem-solving is necessary for the development of adequate self-identities. In the absence of this pattern, the double bind becomes persistent and pervasive as a mode of communication, apparently because it permits individuals to avoid the complete destruction of the self that they believe would follow an unambiguous expression of real feelings and beliefs [p. 402].

Searles (1965), placing more emphasis on the experience of the individual patient and his mother, as well as on the vicissitudes of their symbiotic relationship, believes that it is impossible for both mother and child to express their positive feelings toward one another. The mother has learned through experience with her own mother that such an expression led to withdrawal, anxiety, and rejection; and similarly, the child learns that manifestations of affection and tenderness are met with rejection and withdrawal. However, according to Searles (1965), the schizophrenic child is aware of his mother's extreme difficulties and has intense "compassion, loyalty, solicitude, and dedication" for her:

> It is these feelings, blocked from direct expression except on rare occasions, and their importance to the mother largely denied by her, which are primarily responsible for the child's remaining locked in the symbiotic relatedness with the mother, with disastrous consquences to himself. It is not basically that the mother locks him there with hateful "double bind" injunctions; it is rather that he cannot bear to grow out of the relationship and leave her there, tragically crippled—much as a therapist finds it excruciatingly difficult to leave in midstream a therapeutic endeavour with a patient who is grievously ill with schizophrenia [p. 231].

The threat of death and dissolution associated with loss and separation for both the schizophrenic and his symbiotic partner has been discussed; and the upset in family equilibrium when a patient is hospitalized, family pressure on the patient to remain "sick," and family attempts to remove the patient from treatment once he begins to change in the direction of individuation have been documented clinically (e.g., Lidz et al., 1965). Such reactions by the family seem more comprehensible if the desperate stakes involved in maintaining rigid patterns of interaction, where individuation cannot be tolerated, are understood as reflections of the serious boundary problems of not only the schizophrenic patient but his entire family as well.

Wynne et al. (1958) also stress the importance of family defensive styles, serving either to preserve a constant facade of togetherness and oneness to

avoid inevitable experiences of loss and separateness if differences are confronted directly (pseudo-mutuality), or to perpetuate a sense of vigor-
ousness and vitality through incessant fighting in order to prevent
unbearable experiences of aloneness and meaninglessness (pseudo-hostility). Commenting on pseudo-mutuality, Wynne et al. (1958) state:

> It is only through experiencing the impact of noncomplementarity and articulating
> its meaning that a perceiving ego begins to be differentiated with an identity of its
> own. However, the shared mechanisms operating in these families specifically inter-
> fere with the articulation of meanings that hint at noncomplementarity. For a child
> who grows up and develops his perceptual capacities in a setting in which obvious
> contradictions are regarded as nonexistent, it seems reasonable to suppose that he
> may well come to regard his senses and emotional responses as a tenuous and
> unreliable guide to understanding the expectations he has of himself and others.
> Thus, modes of thinking, perceiving, and communicating built up in such a way
> render unavailable to the person the capacity to attach clear meanings to his own
> intra-psychic states, such as anger at the mother or disappointment [p. 216].

According to Wynne et al., the child internalizes the characteristics of the
family social organization and develops an active investment in continuing
family interaction patterns that maintain his own personality equilibrium.

As Bruch (1962) and others have noted, the preschizophrenic child seems
to have lived in an environment that made it difficult for him to learn to
identify and differentiate between his own bodily sensations, thoughts, and
feelings and those of his family. Thus, he needs external structure to perform basic ego functions, such as reality testing and labeling of feelings,
since he lacks the internal structures and capacities to perform these functions independently.

Lennard and Bernstein (1969) provide some evidence that is consistent
with this hypothesis. As stated above, these investigators compared the interaction of 10 families with a schizophrenic son aged 9–14 years with that
of 8 control families, in a setting in which the families were asked to discuss
three issues relevant to the family. They scored the transcripts of the interaction for Level I and Level II communications—the former defined as
"nonevaluative references to human action, to events, or to other factual
matters" and the latter as references to "an individual's inner states (interpretations and evaluations of feelings, experiences, and so on) [p. 132]."
Examples of Level II communications were: "Did you get any other feelings besides, uh, what was it? Getting mad, or you couldn't stand it? Was
that the sole feeling you had? [p. 130]" and: "I'm sure you don't hate
everybody here [p. 133]." Lennard and Bernstein found that the communications of mothers of patients showed more than twice the proportion of
Level II communications as compared with the communications of control
mothers.

They interpret their findings as follows:

> We tend toward the assumption that the failure on the part of parents to relinquish
> control over a patient-child's inner processes is characteristic of a schizophrenogenic
> context and we believe that the kind of interpersonal environment created by exces-
> sive Level II communications (expecially if they reflect projections and mislabel-
> ings) is contributory to the genesis of the schizophrenic disorder. . . .
> These findings prompt us to offer a few speculative comments about sequences in
> personality and system control processes. We assume that in "normal" devel-
> opment, parents—expecially mothers—through a set of mechanisms not yet expli-
> cated make it possible for a child to learn to identify and evaluate his own feelings,
> experiences, and motives. In time, the child can correctly interpret his own experi-
> ence and is able to reject inaccurate versions when others offer them. Accompany-
> ing this increased awareness of inner states and their appropriate symbolic
> representation is the ability to set adaptive interpersonal processes into motion
> when the relief of discomfort requires actions on the part of another person. Thus,
> the child himself replaces his parent as the "regulator" of system process when
> conditions of intrapersonal or interpersonal disequilibrium require it. If a parent
> fails to induct his child into this control function or the child fails to achieve it, the
> child may remain dependent on the parent (as he has been as an infant) for restora-
> tion of intrapersonal or interpersonal equilibria [pp. 134–135].

Both Lennard and Bernstein and Wynne et al. see the preschizophrenic
child as growing up in a family atmosphere in which he does not learn to
identify and interpret his internal and external experience independently, so
that he needs his family to preserve his sense of equilibrium long after a
normally developing child would have learned to maintain his own equilibrium.

Wynne et al. (1958) also discuss the family's need to maintain interaction
patterns that interfere with differentiation but maintain a sense of relatedness and complementarity:

> The potential schizophrenic typically develops considerable skill and an immense
> positive investment in fulfilling family complementarity and in saving the family as
> well as himself from the panic of dissolution. Indeed, the schizophrenic's ego identi-
> ty often seems to consist of himself viewed as someone who takes care of the needs
> and expectations of his family or family-substitute [p. 217].

Thus, "independent or aggressive behavior is experienced as an impending
disaster (1958, p. 209)." The role of aggression and independent activity in
fostering a sense of individuation developmentally has been elaborated. To
take a somewhat speculative leap, pseudo-hostile families may be seen as
functioning on a higher level than pseudo-mutual ones, for they seem to be
involved in a continuous struggle to maintain their own separate identities
as well as a sense of interpersonal involvement, through conflict and the
expression of differences. Examples from the family treatment of schizo-

phrenics could be cited where overt expression of hostility and differences appeared to coincide with the patient's progress toward separation and individuation.

Searles (1965) has called attention to the defensive function of nondifferentiation, which can be seen as a protection from both the awareness and the expression of violent hostility toward specific objects. Without a sense of other people as distinct from the self and from one another, anger can neither be experienced as a distinguishable emotion the self is responsible for nor can it be directed toward a particular person or situation. Again, in the individual as well as in the family, the development of hostility toward a specific object is likely to coincide with increased differentiation and self-awareness.

Wynne et al. (1958) also refer to the "boundary" between the family as a whole and the larger community, using the concept of the "rubber fence." Relationships outside the family are included if they foster complementarity and excluded if they interfere with it. For example, hospital personnel may find themselves in a position of fostering complementarity if the burden of the decision of no visits from the family is placed on them, relieving both the patient and the family from responsibility for having taken a step toward differentiation and from recognizing that any such step has been taken.

There is growing evidence of systematic differences between the parents and family interaction of patients in the various schizophrenic subgroups. Wynne and Singer present impressive evidence in support of the conclusion that "amorphous" and "fragmented" forms of transactional thought disorder in the parents are related to similar or complementary forms of thought disorder in their offspring. Differences have also been found between families of patients with either good or poor premorbid developmental histories (Phillips, 1953). Thus, Baxter, Becker, and Hooks (1963) scored the individual Rorschachs of parents of hospitalized neurotics and of good and poor premorbid hospitalized schizophrenics on a Defensive Style scale. They found that parents of poor premorbid patients used significantly more primitive defenses (denial and projection) than the parents of good premorbid patients. Farina's (1960) results showed that mothers of poor premorbid male patients tended to dominate in a parental interaction situation, whereas fathers of good premorbid patients were more likely to be dominant. Mishler and Waxler (1968) also found that the interaction of families of good and poor premorbid patients differed along a number of dimensions. For example, families of good premorbid patients were lower on expressiveness, and families of poor premorbid patients were lower on acknowledgment. Very broadly, such studies are consistent with the hypothesis that poor premorbid, or process, patients are more involved with their mothers and have less mature and more "impervious" parents than good premorbid, or reactive, patients.

Certainly, these studies demonstrate that investigations of the family interaction of schizophrenics should take subtype of patient into account. Many more studies of individual parents and family interaction patterns and styles are needed to delineate the differences between families of the various subtypes of schizophrenic patients. Further empirical evidence is required to either confirm or disconfirm the hypothesis that the families of amorphous, process, and poor premorbid patients are likely to show more severe boundary disturbances, manifested in cognitive and interpersonal functioning, than are the families of fragmented, reactive, and good premorbid patients.

This discussion of the relevance of family studies to boundary problems in schizophrenia is primarily speculative. However, some of the phenomena observed by groups of investigators, although interpreted and conceptualized in different ways, seem to be more coherent and understandable if viewed as reflections of boundary disturbance in the family as a whole. Thus, if at least one other family member in addition to the patient experiences separation from and independence of the patient as devastating and annihilating, or if constant arguing and fighting serve to preserve a fundamental sense of individuation, the disturbed patterns of interacting, communicating, and relating found in the family interaction of schizophrenic patients seem to be more comprehensible. Furthermore, the less differentiation there is in each family member, the more intensely would the family as a whole be likely to cling to their rigid roles and distorted interactional styles, since these behaviors may serve to stave off the threat of dissolution of the selves of the family members as well as of the patient.

However, there is a basic limitation to conclusions based on clinical observations and studies of families in which the offspring is already schizophrenic. Such data cannot show whether the family's current behavior is in response to having a seriously disturbed child or antedated the child's disturbance and played some role in its etiology (Waxler, 1974). For instance, Liem's (1974) findings do not support the etiological hypothesis that parents' disordered communications contribute to their offspring's thought disorder. Rather, her findings support the responsive position that parents of schizophrenics may learn disordered styles of communication in response to their schizophrenic offspring. Using a structured object identification task, Liem found that communications of parents of 11 schizophrenic sons were not significantly more disordered than those of parents of 11 normal control sons and had no adverse effect on sons' responses. However, schizophrenic sons' disordered communications had an adverse effect on the responses of both their own parents and on those of parents of normal control sons. Furthermore, Schopler and Loftin (1969) found that attitudes associated with being studied in connection with a disturbed child had a deleterious effect on parents' performance on the Object Sorting test. As will be discussed in Chapter 5, retrospective studies, using data gathered before the child's illness, and prospective, longitudinal studies of children at risk for schizophrenia can help to sort out the relative contributions of parental behavior and the child's genetic and other vulnerabilities to the etiology of schizophrenia. Nevertheless, research on the family interaction of already schizophrenic patients can be extremely valuable in formulating hypotheses about the etiology of schizophrenia and in identifying important variables to investigate in such retrospective and prospective studies.

Summary

In this chapter, we have tried to show that schizophrenic disturbances in the sense of self and interpersonal relationships can be seen as manifestations of early developmental difficulties, particularly difficulty in establishing and maintaining clear-cut boundaries between the self and other people. In support of this hypothesis, we have attempted to integrate psychoanalytic theories of normal and abnormal development with Piaget's views of normal cognitive development, and we have cited relevant clinical research findings on both the individual schizophrenic and his family constellation wherever possible. Psychoanalytic theorists have been primarily concerned with the development of human "object" relationships through interaction with the social environment; Piaget, with normal cognitive development, including the attainment of the inanimate object concept through interaction with the physical environment. However, as a number of writers (e.g., Ainsworth, 1967; Bettelheim, 1967; Décarie, 1965) have suggested, both sets of views may be integrated, so that the development of cognitive capacities, sense of self, and ability to form interpersonal ties can be seen as mutually interdependent, influencing one another in complex ways. Thus, the attainment of the object concept described by Piaget, or of the capacity to maintain a mental representation of an absent (inanimate) object, seems comparable to the achievement of (human) object constancy in psychoanalytic terminology or of the ability to maintain an affective attachment to and a mental representation of another person when that person is not physically present. Bell's (1968, 1970) study provides some empirical evidence indicating that inanimate and human object constancy develop in parallel, and her findings suggest that an affectionate attachment between mother and infant facilitates cognitive development and that consistent human attachment requires some degree of cognitive capacity to represent absent human objects. Otherwise, if there is no mental image of an important person, that person seems to be annihilated when he disappears and is not immediately present—as seems to occur in schizophrenics to varying degrees.

For Piaget, the attainment of the object concept also means that the self is experienced as one object among many, having its own independent existence in a common space and time shared with other objects, with continuity into the past and future. Psychoanalytically oriented writers stress the importance of the infant's interaction with mothering figures in learning to discriminate between inside and outside and between self and other as necessary developmental accomplishments before the capacity for human object constancy can be attained (Jacobson, 1964). According to Bruch (1962), the preschizophrenic child has had difficulty in learning to make these basic discriminations, partly because of inappropriate environmental responses to his expressions of need. Thus, for example, if the mother cannot separate her own needs from those of her child and cannot respond differentially to his various signals, the child will have difficulty in learning to discriminate his own sensations from each other and his own experience from that of his mother.

Many observers have described the symbiotic or undifferentiated forms of relatedness that seem characteristic of the schizophrenic in his relationship with his family, and we have attempted to convey the experience of both the individual schizophrenic and his family involved in such a relationship. Mahler (1968) and others (e.g., Searles, 1965) postulate that a symbiotic stage, in which the child is only partially differentiated from significant figures but differentiated enough to experience severe separation reactions, occurs in normal development. Thus, symbiosis in schizophrenia can be seen as a developmental disturbance, where the patient has never fully established a symbiotic relationship or resolved it in a normal way. Normal resolution of the symbiotic phase seems to involve the attainment of the object concept in Piaget's terms, including the capacity for representational thought, so that constant mental images of self and of others can be maintained and distinguished, permitting tolerance for separation without endangering the very existence of the self or of the symbiotic partner. Degrees of lack of self constancy and of object constancy and inability to distinguish representations of self from those of other people can be seen as contributing to a situation where both closeness and separation involve the threat of psychological death through merging with, or total divorce from, the symbiotic partner. The experience of schizophrenics, noted by many observers (e.g., Burnham, Gladstone, & Gibson, 1969; Rosenfeld & Sprince, 1963), is of being caught in a dilemma—yearning for union, struggling for distance, and unable to tolerate either, since both fusion and separation lead to experiences of dissolution of the self.

We have presented research and clinical evidence showing that the various subtypes of schizophrenics differ in their degree of cognitive difficulty. Special emphasis has been placed on the paranoid–nonparanoid distinction. Consistent with the evidence presented in Chapter 2 that paranoids tend to show more intact cognitive functioning than other subtypes and sometimes sharper cognitive focusing than normals, the extreme constriction and interpersonal distance of paranoids can be seen as exaggerated efforts to defend the self against disintegration and boundary loss. We have also discussed how promiscuity in female schizophrenics, homosexuality in male schizophrenics, and assaultiveness in either can be viewed in part as attempts to achieve separation as well as union. Thus, homosexuality in males may represent efforts to replace the mother with an object different from her, but the major goal can be seen as seeking maternal care from the homosexual partner.

Finally, relevant theories and clinical and empirical findings from studies of families of schizophrenic patients were reviewed, tending to support the hypothesis that degree of boundary disturbance in individual parents, family patterns of role relationships, and overall family styles of communicating and interacting contribute to both the etiology and maintenance of the schizophrenic's difficulties in differentiating himself from his family and establishing an independent existence. The limitations of the conclusions that can be drawn from such studies of families with an offspring who is already schizophrenic were also discussed.

4 / *Clinical Illustrations*

Introduction

Our task in this chapter is to present several clinical cases in considerable detail to illustrate how consideration of boundary disturbances can contribute to understanding various types of psychotic experiences. The five cases presented here were selected because their Rorschach protocols manifested a type of thought disorder indicating a particular level of boundary disturbance. The range of levels included are: contaminatory and vague responses that lack stability and constancy (Patient A); well articulated, but unstable and fluid responses that lack constancy (Patient B); confabulations that indicate difficulty in distinguishing between external reality and internal reactions (Patient C); fabulized combinations that suggest only minimal difficulty in maintaining boundaries (Patient D); and few indications of formal thought disorder, but themes of merging in the content juxtaposed with exaggerated attempts to maintain boundaries (Patient E). For each case, clinical material will be presented first, followed by an analysis of the boundary disturbances in the Rorschach and Thematic Apperception Test (TAT) protocols.* Each case is presented in detail so that it is

* Description of Cards Used in Thematic Apperception Test (from Allison, Blatt & Zimet, 1968, p. 101): 1. Boy with violin. 5. Woman standing by half-opened door looking into room. 15. Man standing in a graveyard. 14. Silhouette of person against a bright window. Line drawing. Two old men in front view, one above the other. (Not in the present TAT series but taken from the first Harvard Psychological Clinic edition of the TAT.) A reproduction of this card can be found in Rapaport et al., 1946, Vol.II, p. 400. 10. Man's and woman's heads in close proximity. Picasso's "La Vie." Depicts a nude couple and a middle-aged woman with baby. (Not in the present TAT series but taken from the first Harvard Psychological Clinic

possible to consider the multiple ways that boundary difficulties can be experienced and expressed not only in psychological test protocols but also in a broad clinical context that includes case histories, current behavior and activities, and the therapeutic process. We also hope to illustrate how boundary difficulties can be manifested in a host of functions, including cognitive and perceptual processes, interpersonal relations, and experiences of the self. In addition, we hope to show that conceptualizing disturbances in terms of boundary articulation is valuable in assessing current levels of functioning of psychotic patients.

We assume that boundary difficulties are related to early developmental disturbances in object relations. The more disrupted boundary articulations occur in more chronic patients who have had a lifelong history of disturbed interpersonal relationships. This genetic reconstruction, however, is most difficult since we must rely on informants who themselves are undoubtedly caught up in the patient's difficulties and may minimize or exaggerate historical details for their own reasons. Our attempts at reconstructive analysis of patients' difficulties, therefore, are presented as speculative and exploratory. Another limitation in these case presentations is that they have been drawn from hospital records prepared by various members of the clinical staff at somewhat different points in the patients' hospitalization. Thus the material varies in detail and sensitivity depending on the skills of the individual clinician and the amount of time available to the clinical staff to come to know each patient. Generally, however, the clinical observations were thoughtful and sensitive, providing excellent material for these case summaries. We are grateful to the hospital administration and to the clinical staff for permission to excerpt from the clinical files and to the many therapists, nurses, social workers, teachers, aides, and activity workers whose acute observations contributed to the richness and diversity of the material. We have, of course, disguised the clinical reports to protect the confidentiality of the patients, but in a way that we hope has not distorted the essential clinical picture. We are also indebted to these patients, and we hope that our work will contribute to fuller understanding of the nature of

---

edition of the TAT.) A reproduction of this card can be found in Rapaport et al., 1946, Vol.II, p. 400. 13MF. Man standing with arm over his eyes, woman on bed behind him. 6BM. Elderly woman with back turned toward younger man. 7BM. Faces of an elderly and a young man. 17BM. Man clinging to a rope. 12F. Faces of a young and old woman, the latter in the background. 3GF. Young woman with one hand against door, the other covering her face. 2. Farm scene, young woman with books in foreground, man working in field and older woman standing in background. 18GF. A woman with hands around throat of another person on a stairway. 7GF. Older woman sitting beside girl who is holding a doll in her lap. 12M. Young man lying on couch, older man leaning over him with hand over young man's face. 3BM. Figure on the floor beside couch, object (revolver, knife) beside him. 16. Blank card.

psychotic experiences. It is only with a fuller understanding and appreciation of these desperate struggles that we, and succeeding generations, can become more effective in aiding our patients to live fuller and more meaningful lives.

The first patient to be presented is A, an 18-year-old high school senior in his second hospitalization; he had been briefly hospitalized the previous year. A was selected for presentation because his Rorschach was replete with responses that were poorly articulated, amorphous, vague, de-animated, and occasionally contaminatory. His responses also often lacked stability and constancy. He was, for example, unable to remember many of his responses once the card was removed, even though the responses had been given only a few seconds earlier. This lack of stability of representations also characterized his interpersonal bahavior on the ward. He quickly became confused when close to others or when he had to participate and interact with more than one or two people. At these times he reported experiences of blurred perception and confused thinking. Clinical reports suggested strong wishes for fusing and merging with important figures, such as his therapist. His difficulties seemed to have begun early, and there were few, if any, reports of meaningful relationships in his life. His current difficulties seemed to have evolved in a slow, gradual, undramatic decompensation over many years.

The second case, B, a 22-year-old, single, female college student, seemed to have been searching for intimacy and closeness for a number of years. Though her hospitalization was precipitated by a dramatic suicide gesture, her adolescent years were characterized by a vague sense of wandering and searching. Her primary relationships during these adolescent years were with two disturbed girls, one of whom attempted suicide. B was selected for presentation because her Rorschach protocol contained beautiful, almost exquisitely sensitive articulations, which lacked stability and began to change as she continued to look at the card. While the responses of both A and B lacked stability, B seemed to be at a higher developmental level because her articulations were not vague and amorphous; on the contrary, they were very well articulated but lacked constancy and stability. Her Rorschach responses also showed themes of union and a wish to "curl up in a central place," but they were juxtaposed with expressions of a wish for separateness and definition, despite the great attraction of union.

The third case is a 20-year-old girl, C, whose development seemed to have progressed normally until she was 13-years old and in the seventh grade. There had been numerous accidents during her early childhood; she had suffered a concussion at one point and had received numerous cuts and bruises and broken several bones. C had always seemed to envy her brother and later she seemed to seek more masculine activity and appearance. C was selected for presentation because her Rorschach was characterized by numerous confabulatory responses and extensive indications that she experienced difficulty in maintaining distinctions between her external perceptions and her internal reactions to these experiences. While there was much joking and humor in C's behavior and in her Rorschach responses, her extensive confabulations indicate that her experiences ranged from extreme elation to feelings of utter doom, desolation, and depletion. While her clinical picture was complicated by neurological difficulties, C's estrangement, feelings of despair, and suicidal preoccupations seem to be predominantly an expression of her long-standing schizoid character structure.

Our fourth case, D, was selected because her Rorschach manifested several fabulized combinations in which the separate identity of percepts was maintained but the spatial or temporal contiguity of the percepts was taken to indicate some type of interrelationship. Of all the indicators of boundary disturbance on the Rorschach, the fabulized combination is probably the least serious. While an extensive number of fabulized combinations can indicate the presence of psychosis, frequently the psychosis is acute and the patient is more readily responsive to therapeutic intervention. When D was hospitalized, there was some concern that she might be borderline or have an underlying psychosis. She responded very rapidly and well to hospitalization and after 6 months was discharged to an outpatient status where she continued to progress. The few fabulized combination responses in her Rorschach indicate some mild boundary disturbances, which seemed to be focused around issues of sexual identity. The test record was consistent with the eventual clinical formulation that D was not psychotic; rather, she was struggling on a neurotic level with oedipal and preoedipal issues of rejection by her father, sexual identity confusion, and depression stemming from an unsatisfying relationship with her mother.

E, a 17-year-old, male, high school student, was selected for presentation because his Rorschach protocol illustrated a variety of ways of struggling against wishes for merging and fusion. E's difficulties apparently began two years earlier, during his junior year in boarding school. While E was hospitalized for a bone fracture, an elderly man sharing the hospital room with E suddenly died. On discharge from the hospital, E became increasingly obsessed with themes of death and homosexuality, and began to experience episodes of depersonalization. In contrast to his marked homosexual concerns and feminine identification, he often reacted with defiance, bravado, mild antisocial acts, and, at times, with violence. He was considered by the clinical staff as being an adolescent in a severe identity crisis and turmoil, rather than as having a schizophrenic reaction.

Case I—Patient A: Contaminatory and Vague Responses that Lack Stability and Constancy

A, a 19-year-old, male, high school senior, was admitted for a second hospitalization. The first hospitalization was for a brief period and had taken place about one year earlier. A had a pale complexion, rigid gait and posture, awkward movements, and a frequently expressionless gaze. He rarely expressed feelings and often gave the impression of being in a daze and not quite in contact with his surroundings. When embarrassed or tense, he would break into an inappropriate and self-conscious giggle. Occasionally, however, when he was pleased by something, he would smile in a warm, childlike fashion. At times, he stared in an intense, scrutinizing way, but more often sat back in a chair as if sleeping, but possibly daydreaming or hallucinating. He rarely spoke spontaneously or answered questions with more than a sentence. His speech was coherent, and his vocabulary and syntax were appropriate. Although he seemed of above average intelligence, he constantly complained of difficulty in concentrating and remembering. He had trouble keeping his thoughts organized or pursuing a topic for any length of time. His discussions of the events of his life were mostly a series of disjointed incidents or fantasies, usually expressed in very concrete, visual terms. He described feelings of confusion when he tried to converse for more than a few minutes or when he was in close proximity with several people. During such experiences, he felt overstimulated, his eyes would hurt, and he would either close his eyes or try to fixate on one specific point, such as a spot on the wall. He also hinted that at such times faces tended to blur and the furniture and walls almost acquired a life of their own. In addition to these hallucinatory tendencies, he also had somatic delusions about the physical deteriorative process going on within him. Initially he had concerns about being subjected to violence or ridicule in the hospital, and he was prone to anticipate criticism, ridicule, or attack and to misinterpret the slightest gesture or alterations in tone of voice. There was no evidence, however, of systematized delusions; nor did he mention any suicidal ideation. His dominant state seemed to be a kind of affectless depression, with constant expressions of a feeling of hopelessness and helplessness (he was born "dumb, inept, degenerate," etc.). He often wished to remain in his bed. He did express, however, a wish to communicate, to have friends, and to be the center of attention. But he felt unable to do anything about these wishes. He repeatedly expressed concern about being misunderstood, and about annoying or boring people. In his more lively moments, his behavior had a childlike, teasing quality, and on occasion he even tried to be humorous, although in a rather weird and self-deprecating fashion.

A was a planned full-term baby. Forceps were used in his delivery, but otherwise it was uneventful. He was bottle-fed. During his first year, A was sickly, with many colds and severe bouts of croup, that required a great deal of his mother's attention, holding and rocking him. She said that she was often afraid they "would lose him." He outgrew this sickliness by the time he was 1-year old, when the family moved to a new home. A walked at 13 months and talked somewhat earlier, when he was around 1 year of age. He never used baby talk and quickly began to use sentences. Daytime toilet training was accomplished at about 2 ½ years, but A remained enuretic at night until he was 10-years old. He was an affectionate, outgoing child until he was 3, when he was sent to nursery school. He was so unhappy and shy that his teacher and mother decided that he should remain at home the following year. At 5 he started kindergarten, with none of the earlier difficulties. This was also the year in which his brother was born. In spite of subsequent bitter hostility between the boys, his mother reported that initially A was delighted to have a baby brother. It was only later, when his brother began to walk and to get into A's toys, that the angry rivalry became apparent to the mother.

A's report of his childhood was mostly a series of concrete, isolated incidents or fantasies with great vagueness as to their location in time. A's earliest memory, which he dated around age 3, was of getting lost and being found a few blocks from home. Most of his memories had to do with feeling scared, humiliated, or being injured. He remembered being scared to be left alone in the house, hearing strange noises and having a hallucination of a monster coming out of the furnace. He would sometimes imagine his parents being changed into Frankenstein-type monsters. He had an imaginary companion, a bodyguard who could summon troops to his defense, a fantasy that he still experienced at the time of his second hospitalization. He remembered being injured in a car because of his mother making a sudden stop. He also vividly recalled a boy having his toes cut off by a lawnmower. He remembered his father as big and powerful, but that his mother did most of the disciplining, frequently shouting at and occasionally spanking him.

His most vivid memories of his early school years were of being slapped by a teacher in the first grade for making noise and of being humiliated by being forced to stand in front of the class. He was occasionally hit or beaten by other boys and would complain to his mother. On the rare occasions when he would fight back and get the best of a fight, he felt very ashamed and worried—a pattern that persisted in later years.

During A's early years the family moved several times. When A was 10, the family moved once again. After this move, A's mother began to work full time. She employed a maid and felt that A continued to see as much of her as before, since he was away at school when she was at work. He apparently did fairly well in the fifth and sixth grades and had several friends, both from school and from his neighborhood. With these friends he shared interests in playing ball, hiking, weight lifting, petty shoplifting, comic books, and other fairly age-appropriate concerns. He also learned about "fucking" from these friends.

According to his mother, A's school difficulties began 2 years later, when he was 12 ½ years. An older boy began bullying and tormenting A, and his life was made miserable. Furthermore, this boy involved all the other boys, even those formerly friendly to A, in tormenting him, so that he was then totally friendless and began to protest going to school. The following year, in eighth grade, the bully was no longer in A's school, and he regained some of his former friends. But his grades did not improve substantially, and he continued to have trouble studying.

He began masturbating when he was about 13-years old. His main fantasy was, and remained, of his watching a girl eating and the girl looking at him. He would draw pictures of his masturbation fantasies, particularly of naked men being watched by women.

He remembered mostly feelings of anger and fear toward his father. He felt that his father was practically never at home and, even when home, not available to spend time with him. His father occasionally slapped him and frequently criticized him for his poor manners, childishness, and so on.

Ninth grade was a "disastrous" year for A. His family moved again, he had no friends, and he flunked all his courses. The other boys ignored him in school, he felt extremely isolated, and he hardly tried to do any school-work. He missed a lot of school, pretending to be sick, and spent a great deal of time in his room, daydreaming or listening to popular music. He also engaged in many sexual and make-believe games with his younger brother. He liked his brother to pretend to be a princess or a baby, and sometimes he took these roles himself. He felt guilty for having instigated these games, which he believed may have contributed to his brother's psychological problems.

The following year his parents decided to send A to boarding school, with the hope that the enforced living arrangements at the school would help him make friends. It was during his second year at this school that concern was first expressed about A's emotional problems. School officials urged psychiatric help, and he entered once-a-week therapy for a year. A felt very angry and hurt about being sent away to boarding school. He was reluctant to talk about his two years there, except for the repetitive themes of feeling lonely, isolated and ridiculed and of doing extremely poorly in his schoolwork. While he was away at school his father was killed in an accident. Beyond the initial shock, A remembered no specific reaction or grief over his father's death. There was no evidence that his behavior changed in any significant way afterward. He felt vaguely guilty about his father's death because he remembered so many angry feelings toward him.

His mother became increasingly more tense and irritable, and there were many squabbles and arguments at home about such issues as his refusal to go to school and staying in his room. It was at this point that the mother sought consultation, and it was recommended that A be hospitalized.

A's difficulties seemed to have developed in a slow, gradual, and undramatic decompensation over many years. Before his first hospitalization, he spent the academic year at a boarding school. He found it difficult to study and failed several courses. Socially, he was quite isolated; most of the boys paid attention to him only to tease or ridicule him. He had several homosexual experiences, which he said he enjoyed. However, he was most distressed by several hallucinatory experiences such as hearing a voice call his name or feeling that a hand was touching his head when no one was around. He was given psychological tests at this time, and the diagnosis was of "incipient paranoid schizophrenia."

At the end of the school year, he returned to his mother's home and spent his time in his room listening to records. His mother kept urging him to go out, and violent arguments ensued between them. With his younger brother also showing indications of severe disturbance, the home situation quickly became intolerable, and the mother decided to hospitalize A. At first A resisted; then, after an incident in which he lost his temper and threw a magazine at his mother, he agreed he needed hospitalization. A was discharged after 2 weeks because "I behaved well and obeyed all the rules." He was sent to a halfway house where he lived for 6 months until his second hospitalization. During this time, he had daily group psychotherapy; but apparently he did not get very involved and felt very tense, uneasy, and at times bored. He was particularly uneasy when his mother attended the sessions and he was encouraged to confront her with his feelings.

While at the halfway house, he was enrolled in a school, but he rarely went to classes and soon dropped out. It was then decided that he should have a job, but he worked for only a few days, as a messenger. Most of his interest during this time was centered around his relationship with a seriously disturbed girl. This was his first involvement with a girl, and they engaged in some sexual activity. Apparently, the relationship involved confusion of sexual identification and roles. At times, A saw himself as the girl's protector; he liked to listen to her and let her cry on his shoulder. At other times, he experienced her as a big powerful, masculine creature or as a mother and himself as a girl or a baby. The relationship ended when the girl was hospitalized. A felt responsible, and he considered his own subsequent hospitalization as partly a punishment for his "degenerate" behavior.

When A entered the hospital for his second hospitalization, he was timid and somewhat confused, but he appeared to be genuinely optimistic about the prospects of his stay in the hospital. During the first few days on the ward, he felt encouraged by the style of the hospital and proceeded to tell various staff members quite a bit of unconnected information about himself—anecdotes from his past, expressions of loneliness, and brief descriptions of family relationships. In general, he was quite candid about his problems as he saw them. Relationships with other patients were much harder for A. During the first week or so, he made attempts to join group conversations and to make friends. When his somewhat awkward attempts at friendliness met with little success, he became more and more isolated, spending as much of each day as he could on his bed. A stated two reasons for spending so much time on his bed—to avoid people and to enjoy his fantasies, for example, of being a strong person and saying "no to a persistent salesman" or alternately thinking of himself as a famous millionaire and an auto mechanic. It was clear that he was also gratified by the attention he received from staff members when they insisted that he get off his bed and do something.

Early in his hospital stay, A became upset about the homosexual undercurrent on the ward, particularly some direct overtures from another patient, who was about his age. Despite A's discomfort about this incident, this patient was the only person with whom A had any real friendship for more than 2 months. A felt somewhat homosexually attracted to him, but stated probably accurately, that the main reason for seeking his company was that the other patient's boisterousness made him feel more alive and that he was one of the few patients who showed some interest in him. A occasionally called him "Dad," and, when confused, he called other patients by the names of boys he had known at school. Gradually, A came to feel that he could no longer confide in the other patient, so the friendship dissolved. Later, A became interested in a female patient, enjoyed talking with her, and was very pleased and sexually stimulated when they both drank soda together out of the same bottle. A began to spend increasing amounts of time with this female patient, and he soon decided that he was in love with her. This one-sided romance was very painful for A, and he found it difficult to refrain from pestering her to spend unreasonable amounts of time with him. Traumatic as this experience was, it seemed to help A break out of his pattern of isolation. He spent less time daydreaming on his bed, stayed up later, and was generally livelier in his activities on the ward.

A's timidity and lack of self-assurance affected a number of aspects of his life on the ward. For instance, he had great difficulty sustaining normal conversations. On one occasion, he asked to talk to one of the aides, and, after a period of silence, abruptly asked, "What do you think of the possibility of a future merger of China and Russia?" He later explained that he was trying to make small talk. A entered the hospital's high school to complete his senior year and graduate. When he first entered classes, he was quite explicit about his problems with school. However, shortly after the class began a sex education unit in biology, he stopped participating and gradually became stuporous and monosyllabic. He would do an assignment only if the teacher insistently told him to do it. A's problems with passivity and his difficulties in concentrating and maintaining focus were so great that without some compulsory, clear, structured activities, school was very difficult for him.

In the first few weeks of therapy, A seemed pleased to be in individual therapy and was relatively active in talking about himself. He talked in rapid succession about a variety of themes, including his problems with "identity," his guilt about his father's death and his brother's condition, and his strong dependence on his mother and his wish to be babied by her. He spoke of his sexual problems and his difficulties with girls. He considered himself "bisexual" at best and was convinced that he was born with inadequate genitals. He also mentioned that he had been going downhill physically, that he was fat and flabby, and that some vague pains in his leg might indicate that it would have to be amputated. While the extent of his psychotic thinking was evident early in his hospitalization, the intensity of his passivity, inertia, and withdrawal became apparent only later.

In therapy, he talked more and more about his feelings of discouragement. He talked about not being able to make any friends among the patients, of missing the halfway house, and of wishing that he was at home with his mother. He constantly apologized and blamed himself for his inability to communicate. It was pointed out to him that initially he seemed to have expected that the new therapist and the new hospital would result in some sudden magical change in his condition, and that he was disappointed. He was also concerned that he was making the therapist somewhat discouraged and wanted to know whether he was a "heavy case." The therapist agreed that A had been seriously incapacitated for a long time and that he had experienced his life for many years as merely being pushed around from house to house, school to school, and hospital to hospital, so that he felt he had no will or initiative of his own. But the therapist stressed that he was not as hopeless or helpless as he presented himself, pointing out that he was withdrawn and passive from a sense of discouragement and fear and from an attempt to gain some satisfaction from his fantasies. The therapist also hinted on several occasions that there might be a good deal of anger behind his attitude. While this made A anxious, he increasingly talked about feelings of resentment toward his mother, particularly at her emphasis on good manners, the importance of school achievement, and so on.

The therapist was quite active during the sessions, making comments in a spontaneous and direct fashion. A was encouraged to experience the therapist as a real person, interested in helping him, but with limited powers either benevolent or malevolent. With his relationship to his mother in mind, A was told that the therapist could not and would not manage his life and would not be drawn into a battle between an irresistible force and an immovable object. A agreed that this statement made him feel both safe and disappointed. He told the therapist at times that he considered himself "tough." Yet it was pretty clear that, for him, the highlights of the sessions were the moments during which he found that he and his therapist had something in common—for instance, when they were both smoking or when the therapist expressed knowledge of places where A had been. These occasions probably triggered some fantasies of merging, and he would beam with a blissful, childish smile and tell the therapist that he liked him. At the other extreme, he expressed some anger toward the therapist, in mild words and by pretending to fall asleep, when the therapist said that he did not share A's conviction that defective genitals were the cause of all his problems. A also reported several dreams. The more salient of these dreams included looking at himself in the mirror and seeing, instead, the face of another "rugged" patient; seeing himself sitting on a giant tape recorder and flying through the shell of a building, sleeping next to his mother on top of the mast of a ship and being frightened of falling down, and a nightmare about watching a parade by people stacked on top of each other and of feeling trapped and running.

From A's account, the events of his early years, the personalities of his parents and brother, and the nature of his interactions with them remained obscure. It can be speculated that this lack of information in his account reflected, in part, difficulties in establishing and maintaining stable self and object representations, so that he was unable to describe himself and other people as having clearly differentiated characteristics. The mother's account of A's history, up to his adolescence, was also uninformative. A's selection of memories from his early years stressed his constant fearfulness and expectations of injury, humiliation, and ridicule. He gave the impression that most of his early relationships were strongly sexualized, but at a very early oral level; and he showed a massive confusion of sexual identification and an absence of relatively conflict-free areas of competence and achievement. It seemed as if early in life he had acquired the conviction that any activity on his part could end only in failure or ridicule or in damage to himself or to others. It appeared that with the beginning of adolescence, A's development practically ceased, and he began a downhill trend. His capacities for schoolwork and social relations lessened, and he withdrew more and more into autistic fantasy life. His activities seemed to have consisted mostly of getting himself into the role of victim or scapegoat for his peers and of defeating, in a passive–aggressive fashion, his mother's demands and expectations. A's very infantile and clinging, but also fearful and angry, relationship with his mother seemed to be central to his emotional life. He described his mother as intrusive and seductive, but also as confusingly demanding and threatening. It appeared that one of the functions of A's passivity was an angry pulling back from his mother, at the same time drawing her attention to him and maintaining his dependency upon her. It also seemed that the competition with his brother had turned into a competition for pathology. A seemed to have experienced his father as alternately threatening or shadowy and weak. His homosexual trends seemed to involve a lack of any differentiated sexual identification, rather than a definite feminine identification. They probably also represented attempts to gain, by a sort of osmosis or merging, some sense of masculinity and liveliness through physical closeness to males. It was difficult to assess what role the relatively recent death of his father played in A's difficulties, but the lack of any overt reaction or change seemed troublesome.

A's thought disturbance—his impaired reality testing and his inability to tolerate any steady interaction or stimulation without becoming disorganized and confused—suggested serious ego defects that had been present from early childhood. Diagnostically, A was considered to be schizophrenic with marked paranoid and passive–aggressive features. His difficulties seemed to have had a slow course, with no clear precipitating events. In his overt behavior, he never acted in a way that was grossly bizarre, violent, or self-destructive. Yet there seemed to be few areas of intact functioning and no developed skill to give him a sense of competence, self-esteem, or gratification. Insofar as he had any sense of self, it seemed to be the negative identity of a doomed patient who was born defective—an identity that was stubbornly defended and also put in the service of his passive negativism. The possibility of further growth for A seemed to depend on his reaching a level where he could express hostility and rage in a more direct and active fashion.

```
RORSCHACH--PATIENT A

Card I.   [5 sec]

  1.  Looks like a mask.              1.   (Mask?)  The two halves in
                                      it, the two spaces look like eyes.
                                      (Impression?)  Looks like a grimac-
```

	ing mask. (Grimacing?) Because of the lower spaces look like a grin or a grimace. All of it.
2. *Looks like a couple of sphinx with wings (yawns). That's all I can see in that.*	2. (Sphinx?) I forgot, no I forgot. (Gives him the card and shows it to him.) Almost all of it looks like a sphinx. (Impression?) It's hard to describe all of it. Just the outline.

The opening response to Card I is an animate–inanimate blend, since the response of a grimacing mask implies that an inanimate object can have animation and life. While responses of masks with grimacing or grinning expressions are not uncommon, the verbal construction implies that the mask itself is actively grimacing. Also, the opening comment to the first response is about the two halves in the mask. While this is not elaborated, it suggests possible concerns about separation and, alternately, fusion.

Response 2 to Card I is another animate–inanimate and animal–human blend: a "sphinx with wings." A sphinx is implicitly a blend of human, animal, and inanimate features, but it has an appropriate cultural reference. A, however, compounds this issue further by giving the sphinx a set of wings. In addition to the blending of human–animal and animate–inanimate features in both of the responses to this card, A also loses the image of the   second response during the inquiry. This is particularly noteworthy, because the Rorschach was administered according to the Rapaport procedures (Rapaport, et al., 1945), in which the inquiry is conducted immediately after each card.* At the end of Card I, after the two responses were

* The Rorschach protocols presented in this chapter were administered according to the procedure of Rapaport et al. (1945) in which inquiry into the responses is conducted after each card is completed. This inquiry is conducted with the card out of sight. Thus, in taking the Rorschach, the subject is presented with the card and asked, "What does it look like?" or "What could it be?" After the subject has finished giving his spontaneous responses, the card is removed, and he is asked—through one or two indirect questions—to elaborate his responses. This inquiry into the responses is kept to a minimum and leading questions are avoided. The standard questions asked in inquiry are, "What made it look like that?" or "Was there anything that made it look like that?" Inquiry into unusual verbalizations or details is conducted by indirect questions such as "What do you mean by . . . ?" or "I don't quite understand what you mean by . . . ?" or "What made it look . . . ?"

The Rorschach protocols are presented in this chapter card by card. The time elapsing between the presentation of each card and the subject's initial response is recorded above the initial response. The spontaneous responses for each card are presented in the left-hand column with the inquiry for each response presented in the right-hand column. Standard questions asked during inquiry are indicated by the notation (?) and when more specific questions were asked, they are indicated in detail. An interpretation of the responses for each card appears after all the responses and their inquiry elaborations have been presented.

given, the card was removed and inquiry was made about both responses. A forgot his second response, a "sphinx with wings," even though the inquiry followed immediately. This fluidity could be a function of organic impairment, hypomanic distractibility, the use of repression, a lack of stability of representations, or an undifferentiated level of psychological organization characterized by amorphous and diffuse experiences. A's forgetting occurs in the context of a very sparse record, with relatively little time intervening between response and inquiry. Also, there seems to be no indication that the response was particularly conflict-laden. Thus, it seems unlikely that the forgetting was due to hypomanic distractibility or repression. Rather, the forgetting seems to be a function of organic impairment or a diffuse, amorphous level of psychological organization, with a very limited capacity for object constancy. Even when the card was returned to view, A still had difficulty describing his response.

Card II.   [10 sec]

1. Looks like a face because you can see here looks like eyes, the red marks, and this could be the face and the mouth is wide open and here the chin seems to be struck by something and it's bursting into blood.

1. (What made it look like a face?) Eyes, mouth. (Eyes?) They were spaces. (Mouth?) Large space in the middle of the picture of the ink blot. The thing in the middle, the blood is red.

2. Looks like two bears kissing because you see without the red mark this looks like a bear. Just the head of the bear and the shoulders. That's about it.

2. (Two bears?) Everything, except the head looks like a profile of the two bears. (Kissing?) Fact that the bears were pressed together.

There are relatively few indications of boundary disturbance in the responses to Card II; but there is a suggestion that A may have some difficulty in establishing distance from frightening, aggressive fantasies. In his first response, he uses the present tense to describe a face bursting into blood because the chin is being struck by something. The use of the present reflects the immediacy of his experiences and suggests that he may lack capacities for the delay, control, and modulation of his impulses. In the second response to this card, "two bears kissing," there is an attribution of some human qualities to an animal, but this is not atypical. However, there is some indication in the inquiry, of a possible tendency toward fusion and merging in his comment that the bears seem to be "pressed together." A profile view is not unusual on this card, but it will be of interest to see if this occurs in less appropriate contexts.

Card III.   [15 sec]

1. I've seen this before, looks like two people ripping a crab apart and that's a butterfly in the middle.

1. (People?) Their head was vaguely outlined and the bodies were outlined. (Ripping?) The fact that they're holding on to something, a crab. (Crab?) Claws and the various parts, the legs.

2. (Butterfly?) Had wings, it was the red spot, it was colorful.

3. The red up in the corner looks like an old man, primitive, it's upside down, the picture is upside down.

3. (Man?) The two red spots in the corner look like old men, the way they were huddled over, that's all.

4. And upside down the black part looks like an insect or crab, part of an insect or crab.

4. (Crab?) I forgot, have mandibles near the head or something. And looks like the whole shape of the crab the way the claws were formed and everything.

On the third card, A gives further indication that his experiences are vague and poorly defined. A gives a popular response of two people, a response that is usually experienced as well defined and articulated. A, however, comments that their head was "vaguely outlined." The fluidity noted on Card I and the vagueness of portions of this response suggest that his difficulties are most likely a function of amorphous and diffuse experiences, particularly around the representation of people.

In his third response to this card, A comments that the men are "huddled over," that the picture must be "upside down." Rather than altering his environment—rotating the card so that the men are in an upright position, he passively accepts the world as it is presented to him and feels relatively helpless to change events; all he can do is simply experience things. Also, on this card he again forgets a response, one that emphasized a head, mandibles, and claws.

Card IV.   [15 sec]

1. Looks like an awful monster's head.

1. (Monster's head?) Now I can't remember it, just tried describing it because I couldn't do it unless I was looking at it. The shape of it, the shape of it, too.

2. There seems to be pigs' heads going out on the sides.

2. (Pig?) Just the head just shaped like the profile of a pig's head.

On Card IV, A gives further evidence regarding the nature of his forgetting and his inability to remember a response. He seems unable to maintain a mental image. He needs constant perceptual input in order to describe his experiences. For him to describe something, it must be directly present in his perceptual field. The instability of his representations is expressed both in his experiences of things being vague and poorly defined and in his difficulty remembering a response only a few seconds after the card has been removed. His impaired capacities for articulation and constancy leave him feeling lost and at a distance from others. It is important to note that his vagueness and difficulty remembering responses usually involve "heads." His emphasis on the vagueness of "heads" and on profiles suggests an emptiness and a lack of vitality in his interactions with others.

Card V.   [2 sec]

1.   The entire thing looks like a bat.   Shaped like a bat, the entire thing, there's the wings. Here are the wings.

1.   (Bat?)   The shape, the head of it, had legs.

2.   Vaguely looks like faces. The wings do when they are upside down.

2.   (Faces?)   The wings then when they were upside down looked like faces.   The nose and the chin.   They were part of the wings. (Did you see them at the same time?)   Yes.   The bat looked a little bit weird.

On the fifth card, A again reports that his experiences are vague and poorly defined, and again this occurs around a representation of a human head. In addition to the vagueness, the response of faces is unstable, and there is a tendency for the faces to merge with the perception of a wing: "The wings then when they were upside down looked like faces.   The nose and the chin. They were part of the wings." While this response is not a full contamination, there is a strong tendency toward contamination. He is unable to keep the two responses independent, and they tend to merge. The second response is prefaced by the word "vaguely" which A used earlier in several other responses. The word "vaguely" seems to characterize his general amorphous level of functioning.

Card VI.   Oh, I remember this from before.   [10 sec]

1.   Looks like a cat skin.   The skin of a cat or a rug.   Here's the head and the whiskers.

1.   (Cat?)   The head with the whiskers particularly.   (Skin?) Because of the sides, they look

like they were fringed. Ragged,
the outline of it.

2. And this is a face, design
of the cat, with a beard. That's
it.

2. (Face?) This here and the
beard, and the eyes. (Beard?)
Part of the area of the side. The
side of the cat. Because it was
there. I saw them both together,
when I turned the card upside down,
yeah, but it wasn't conspicuous,
it was all blended together.

Again on Card VI, as on V, after A gives a popular response, his subsequent response shows indications of boundary difficulties. In his second response to Card VI, he clearly demonstrates difficulties in maintaining boundaries between independent percepts. In addition to a tendency to blend animal and possibly human features, a cat with a beard, he comments that he saw the side of the cat, the cat's face, and the beard together, and when he turned the card upside down, "it was all blended together." In addition to showing contaminatory thinking, the second response is another expression of his tendency toward de-animation. He talks of a "design of a cat" and of seeing "the side of the cat." Like his earlier profile responses, these responses suggest his tendency to devitalize interactions.

Card VII. [10 sec]

1. Looks like vaguely two
little girls with their hair
flying up in the back.

1. (Girls?) The head in particular, that's about it, it was the whole card. (How much of the girls?) All except for the legs.

2. And there's something that
looks a bit like a moth in the
middle.

2. (Moth?) The middle part, the way the wings were shaped, nothing that I can remember.

3. Very strong faces down
here. That's it.

3. (Faces?) The torso of the girls. They were the faces. (Faces?) There were eyes and mouths. Don't know any more about it, that was rather strange. (Part of the girls' torsos?) Yeah, saw it at the same time. The girls didn't look like real girls but like caricatures. They were ugly.

They were ugly because their heads
were jutting out, there weren't
any logs. They were roughly drawn.
This test is really unreal. (?)
The fact that you're writing down
stuff. (Uncomfortable?) A little,
not that bad.

On Card VII, he gives a vivid and popular response of human figures, but later in the inquiry he comments that they are only torsos, rather than real people, that they are not like real girls, but caricatures. He indicates that his experiences, particularly of people, are not well articulated: the card "vaguely looks like two little girls," it is "roughly drawn," and "this test is really unreal." The vagueness of his experiences, the instability of his object representations, and his de-animation of human figures are all evident in this response. It is important to note, however, that despite these difficulties, his perceptual processes are reasonably accurate. The fact that his vague and unstable representations have not seriously interfered with his perception of reality suggests that considerable ego resources have remained intact, and these may facilitate his response to therapy.

Card VIII.   [8 sec]

1. *Looks like beavers. Nothing particularly interesting about it, it just looks like that.*

1. (Beavers?) The side, the pink globs that were on the side. They just look like beavers, that's all I can say.

2. *Looks like a face, the eyes, rather skull-like, nose and mouth, that's the mouth and nose.*

2. (Face?) The eyes and the mouth. (Mouth?) I have to see the card again. I don't know what I saw without seeing the card. (Card given back.) Oh, the mouth and the nose appear to be skull-like because they were empty. They were just spaces.

On Card VIII, A again comments about the instability of his response and of his need for direct perceptual experiences in order to maintain the representation. Throughout the Rorschach, we see numerous statements about his difficulty with object constancy around animate figures, particularly perception of humans. Again he indicates a move toward de-animation when he describes the face as "skull-like." It is impressive that many of these responses of faces involve the white spaces of the card, suggesting the speculation that the white spaces stimulate feelings of emptiness and of a void, which resonate with his experiences of people.

Card IX.   [5 sec]

1. *Oh that looks like some kind of faces. The orange faces. The noses are connected by some kind of orange filament. Again there are faces up here that seem to have fangs. The pinkishness on the shading made it look like babies, babies' heads and shoulders and that's about all.*

1. (Faces?) Just the way it was shaped, the profiles, it goes for both faces, the baby faces and the orange ones. The orange faces were connected by an orange filament between them.

2. (Faces, baby faces?) Well they had a profile outline and looked like fangs. The pinkishness made it look babyish and the shading made it look like the very delicate skin of a baby.

On Card IX, there are several animate–inanimate blends and primitive and devitalized object representations. Faces are "connected by some kind of filament," and again these faces are profiles. In addition to the devitalization, there is a theme of people being "connected" in bizarre ways. The second response of baby faces is a profile, and it has a quasi-human quality because of the "fangs."

Card X.   [10 sec]

1. *I see a face in the middle of it all, there are yellow eyes, greenish moustache.*

1. (Faces?) In the white spaces, most of it. (Eyes?) The eyes were yellowish and the moustache was large and unrealistic because it was way too large to be anybody's moustache. Green seemed to be dark so it could have been the green which made it look dark, and made me think of moustache, because they are dark usually.

2. *There seem to be crabs and insects all over the page. There is a blue crab or crabs because of these two. It's double focus. That's all I can say about that.*

2. (Crabs?) Just the way they were shaped. (Double focus?) That there were two sides of the card and they both had the same thing that was going on, as in all of them, that's all that I meant.

On Card X, a human face is seen in the white spaces, and once again it is a distorted representation of a human head. He comments on the instability of his perceptual experience in his mention of the "double focus" of the card and the way that the "two sides of it have the same thing going on," which seems confusing for him.

Despite the unstable, vague, and distorted responses, there are a number of constructive features in this Rorschach, including the perceptual accuracy and the involvement with people shown in his—albeit distorted—human responses. While there seem to be serious impairments in ego functions, there appears to be some potential for therapeutic progress.

TAT--PATIENT A

1. *(Card 1). There's a young boy, probably about 10 years old, looking at the violin, the music sheet is underneath the violin. He looks quite discouraged with the situation. Before he was playing the violin, taking his lesson, and he began to have trouble with some of the chords. So he put down the violin. (Outcome?) Outcome will be that he is going to put the violin away and not practice anymore.*

2. *(Card 5). It's a lady standing by a door--she looks about 50, she's looking out into a room. Apparently she heard a noise from the room, she wanted to see what was going on. She is going to walk into the room, look around, and I have no idea what will happen after that. (Thinking and feeling?) Feeling apparently about the noise and a little frightened. (?) She thought she heard someone making noise. That's all I can think of.*

3. *(Card 15). It's a picture of a graveyard and there's a man standing in the middle of the graveyard apparently praying. I assume that a close friend or relative had died and he's come here to pray for the relative. He's feeling grim about the whole thing. After praying for a while, he's going to go where he lives. That's all I have to say about that.*

4. *(Card 14). It looks like a photograph, apparently, this boy is looking out a window in a house, I don't know what he's doing there, but I imagine he's trying to see how the weather is. When he's done looking out the window, he'll go back and decide if he's going to go outside or not. That's about all I have to say.*

5. *(Line drawing). This is a bizarre picture. An old man seems to be physically hurting another old man. I don't know if they're fighting, but they must have had some kind of disagreement. I don't think I have much more to say. It doesn't look like an entity is what I'm trying to say. They might be a portrayal of the downfall of the old man who has another old man on top of him (looks under the card).*

6. *(Card 10). It's a picture of a man with a woman, and the woman is leaning against the man's shoulder and I would imagine the story involved a man beginning to go off on a mission of some sort and the*

woman beginning to see that he's all right. (Mission?) Well, it's likely the man was trying to help somebody out of a fire. The woman is glad to see that he is alive. (Outcome?) Go home and have dinner.

7. (Picasso "La Vie"). It's hard to figure this out. It's a man and two women. One woman is holding a baby. I really don't know what to say about the story. (Make up one.) Well possibly, it's really hard to figure out what this could be. (?) Well possibly the baby is the son or daughter of the couple that are close to each other, the woman holding the baby could very well be taking care of the child for them. I must say I am surprised at the expression of the woman who is holding, who is leaning against the man. (?) Because she looks so depressed and maybe it's because she is losing the child. It's her baby, looks like as if the lady who's glad, took the child away from the couple. That's all. (Outcome?) Well, because the young man, who looks like Jesus Christ, will take his bride elsewhere.

8. (13MF). It's the picture of a woman lying on a bed and there's a man standing above her. Hiding his eyes with his arm, it seems likely that the woman committed suicide and the man found her there. The man will probably call the police, that's about all I have to say. (Why committed suicide?) I have no idea, I have no insight into that sort of thing. (?) Ugly people commit suicide.

9. (12M). That's a drawing of a young man asleep. And an older man is kneeling near the bed, partly on the bed. (?) And it looks surprising enough, like the old man is going to strangle the young man. I think the young man will awake and defend himself. That's about all I have to say about this picture. (What led up to the story?) The young man was rude with the old man (laughs), so to get his revenge the old man is going to try to kill him.

10. (6BM). It's a picture of an old woman, a young powerful looking man, apparently the young woman, the old woman, excuse me, looking out of the window. I don't want to say apparently for the fifth time, so I'll try not to. She looks fairly distressed. The young man has brought her bad news, he might have to tell about a death. Or some kind of intrusion such as a part of the lawn may have to be used in making a highway. (He asks if this will be discussed with his therapist.) (?) Thing will be that they build a highway through the garden.

11. (17BM). I've seen this one before, this one reminds me of the ones I've had before. Man seems to be going down the rope of a building, from the building. I don't know why. (Make up a story.) Could have been a fire in his apartment, he's trying to get down from his apartment by a rope which is dangerous, but he looks quite muscular so he'll manage. I find it surprising that he's looking off to the side, would be more rational if he were looking down. (?) He must be seeing something, something must have caught his attention. (?) Possibly because something going on in another apartment.

12. (7BM). Picture of two men, the older man has a moustache, and we see the profile of the young man. They're probably making some kind of deal, business deal. I suppose, oh the younger man seems discouraged

or disdainful, the older man looks pleased and cunning. That's about it. (Pleased?) I guess because he got the better half of the deal.

¹⁹ (16). Nothing, I refuse to make a story to this because there's nothing on the paper and I'm not going to make up something that I can't draw with a pencil and a paper. (Pencil and paper?) Drawing is the only way I can get something prepared for you to hear.

It is impressive how A is able to organize and limit his responses to the TAT. With more structured and well articulated stimuli continually present as he gives his responses, he can utilize the reality support and maintain contact. However, for the most part, his stories are only descriptions of the cards, and he rarely extends his stories beyond the immediate perceptual details of the stimuli. Like his opening responses to many of the Rorschach cards, his TAT stories are often obvious and unelaborated. As he indicates in his second TAT story, unless something is directly represented, he has no way of knowing what will happen and is unable to extrapolate or imagine a situation that is not immediately present in his perceptual field. In story 4, there is a tendency toward devitalization when he talks about a picture as a photograph. While this is not an inappropriate comment, it does suggest that, for some reason, this stimulus has to be made less vivid.

Story 5 is a response to a more abstract and less realistic card. The two figures depicted on the card are not well delineated, and they are close to one another, almost superimposed. On this card, there are suggestions of fusion tendencies in his response that one old man is part of the other old man and in his comment that "it doesn't look like an entity." While this card generally stimulates this sort of response, the statement from A is more extreme than usually expected on this card. His tendency to see figures as merged and fused emerges when reality is less clearly defined.

In story 7, he again has difficulty in extrapolating beyond what is directly portrayed on the cards. Those inferences or interpretations he allows himself are based almost exclusively on his understanding of the facial expressions of the figures on the card. While there is some grandiose thinking expressed in this story when he says that the man "looks like Jesus Christ," in stories 9 and 10 the sense of absurdity and danger he must experience in his interpersonal relationships becomes apparent. A young man is killed because he was rude to somebody, and the theme of death is seen as equivalent to a road coming through a lawn or garden.

On the blank card (16), as would be predicted from his unstable object-representations on the Rorschach and his difficulties thus far on the TAT with extrapolating beyond the immediate stimulus, he refuses to make up a story because "there's nothing on the paper." He cannot make up a story without a tangible stimulus. As he states, he needs to draw a visual stimulus before he can begin to speculate or allow himself to consider a situation.

The report in his case history of his need to draw his masturbation fantasies is consistent with the test indications of his inability to establish adequate mental representations.

Summary

These observations from the test data are consistent with the clinical reports, which suggested that he had difficulty keeping his thoughts organized and pursuing a topic for any length of time. His description of his past life was presented as a series of disjointed incidents, which were usually expressed in "very concrete and visual terms." Participation in a conversation for more than a few minutes at a time or in a social situation in which he was close to people caused disruption and feelings of confusion. He contained these feelings of confusion by fixating on one point or particular perceptual feature. His difficulties with representations and object constancy were clearly evident to the school teacher who commented that he needed clear, structured activities in order to facilitate his maintaining focus and concentration. A also commented in therapy about faces being blurred, which was another expression of the vagueness of his perceptions. The therapist also observed that, often for A, furniture and walls almost acquired a life of their own, an observation consistent with the animate–inanimate blends shown on the Rorschach. As suggested by the findings of Blatt and Ritzler discussed in Chapter 2, the blending of human and inanimate features occurs most frequently in patients with more serious boundary difficulties. The perceptual passivity observed on A's Rorschach is consistent with his constant expression of feelings of hopelessness and helplessness and his wish to remain in bed. The vagueness and devitalization of his human responses on the Rorschach and his perceptions of profiles are indications of his severe isolation, loneliness, emptiness, and inability to establish contact.

A's preoccupation with merging and fusing was suggested, for example, in a report made by the nursing staff that in one attempt to talk to an aide, he abruptly asked, "Well, what do you think of the possibility of a future merger of China and Russia?" A tendency toward fusion and merging was evident in the therapist's observation that A felt most comfortable when he and the therapist were engaging in the same activity, such as smoking a cigarette, or when the therapist indicated that he had had similar experiences to A. A similar tendency was also expressed in a dream in which he looked at himself in the mirror and instead saw the face of another patient.

A's difficulty with maintaining object constancy, his tendency toward merging and fusing, his extreme passivity and isolation, the vagueness of his experiences, his difficulty with sustaining concentration and focus, and his devitalization of people all suggested serious ego defects, which were probably present from early childhood. While the test data were quite consistent with the other clinical material in suggesting serious impairments, the test protocols were by no means bleak. They showed that A was capable of establishing adequate reality contact at times and that he was able to maintain some degree of investment in people. While in the initial clinical impression it was thought that therapy would be a long process resulting in only limited improvement, the test data suggested that he could be responsive to therapeutic endeavors. After several years of therapy, he was discharged from the hospital. At last report he was in outpatient psychotherapy, enrolled in a junior college, and doing reasonably well. He continued, however, to live within a few miles of his mother's home.

Case II—Patient B: Well Articulated, but Unstable and Fluid Responses that Lack Constancy

B, a 22-year-old, single female was admitted to the hospital after she tried to drown herself by swimming far from shore. She stated that she did this "not to kill myself, but to get out of an impossible situation. I was messed up. I could not stay at home, but I had nowhere to go." During the first two weeks in the hospital, she was noted to be catatonic in appearance. It was difficult to engage B in talking about herself, particularly about her experiences prior to her senior year in high school. However, she spoke in some detail about her life since that time. She described her desperate search for some type of closeness and intimacy during the 4 years preceding her hospitalization.

It was difficult to date the onset of B's illness. She apparently was rather isolated for many years. However, she stated that things became difficult for her in her senior year in high school, when she was 17-years old. She stated that she "died in April of that year." When asked what happened at that time, B listed a number of problems: a close girlfriend was admitted to a hospital because of being withdrawn and suicidal; a teacher to whom B was quite attracted would not see her outside of the teacher–pupil relationship; her sister had a "breakdown" and began outpatient psychotherapy; and her parents started to talk openly about a separation. Prior to this time, B apparently had been able to deny any marital discord: "My parents' anger toward one another came as a complete surprise to me. I guess in some way I knew they were unhappy with one another, but I couldn't face up to that fact." B could not identify any one of these issues as being more important than the others.

B experienced quite a bit of difficulty in trying to communicate some of her thoughts and ideas. This did not appear to be blocking, but rather, that words meant something very peculiar to her. Often, in trying to describe something, she used her hands as a way of expressing what she was trying to get across. Also, B was at times quite suspicious and guarded. There did not seem to be any loosening of associations or tangential thinking, and she denied having hallucinations. She did admit, however, to having delusional ideas about being a "medium through evil." Her affect was flat except for occasional flashes of humor. She was fully oriented and memory was intact. Insight seemed quite good at times, and judgment was fair. Her intelligence appeared to be above average.

B was the firstborn, and her mother described the labor and delivery as difficult. However, there appeared to be no problems after birth, and her mother said that she "took to" B at once, "she was very active and alert." During the first few days in the hospital, B was breast-fed. However, the breast-feeding was stopped because the doctor thought the baby was not getting enough milk and was not gaining weight.

During infancy, B was cared for primarily by a nurse, because her mother felt that she did not have time to care for B herself. The nurse left after several months, and a young housemaid was hired to help with B and other household tasks. Both parents described B as "relatively normal" between the ages of 1 and 5. There were no problems with feeding or toilet training. B was a rather quiet child, and there was no history of temper tantrums. The family described her as being "thoughtful" much of the time.

The birth of B's brother, when she was 4-years old, was difficult for her. After the baby was brought home, she began to wet the bed and was quite upset by her wetting. The family handled B's enuresis by restricting fluids at night, and it cleared up spontaneously after some time. B also began to have nightmares and was afraid of sleeping in the dark. The mother spent a great deal of time with the brother and rarely spent time alone with B.

B started school when she was 5-years old. She attended the same school until the third grade, when she asked to be allowed to change schools. When asked why B had wanted to change schools, her mother replied that "she got tired of the school. The other girls began to get feminine—dressing up in dresses. B liked jeans." At the same time that B changed schools, she became involved with a group of children in the neighborhood who spent a great deal of time together running and playing. B was designated as the leader of the group because she "could run faster than the others. Also I had a cruel streak in me where I wanted to use power." B remained with this group of children until she entered seventh grade.

B recalled that during the seventh grade she began to develop sexually.

She said that she had been prepared for menstruation by a movie that was shown in school and that her mother had told her little about sex except to complain how difficult it was to be a woman.

The ninth grade was eventful. She was friendly and outgoing, attended a number of dances during the first few months of school, and was enjoying herself. However, several friends teased her about being "too sexy." Apparently B herself had similar concerns and had been thinking about how she did not like being an adolescent. After being teased about being too sexy, she began to restrict her social life and to spend an increasing amount of time studying. She recalled that she retreated into an interest in nineteenth-century novels and spent many hours in her room alone. Although she had many boyfriends during her high school years, she did not feel particularly close to any of them.

In the summer after her sophomore year of high school, B went to the West Coast. This was the first time that she had been away from home for a prolonged period. During this trip, she wrote her parents and told them that she wanted to transfer schools. The new school she wished to attend was liberal and the students were involved in social activism. Although her parents did not approve, they allowed her to transfer. B continued to be isolated; she was not involved in any extracurricular activities and had few social contacts. She dated infrequently and had only two close friends. It was in her senior year at this school that she stated she "died for the first time."

She first became involved with drugs while in this school. Since that time, she had smoked marijuana and hashish on numerous occasions and had also taken LSD many times. She denied having used hard drugs and stated that she was not a habitual user of marijuana. In fact, she felt that it would be a misuse of any drug to take it on a regular basis and opt out of the environment.

B entered her freshman year at a college her mother had insisted on her attending. While she had looked forward to leaving home, she did not enjoy living in the dorm. She felt lonely and isolated and was disinterested in most of her studies. During this year she noted that her mother was complaining more and more about her father, which made B uncomfortable, so when she was home for school holidays she spent less and less time at home. She began to experience "panic attacks" and would talk with her sister in an attempt to alleviate the panic. Sometimes the panic was alleviated and sometimes it was not. Her sister suggested that she see a psychiatrist. She went to the student health department and saw a therapist for 10 sessions. But she terminated therapy because the doctor "was always late and would sit silently, he never asked me any questions." The panic attacks seem to have begun to occur shortly after B's father left her mother on a permanent basis. B was rather vague about the effect the separation had on her.

B began experimenting with LSD during that school year. She and her boyfriend sat in her room and listened to music, and both found the experience generally enjoyable. In addition to dating this boy, B went out with another boy. She maintained relationships with both boys for 4 years, and both relationships seem to have been platonic and intellectual.

At the end of her freshman year, B did not wish to return to school. She decided to live in San Francisco and study sculpting. In San Francisco, she did some sculpting, but her life was generally unstructured, and she did not take any courses. She stayed in a kind of halfway house. Many of the residents were artists and musicians, and there was considerable camaraderie in the house. However, there was seldom enough food, and the house was poorly heated and cold. Despite these adverse conditions, B began attending two courses. This was her first attempt at education in over a year. She enjoyed the courses but at the same time became increasingly withdrawn from the other people in the house. She stayed in her room for long periods of time sculpting and went out only for classes and meals. Finally, feeling disappointed in the house and in herself, she left. "I had to go where things were alive and growing, where the soil was warm." She began to travel, and it was during this time that she had her first experience with sexual intercourse. She had intercourse with several different boys, but "didn't enjoy it."

During the summer, B stayed with a friend in a house along the Big Sur, and she and her friend believed that the house was haunted by some evil presence. In the fall, she returned to San Francisco and found a room. B continued to feel dissatisfied with herself. She felt that she wanted to be alone, but at the same time needed people. Shortly before Christmas, she flew home to spend the holiday with her family and began to consider the possibility of remaining at home. This was the first time she had seen her family since her departure for San Francisco 2 years earlier. She stayed with her mother but was uncomfortable living with her. She spent as much time as possible visiting old friends and keeping away from her mother who, she said, complained constantly about her father. B finally flew back to San Francisco on Christmas Eve, not being able to tolerate the family dissension any longer.

B found a new apartment, began taking a course, and continued to see her friends occasionally. She felt that a new chapter in her life was starting; she was beginning to feel at peace with herself and also somewhat more comfortable with other people. In order to help herself achieve these feelings, she visited a monastery for one week. She found living at the monastery a very enjoyable experience. "It was so peaceful. Everyone could be close to one another and be quiet at the same time. We spent several hours a day in meditation." Several weeks later, she heard that a priest from the monastery had been killed in an automobile accident. This was the first of what B called her "dangerous coincidences." She recalled that during the weekend of the accident, she had had a dream that included a car being in an accident. She began to feel somewhat frightened and concerned that somehow she was indirectly responsible for the accident and to be more attentive to other "coincidences."

During the summer, many of B's friends left town for vacation. At this time she became even more aware of "coincidences" and began to feel that she was a "medium for evil which can be passed through me and be dispersed onto a variety of people." She felt that bizarre things were happening in her apartment house. She felt that some of the people living in the house were working for the police department and wondered whether they were following her for some special reason. She wished desperately that her friends were around so that she might talk to them about the peculiar experiences that she was going through.

B became so terrified and unsure of what was going on that she rarely left her apartment. Finally one day, feeling that she could no longer tolerate the situation, she knocked on a neighbor's door and began to explain her fears about "coincidences." The neighbor became quite concerned and called B's mother. B's mother telephoned, and B assured her that she was all right. Several days later, her mother appeared and stayed with B in her apartment for about 2 weeks. Finally, her mother persuaded her to return home. On arrival, B's father met them at the airport. Her parents fought, and B was quite upset, feeling that she was in the middle of an all-out war between her parents. B was seen by a psychiatrist, who suggested that B live with her mother for a while. B went along with the suggestion, but she found that staying with her mother was intolerable. At the same time, she felt that if she were to live anywhere else, she would be betraying her mother. This was the bind in which B found herself when she finally tried to commit suicide as a way of escaping.

While B changed subtly but significantly in the hospital, she did not go through any marked fluctuations in mood or outward behavior. A gradual unfolding left her less tentative than when she came in, less of an observer and more assertive. When first admitted, B was described as "trying to look as mousy and inconspicuous as possible." She had a ragged appearance—roughly cropped hair, a sweater, pants, and a turtleneck blouse—and looked like a sexless waif. She seemed very alert and able to talk clearly when approached, but she always remained on the "fringe" of groups. She described herself as "filling myself up with other people's activity." A great part of each day was spent alone in some quiet corner.

At the onset of hospitalization, B presented herself as a very gentle, quiet, thoughtful girl. She was quite bland, rarely spoke above a whisper, and at times seemed out of touch or indifferent to what was going on around her. She was reluctant to make requests and would often wait several weeks before approaching anyone about something she wanted. She never initiated a discussion. When asked direct questions, she would often pause, seem confused, and then either dismiss the question or request clarification. At the same time, she related in a quite eloquent, almost poetic fashion how impossible it was for her to use words to talk about herself. For a long time, she remained isolated and seemed to have little contact or interaction on the ward.

After a few weeks, a very subtle change began to be noted in B's demeanor and availability. She seemed to have resolved the problem of whether or not to stay in the hospital. She began to be a little more assertive. She became mildly enthusiastic about her plans and showed some initiative. She even attempted to interact with newer patients and seemed rather interested in other people and in getting to know them. Her role with them seemed to be primarily that of listener and confidante. On one occasion, a patient came up to her and said, "It's time for our therapy session." In a quiet, reserved fashion she seemed to move toward a commitment both to therapy and her hospitalization.

However, B also seemed to feel some kind of "cultural barrier" between herself and the hospital. Although she was continually encouraged to participate in groups, she described a fear of being "swallowed up" by any group and felt unable to share and communicate her experiences and problems. She often accused the staff of being "complacently egotistic" and of not being willing to question their "basic assumptions." She was very candid about offering rather keen observations to the staff concerning the way they came across to the patients and about questioning their motives. This behavior did not seem to be an attempt to put her problems outside herself, for she was equally candid about herself. She seemed to use the staff as a mirror to find out how she appeared to the world. For example, she asked whether another patient found her "threatening." She seemed attentive to comments made about her, often approaching a staff member to discuss a remark she had been mulling over.

There was a careful, planned quality to much of what B did on the ward. She wanted long stretches of quiet in which to read, and she sought out a spot where she could read steadily, not liking to leave a book unfinished. In many ways, her behavior and conversation seemed almost painfully meticulous, with each graceful gesture exactly right for each situation as it arose.

In therapy, B made frequent use of metaphors in trying to explain something. It became clear that in some ways this was a diversionary tactic. The therapist found himself so caught up in trying to figure out her latest metaphor that he was no longer listening to her but rather, trying to solve a puzzle she had presented. The therapist began to experience more and more frustration as she continued to bombard him with her metaphorical language. At the same time, the therapist felt that she was trying to let him know how difficult it was for her to communicate.

From the available history, it appeared that both in early adolescence (ninth grade) and in her senior year in high school, marked changes had occurred in B. It was unclear whether these changes were merely schizoid withdrawal or frank psychotic episodes. Despite her schizoid life style, she had been able to maintain herself out of the hospital and essentially had lived in an independent fashion. In many ways, B's history seemed to be a search for some type of constant object relationship. This search was understandable in terms of her lack of such a relationship with her mother. Apparently B's mother was almost entirely absent during B's early infancy and childhood. It was only when a male child was born that her mother was able to relate to him. Despite this lack of a maternal figure, B did fairly well until reaching puberty. At this time, the increasing demands on her for separation and individuation brought on by her emergent sexuality were apparently overwhelming. This resulted in B's retreat into her studies and into reading novels. She emerged from this withdrawn, schizoid position only in relationship with a girlfriend during her last 2 years of high school, but this girl was seriously disturbed. At this time, further stress was placed upon B. She felt a need to flee from her mother and her parents' marital discord, but she had nowhere to go and no stable figure to whom she could turn. In addition, she was faced with the challenge of entering college and leaving home. She became increasingly isolated and frightened and was able to maintain relationships only with her sister and two boyfriends with whom she had platonic relationships. Since B's freshman year in college, she had been in constant flight, going from place to place, from group to group, and person to person. She achieved no satisfaction from any of these relationships, and she seemed to be desperately searching for intimacy, yet also fearing it.

The picture was of a longstanding schizophrenic process with depression and paranoid features. An earlier obsessional adjustment seemed to have given way to a more openly fragmented state. At best, her sense of self was of a somewhat artfully contrived observer of life. At worst, she saw herself as being a destructive person who was a loose conglomeration of odd parts, slowly petering out and retreating into herself.

RORSCHACH--PATIENT B

Card I. [5 sec]

1. First I saw two dancers. Folk dancers, Slavic. I saw the picture back there (pointed to a picture on the wall). They also looked like, reminded me of a dance where they get down like that (illustrates). Part of the costume is flowing out back.

1. It's as though they're probably holding hands and spinning around going around quite quickly as if the scarf is flowing out in back. Is that a particular person (referring to the picture on the wall)? Dostoyevsky? The quality of big, brutish, peasant heaviness about the bodies--also maybe because of the folk dancers I saw last month.

2. Even though someone couldn't be standing in the center if they were dancing around, it looks like the figure of a woman in the center. She could be standing in the background. Her dress is also peasantlike.

2. They're standing quite upright and still. (?) Sort of peasantlike dress, but she's a bit bulky. (?) If they actually are spinning around, she couldn't be in the middle. Also the legs come down to a point lower than theirs so she could be in front of them, perspective-wise, but it's also sort of mingling--her hands could be the dancers' hands--or hers. I don't care to separate them.

3. These little spots quickly look like musical notes accompanying their dance.

3. They don't even look like notes. If someone writes a birthday card with singing words, they put notes around, notes sort of to indicate the motion of the figures, sort of flung off figures.

4. As I look, things change. Should I bother with that? The posture of the two figures now is like a Minoan statue--has a strange rigidity and sway-back quality. Is that sort of the typical length? Can you tell me how it feels to you to hear this kind of description? These two (response 1) become much more majestic than in the beginning. They keep changing, I might as well stop.

4. At first they were moving Slavic dancers, then I also see them as stationary and stylized, like Minoan painting, the sway-back curved lower part of the back. (?) The reason they look like Minoan figures, then they became more like statues, indicating a figure of a woman. The statues stand together, the profile is more majestic seeming. The thing that flew out in back like a wing could mean demigods or kinglike figure.

Card I of B's Rorschach is replete with indications of boundary disturbance. Her opening response of two dancers is precise and well articulated.

But, during the inquiry to this response, there is an indication of boundary disturbance when she relates the perception on the Rorschach to a picture hanging on the wall in the office. She is unable to limit her attention to the task but begins to respond to stimuli from several dimensions and then to interrelate them. She says that the card and the picture on the wall look alike; they both remind her of a dance she had seen a month earlier.

She then indicates that she is puzzled by the fact that there is a figure of a woman in the center. This is an accurate perception, but somehow B feels that there could not be a woman standing there between the other two figures who are dancing around. She then states that the woman in the center could be in the background, raising the question of whether the theme of background is related to her looking at the picture in the back of the office.

She then shows that her percepts are quite fluid. They seem to have relatively little stability and to change their characteristics as she continues to look at them. She sees little spots that "quickly look like musical notes" accompanying the dance. This response suggests a looseness of associations and the possibility of auditory hallucinations. Her following comments show how fluid her responses are. She says, "As I look, things change," and then talks about how the figures she first saw as dancers have a "strange rigidity and a sway-back quality." Then she asks how the examiner feels about these kinds of descriptions, as if seeking some reaction to her strange experiences and help in stabilizing her perceptions. She comments that the figures are "much more majestic than they were in the beginning" and that they "keep changing." The instability of her representations and their relative lack of constancy leave her vulnerable to distraction and a loss of focus. Her responses can include, for example, features of the card, a picture in the room, and a memory of a dance she recently attended. Her responses vary from one extreme to another—from graceful dancers to statues, from spinning around to being rigid and sway-backed. The phrase "sway-back" may be an association stimulated by the image of the dancers. As her responses become more fluid, their content becomes more grandiose. She attempts to achieve stability in a somewhat grandiose, confabulatory, and static perception of Minoan statues which are rigid and "majestic," like "demi-gods or king-like figures." However, her perceptions continue to be fluid.

Themes of merging and fusion are indicated in the inquiry to her second response, where she discusses the relationship of the central figure to the two figures who are dancing on the sides. In discussing the perspective and the relative positions of the figures, she indicates that there is a sort of "mingling" in which the hands could be the dancers' hands or the hands of the person in the center, and "I don't care to separate them." There is also a tendency toward animate–inanimate blends; dancing figures become stationary—stylized paintings or statues. Her use of the profile view also suggests a tendency to de-animate figures in an attempt to gain some distance and control, as well as expressing her feelings of depersonalization and estrangement.

In general, her responses are very well articulated, but they lack stability and constancy. Her manifestations of boundary disturbance do not seem as severe as those noted in the amorphous, diffuse, and vague responses of patient A.

Card II.   [15 sec]

1. *I get Slavic things again. Two large bears slapping each other, hunched over, big bears.*

1. Their heaviness, largeness, stooped over, also symbolic of the Russian bear. (?) I think I've got Russian things on my mind. Like in Gogol's Cloak--illustration of that sort of heavy figure going through heavy snow as in darkness. You don't really see the other person--reach out your hand--that sort of gesture--more Slavic-- making gestures is not very American or English. (?) The gesture of raising the hand like that (illustrates)--like in all sorts of cultures--maybe not so peacelike as greeting.

2. *Two red things (upper red) look like two cats' faces looking at each other. This isn't very coherent to me.*

2. The profile--two profiles-- they were incomplete. Only the front part of the face is there. The eye, only part of the mouth, sort of obscured. (?) Just looking at the bottom part--two legs coming out look very much like cats' paws stepping. (?) When I saw the legs, I no longer saw the face, but it didn't really bother me--it could be both.

3. *(Lower red) This looks quite like some sort of beetle or horseshoe crab. That's it. The bears do have a somewhat human aspect to them. This could be the cloak--it could be some sort of greeting, or peacelike gesture. Again, heavy set, in*

3. Could be moving downwards, the front part had lots of protuberances--actually only one. (?) Pointed that way--headed that way.

winter's clothing, as if they met
on a winter's evening.

1. Looking at it more closely,
I see another figure standing
like this (illustrates) sort of
a peace stance (inner lower red).
It's changing too, of course,
right now the peace figure has
leather pants, the leather pants
that cowboys wear, but they're
red. That gives it a warlike
aspect or courageous--more that.
Do you know what those things are
called? Now up in the cat's head,
what was once a chin is becoming
two legs, one setting forth quite
gracefully. (Let's go on.)

On Card II, her perceptual experience continues to be quite fluid, and her responses still lack stability and constancy. In addition to the fluidity, there are also blendings of animal and humanlike features. The two large bears of her opening response are "slapping each other"; and she comments quite spontaneously that the bears "do have a somewhat human aspect to them. It could be some sort of greeting or peacelike gesture." The looseness of her associations and lack of a clear separation between different concepts are indicated in her last response, in which she follows up on the peace theme and talks about seeing another figure in a "peace stance." But then the peace figure changes. It has "leather pants, the leather pants that cowboys wear, but they're red. That gives it a warlike aspect or courageous." Then she goes on to elaborate how an earlier response of a cat's face is now changing into two legs, "one setting forth quite gracefully."

In this series of responses to Card II, there is great instability of her representational processes, not only on a perceptual level, but on a conceptual level as well. The percepts are well articulated, but they lack stability and constancy. This tenuousness of her object representations, the instability of perceptual and cognitive processes, permits ideas to merge with one another. Thus, her associations are loose when a peaceful gesture of Russian bears becomes the "peace stance" of a figure, which then develops into cowboys' leather pants, which are red, giving it a "warlike aspect," which then becomes "courageous." She comments on how things lack coherence, but she is very quick to assure the examiner and herself that this does not really bother her.

Card III.   [7 sec]

1. Again two people in a stylized position leaning over a pot, a cooking pot, an open fire, first suggestion Indians, not India, American Indians. Kind of a humorous posture. Obviously it's an unnecessary way to stand. The quality of theater about them as though somewhat acted. Funny faces--could mean masks, birdlike masks. I think it reminds me of Woody Woodpecker. That's going a long way back. I find myself having to look at these (upper red).

1.   I don't know why unless it's a hangover from the cowboy figures. I don't know very much about Indians or art. Maybe the zigzag or the posture and thinness. (?) Probably because of lack of clothing, very little clothing. (?) I don't see the fire, but I saw the pot. It would be over a fire. (?) Cartoon Woody Woodpecker had a strange tall posture (gestures with her face).

2. I wonder what they could be. Nothing pops into mind. I wonder if in doing so, I'm retreating from involvement in things. (Anything else?) As opposed to the grayness, these look (upper red) like some sort of spirit doing somersaults in the air. Maybe they have something to do with my immediate idea of an Indian setting. Spirits may have to do with ideas of cooking and the whole way of thinking. Like Indian drawings, drawing to represent something. It isn't so much like a somersault as drifting down, down. (Tester stopped subject.)

2.   Partly the different color, partly as though floating in air. (?) Because lighter than gray as though it suggested different quality, lighter, more transparent, also smaller.

On Card III, B sees the usual popular response of two people, but she dehumanizes them by commenting that they have a quality of the theater about them, as though they were acting, and that they have "funny faces" or "birdlike masks" that remind her of Woody Woodpecker. In addition to the figures being stilted and having birdlike masks, the association of Woody Woodpecker, a popular cartoon figure, is an animate–inanimate blend. Though she comments on the humorous quality of this response, she also indicates that she is blocking, and then makes the observation that she seems to be "retreating from involvement in things." She goes on to give another animate–inanimate blend, which concerns spirits doing somersaults in the air, followed by the loose association that the spirits may have something to do with the cooking mentioned in her first response. She demonstrates even more clearly how her inability to maintain separations and distinctions leads to loose associations when she says that her response of Indians on this card may have been "a hangover from the cowboy figures" seen on Card II. It is impressive that, despite the fluidity of her representations, she can reflect upon and be aware of some of the factors that influence her thinking. While she attempts to be humorous in her responses, she comments about her tendency to retreat from involvement. Likewise, while she elaborates a grand and mystical response about Indian spirits, it turns out to be something "drifting down, down."

Card IV.   [5 sec]

1. *This one looks like some sort of animal. It's changing already. I at first saw a great big leg, great big legs, huge feet, out-stretched legs, arms, somewhat funny posture, head ends up as a delicate deerlike face, peculiar in connection with the large body and legs. The legs give a Peter-and-the-Wolf-like quality. Again I'm thinking of a picture I probably saw like that in the Wolf, in Peter and the Wolf.*

2. *(Lower center D) This reminds me of a skull, some sort of head with tusks. I don't see them as horns, ears, view from the top of the head, looks prehistoric. A view of skulls prehistoric--I don't know if it's a head or a skull. The eyes make it like as if it's not a skull. My feeling is this is in a forest--this one is in a forest (lower D) from its slight-ly inquisitive look. The arms are rather treelike, the whole thing suggests an atmosphere in which the animal is very much a part of the forest and vice versa. (Anything else?) The plume around the head (response 1) is like a collar. The way the ink is sug-gests delicate markings on the animal's fur, the way colors and patterns change on some animals. (Tester stopped subject.)*

2. It's hard to tell. Any sort of head of reptiles not a skull or head of a mammal and a skull. (?) Plainer surfaces, smoothed over by skin and fur. (?) It doesn't look like any kind of ani-mal I know about that's not pre-historic--resembles a picture of a prehistoric animal drawn from above, for example, two tusks like horns out in front or points over eyes. Prehistoric animals have more things like that.

On Card IV, B comments almost immediately that "it's changing" as she looks at the card. Her second response is a skull, but she is uncertain whether it is a skull or a head. Again there is a blend of animate and inanimate, not only in her indecision about whether it is a skull or a head but also in her comment that it has a "slightly inquisitive look." She then says that the arms are "rather treelike" and proceeds to elaborate in a confabulatory way that this suggests "an atmosphere in which the animal is very much a part of the forest and vice versa." Thus, the animate–inanimate blends are accompanied by a theme of merging in which the animal becomes part of the surrounding context of the forest. She attempts to resolve the head–skull contradiction by saying that it "looks prehistoric"; but the attempt is unsuccessful and she proceeds to give another animate–inanimate blend.

Card V.   [10 sec]

1. *Another animal, perhaps found somewhere between the plains and the jungle in Africa. Probably lived in both. Sometimes you see it running across the plain--sometimes in the jungle, graceful. Obviously it doesn't look like a real animal--a combination of different wildlife features. These two (lower protuberances) look like legs. They don't especially look like bird legs. Even though they are gazelle legs, the fact that there are only two and that these two look like wings, makes it look much more like a bird. It is somewhat disturbing to have this mixture. Because I have to think how it would move--it's difficult to decide whether it would be like a secretary bird and run very swiftly and not be able to lift itself off the ground--that might not be necessary--or whether it actually flies with a large wing spread--I imagine it flying in slow movements of the wings (illustrates). It makes movements of air currents slowly. The discrepancy between the gazelle and the secretary bird and the slow flying motion. (Tester stopped subject.)*

1. Maybe not so much of wildlife maybe because so much of the wildlife photography is done in Africa. (?) Legs like a gazelle, a lot of deerlike animals in Africa. Thin legs run very fast. (?) A large bird, in South America. It eats snakes and makes strange noises.

On Card V, again the instability of object representations is seen in her perception of an animal that is not a real animal but "a combination of different wildlife creatures." She comments that the legs look more like gazelle legs than bird legs; but because there are only two legs and because it appears to have wings, it looks more like a bird. She finds it "disturbing to have this mixture" and concludes that it would be like a secretary bird. The gazelle-secretary bird is an amalgam of an animal and a fowl that belongs neither on the plains nor in the jungles of Africa, but probably lives in both. She talks about it flying slowly, yet running swiftly, of having properties of animals that live in Africa, yet like a large bird from South America. The general tone of this response is of a strange amalgam that lacks stability, constancy, and relevance—that belongs everywhere and yet nowhere.

Card VI. Phooey! [20 sec]

1. Humorous image of an animal sitting down in a way animals don't sit, the way humans sit on the floor, with legs out in front slightly to the side. An unrealistic position and an unrealistic animal sitting very strange--head high in the air. Cartoon of a tiger because the head and whiskers are coming out--a few from the back. I'm tired of all these animals. It's facing in front of itself, away from us. Something royalistic--somewhat royalist quality, maybe a mockery of that. A tiger is a kinglike animal among the animal kingdom. This one seems tainted by domesticity or it has a human nature about it. When I'm looking at it, seeing something more characteristic rather than looking for more sights about it. (Anything else before you stop?) I'd describe it as a living thing being there, also, it's also showing itself as an animal skin, like you get in the store for a rug. It's losing its humorous quality, becoming much more flat than before. (Tester stopped subject.)

B's response to Card VI involves a human–animal blend: an animal sitting "the way humans sit on the floor" with legs stretched out in front—an unrealistic posture for an unrealistic animal. She attempts to tone down and deal with this peculiar percept by calling it a "cartoon of a tiger" and comments that she is "tired of all these animals." She also tries to cope with it through humor by making it "royalistic," or a "mockery" of that; and she talks about a tiger as a "kinglike animal." But this one is "tainted by domesticity" and has "a human nature about it." Then she comments that it is "a living thing," but "it's also showing itself as an animal skin, . . . losing its humorous quality and becoming much more flat than before." Here, there seems to be a decline in level of organization and functioning as she moves from human–animal blends to blends of animate with inanimate. She uses humor, grandiosity, and mockery to defend herself against the painfully dysphoric feelings stimulated by her confusion and by her experiences of estrangement and isolation.

Card VII.   [25 sec]

1. Sculpture, the figures on either side related to one another, balanced on a form. Could be abstract and stylized figure that I saw at first. Mainly a motion of human form is presented in an abstract way, since being able to make out the actual position and who and what the person is, isn't very important.

2. I saw these two figures becoming more defined, dressed in belted monks' robes, coming down to their ankles, a hood up top. Flowing up as if they were running, maybe even dancing.
The ink looks very, very--no, the ink looks like clay--it's been pinched--thin toward the edges.

2. Could be part of the robe, I don't see how it could be so much extra material. Probably an arm reaching back.

3. Well talking--two fishes coming down (upper third), looking at each other, the eyes of wisdom, a Buddhist symbol.

3. I don't know if it's the way it's placed, two fish, tails in the air looking at each other, eye of wisdom.

4. As I saw, a profile of a forehead and nose. I thought of Gogol's story of the nose, with a fish, or noses has the quality of 3D. (Tester stopped subject.)

4. Nose I began to see, profile doesn't stretch too far up or down very distinctive nose. It brought Gogol's story to mind.

On Card VII, there is another human–inanimate blend when she talks about a sculpture of an "abstract and stylized" human form. It is important to note that these responses are popular figures; but she covers them with monks' robes and de-animates them by making them sculptures and then by attending to the texture of the ink or clay. She then gives another human–animal blend in her response of two fish "looking at each other" with "eyes of wisdom." Again this response declines to an animate–inanimate blend, for the fish become a Buddhist symbol. All the indications of boundary disturbance noted earlier—the animate–inanimate blends, fluidity, and loose associations—are present in the responses to this card. Devitalization is suggested again by her comments about the profile of a human head.

Card VIII.   [25 sec]

1. I recognize this. It makes me think that I saw all of them before, I suppose I have. Two animals, before I saw large ani- mals--now the face looks like as though it's become that of a smaller animal. The head is al- most chipmunk. The last time I looked more at the body, saw a strange animal, the family of cows called the tapir. It definitely isn't a cow, something between a cow and a pig.

2. They're climbing up this central place--it's in a slightly unnatural environment animals are kept in, not a zoo, but an area where a farmer might pen it off for animals to climb around in and curl up in. There was such a place that I saw with rocks to climb on. The colors are nice, especially here. (Referring to response 1.) I guess not so much chipmunks, they seem to be aware of each other, not alone, I guess it's because it's symmetric.

3. On the other hand, I see something without the animals in the pen sort of like--not so much, not so strong as an explosion-- expanding, coming apart of what was once all together, smoke curl-

> *ing up, essences of the original*
> *center. Partly because it's dif-*
> *ferent, partly because it crowns*
> *it on different levels, crowns it,*
> *shelters it, forms a rooflike*
> *structure--shells progressingly*
> *coming out of the center. Two*
> *ideas; one of the animals coming*
> *together, the idea of creation*
> *from the center, come forms and*
> *then animals, rocks, maybe trees,*
> *all as though it was expanded and*
> *created from what was central.*

On Card VIII, B again gives a response that is a blend of several types of animals, "something between a cow and a pig." Then she moves to a second response of a "central place" in an "unnatural environment animals are kept in," which is like an area penned off for animals to "climb around in and curl up in." In the central place, there is something which is "not so strong as an explosion—expanding, coming apart of what was once all together, smoke curling up, essences of the original center." Then she comments that she has two ideas: "one of the animals coming together, the idea of creation from the center, come forms and then animals, rocks, maybe trees, all as though it was expanded and created from what was central." In this response, she shows her preoccupation with themes of fusion and separation and her struggles around these issues. The regressive, undifferentiated union is a safe position in a central area where one can "curl up." But it is also an "unnatural" penned-in position. On the other hand, when the union fractionates into parts, it is almost like an "explosion." However, the parts are still interrelated because they emerge from the same central core.

> Card IX.   [25 sec]
>
> *1. A museum piece, maybe Chi-*
> *nese, an old valuable Chinese*
> *vase, a combination of vase and*
> *sculpture. The green looks like*
> *jade. I don't know whether it*
> *would still be jade. It comes*
> *in orange. The material changes*
> *color but retains its shininess.*
> *Out of the green rise figures*
> *like, somewhat witchlike, dressed*
> *in robes, but less witchlike than*
> *something else. Some other kind*

> of person, robed figures, peaked
> hats. The whole thing is mounted
> on a pink pedestal. I'd almost
> ****** *** it as ink on a dirty
> white background. (?) I won-
> dered why it was dirtier than the
> others. I don't like the colors
> together. That sort of Chinese
> vase and sculpture never appealed
> to me. Drip sculptures made out
> of sand looks like that sort of
> slippery when it's wet, you know,
> if it's jade.

B's response to Card IX is a very well articulated and sophisticated response, an "old jade Chinese vase," But out of the vase rise figures that are
"witchlike" or maybe "some other kind of . . . robed figures wearing
peaked hats." She is troubled by this response, saying the card was "dirtier
than the others," that she does not like "the colors together," and that this
kind of Chinese vase and sculpture never appealed to her. Here again is an
animate–inanimate blend in which human figures or quasi-human figures
arise out of a basic unity with an inanimate object. But this time, she seems
to indicate that unity is an unpleasant experience for her.

> Card X. [5 sec]
>
>   1. A birthday party, lots of
> colors, balloons, somewhat explo-
> sive, too noisy. I'd like to do
> something to it so I'd like it
> better. I don't really like it.
> Looks like, I like bits of it.
>
>   2. (Side down) This looks
> like an animal, stylized, reaching
> out to get from one stone to an-
> other. All sorts of animal things
> appear, whimsical.
>
>   3. More creatures up top,
> funny things (upper green).
>
>   4. That looks like the head of
> a rabbit.
>
>   5. Horned animal, gazelle,
> sort of leaping (upper green).
>
>   6. Wishbone of a chicken, the
> colors in that are so unmixed,

*so elementary, so many different
colors makes it splashy.*

*7. The blue thing, kind of a
creature with lots of appendages,
taking a step, the way in which
it's all going (gestures upwards
with hands) this jumping on this,
this holding onto that. I find
the animals look contrived. If
it were a painting, you would say
that it doesn't hold together,
that it doesn't have a lot of
coherency, that kind of criticism.
If it's all going up in that
direction, that adds some unity
(referring to #3). These have
something medieval about them.
(Tester stopped subject.)*

Card X is the most fragmented of all the Rorschach cards; and B soon says that she does not like this card. Even though she sees the whole card as a birthday party with lots of colors and balloons, it is also "somewhat explosive" and "too noisy." After giving several different types of fairly conventional animal and animal detail responses, she comments that the card "doesn't hold together" and lacks a sense of "coherency" and "unity." She seems troubled by the lack of integration and cohesion and by the fragmentation and separation of the stimuli on this card. Thus, she seems to experience more comfort, peace, and safety in unity.

In summary, themes of intense ambivalence about union are expressed in this Rorschach protocol. While several responses indicate a wish to separate and achieve individuation, there is great attraction in union and "curling up" in a central place. Her cognitive processes express this lack of individuation and separation. There are many responses showing human–animal and animate–inanimate blends, loosening of associations, and marked fluidity of perceptions, indicating that her representations lack stability and constancy. Her percepts are often accurate and well articulated, at times even creative, but they lack stability. For her, reality seems to be in a process of continual change, and these changes occur even while she looks at an object. She tries to cope with her impaired capacity for constancy by attempting to appear creative, artistic, humorous, mystical, and sometimes even grandiose but these maneuvers seem unsuccessful, offering her relatively little protection and comfort. She feels confused by the lack of coherence in her experiences, is flooded by a wide range of associations and memories, and attempts to retreat from involvement as a way of handling this sense of confusion and instability. This retreat seems to involve fantasies of merging, such as getting lost in a forest or "curling up" in a central place.

```
TAT--PATIENT B

  1.  (Card 1).  (pause)  I don't really feel like story telling.  Just
any story?  A boy was told to make a sketch of a violin and bow for a
class in school.  All the children in the class had to do this assign-
ment but could use different instruments.  He has a violin that's been
in the family for quite a few years but no one has been playing it.  I
suppose his grandfather played it when the boy was much younger.  I'm
not sure if he's remembering or remembering being told about it.  He's
taking it upstairs to his room, got out the drawing paper, a large piece
seen in the picture and started to draw and felt discouraged because he
couldn't get it to look right.  He stopped, started to think about music--
what makes such a thing have sound and a special kind of sound so that
one can play tunes on it.  He's drawn it closer to him, brought it over
on the papers.  (Finish?)  He seems not at all interested in trying to
draw it now, at least for the time being.  He is carried along by the
thought of music and his grandfather.  He's still pouting and knowing
his mother will be up soon to check if he's done his homework and he
knows she will find him not having done it.  Possibly he's becoming
interested in learning how to play it and maybe will tell her and it
will serve as an excuse for not having done the drawing.  (Finish?)
Yeah, I suppose I could go on and on.  It's not really a story.  I should
finish it up by now.  One thing has always been the issue is that he
started out and they never changed him from being left-handed.  People
felt he'd be better right-handed, and he'd better change now and this
had something to do with how he was discouraged about drawing because
he's discouraged about anything he does.  Maybe he'll stop wondering
if being left-handed will interfere with playing that instrument.
```

The first story has a unique twist about a boy who is trying to draw the violin and bow, rather than to learn to play the violin or to practice. He stops and is thinking about how such a thing has sounds, and a special kind of sound, so that one can play tunes on it. This emphasis on sounds and special sounds raises a question about the possibility of auditory hallucinations (see also the responses to the first Rorschach card). The boy is carried away by thoughts of music and his grandfather; but suddenly the story shifts to the boy being left-handed, feeling discouraged, and being shifted to right-handedness. Suddenly the story takes on a strange quality about the relationship between handedness and drawing, rather than a child trying to play a violin. She saves the story by wondering if being left-handed interferes with playing that instrument. While there are no boundary disturbances of note in this story, there is a looseness of associations which suggests disordered thinking.

2.   (Card 5).   It's as though they were made to look gloomy so that
you'd tell gloomy stories.   (long pause)   The scene of a play.   The
author and title I don't know about.   It isn't Molière, but that sort
of thing.   At this point, someone said to the maid early in the day
that the gentleman of the house would have a visitor in midday, and
both are going out together and that she should clean up so that after
they come back in about three hours the tea things would be cleared
away.   The gentleman comes to visit--he's a dealer in pigs.   The owner
of the house wants to buy one when it's small, raise it--that's what a
lot of the people in the area do.   This particular family doesn't have
their animal.   Out of the blue, the husband-father decides to get a
small pig and raise it.   This alarmed the rest of the family.   The maid
thought that she was working for a more distinguished family because
they didn't have animals and was displeased because it would make her
prestige go down.   She's trying to think of a way to interfere.   With
the stern master, she'd get nowhere--just get into trouble.   At this
point she's coming into the room just as they're leaving--they've gone
out the other door.   She was probably listening to the discussion.
Beginning--middle, and end.   (End?)   (long pause)   I guess that there's
a change of scene when they go out.   I'm avoiding the issue.   (Bring it
to an end.)   The maid, having listened to the conversation through the
door, decided to leave and not work for a family that has pigs and probably won't bother to clean up the tea they had.   Eventually the rest of
the family will be angry at the father for deciding that a pig would
take the place of the maid.   I think that's enough.

In the second story, again there is a strange response, this time about a
man deciding to purchase a small pig for this distinguished family to raise.
The suddenness of the fabrication about the husband–father's decision to
acquire a pig is like the surprise shift in the first TAT story. It may be
another manifestation of the fluidity of her experience so vividly apparent
on the Rorschach. She attempts to end the story in a humorous way by
saying that the father decided that the pig will take the place of the maid.
Here again animals and humans are interchangeable. In addition to the
personal meanings that the content of this story has for B, there are indications of boundary disruptions, particularly in the conceptual realm of human–animal objects. While the story has a humorous, almost
tongue-in-cheek quality, there is an all too easy blending of animals with
humans.

3.   (Card 15).   (long pause)   (Can you start?)   Once upon a time a
man was always in a bad mood.   He was born among high society, expected
to please his parents, take part in social events, learn the art of
entertaining and good manners, and all he could do is complain about
this and be full of spite toward his parents and the society involved--
a Hamlet type.   He used to go to parties and stand around and make snide
remarks, wishing that he wasn't there--disgusted with all the people.

> One night he was at a party and suddenly all the people turned into gravestones. He blinked, realized he was in the middle of a vast graveyard--no one else but him, and nothing much to say to himself.

In the third story, which is very similar to Dostoyevsky's short story "Bobok," she expresses her difficulty with boundaries even more clearly. At a party one night, suddenly all the people turned into gravestones. Once again there is an animate–inanimate blend. The theme in this story, much like the preceding one and the Dostoyevsky short story, is about the absurdity of life, the hollow, pretentious concern with appearance, prestige, and good manners which covers an inner emptiness, depersonalization, and utter estrangement.

> 4. (Card 14). (pause) Once a man had a flower shop in southern France. He had it for a few years, since he was in his late teens. His parents had died when he was small and he had been brought up by relatives. Quite young he was on his own, had an opportunity to set up a flower shop. On top of it there was a small room which he lived in with one window overlooking the village. He lived on the edge of the village and liked taking care of the shop. Every winter was hard for him. He didn't have too much to do--business and the little room got pretty cold. The elements were very much a part of his life. He couldn't really keep them out of his room and sort of liked that--could tell when spring was there--could watch it coming. He's watching it come in this picture-- noticing that the village is changing over the years. There are more tourists, more business, and next winter would be less difficult. This doesn't please him very much. This year when he sees spring come, he wonders if he will last the year and maybe move on.

Although loneliness and isolation are expressed in this story, it seems to be an intact response. While the changing scene over seasons may reflect an instability of object representations, this theme does not become disruptive and she seems to manage the story nicely. There are some minor peculiarities in the story about how he "couldn't really keep [the seasons] out of his room. . . ." There are also some suggestions of loose thinking as when the man shifts from thinking about the changing seasons to reflecting on the changes over the years. But generally the story is intact and organized, with only hints of boundary disturbances.

> 5. (Line drawing). (pause) On one island in the North Sea, a small island, people from the outside rarely come, and it has become less populated than it used to be. There's still some farmers and other families living there. They're very conscious of family clans--histories of what went on on the island--a strong sense of their island having had a catastrophe--afterwards more and more islanders began to leave.

Eventually two main families--clans on the island that used to get along
and interact, one farming, the other running the port and fishing. But
eventually they began to interfere with each other and doing it differ-
ently and began fighting and doing all sorts of wicked deeds to each
other. About when the trouble began to happen, one of the landmarks
on the island, a huge old tree, one night in the storm, split down the
middle--a symbol to the islanders that it wouldn't be the same anymore.
When it split, it let out all sorts of evil mysterious forces. People
who look back wonder if it was a sudden catastrophe like the tree broken
in the storm or whether it happened over time. Since the people were
suspicious--the outcome of natural progress of time the way things
change but since they were suspicious they thought it had something to
do with the storm.

The story told to this card (line drawing) shows the same theme of isolation as the story told to the previous card. The island is less populated, and
there are serious ruptures in interpersonal relations. These responses, like
the closing responses to the Rorschach, raise questions about the extent of
her withdrawal and the intensity of her feelings of estrangement and alienation. As discussed in the case material, her continual investment in mystical
experiences is elaborated in this story about evil, mysterious forces that
cause people to fight and to do "wicked" things to one another. Her confusion over the strange and sudden disruptions in her life may be reflected in
this story. While this card often elicits responses in which there are themes
of merging and fusion, B's story seems relatively free of these issues. Quite
to the contrary, there is an emphasis on a tree being split down the middle
in a storm. B's ambivalent struggles for separation from her mother may be
achieved in part through aggressive action and paranoid ideation.

Summary

B's psychological test protocols present an interesting picture of a young
woman whose responses can be sharply defined, well articulated, and even
creative and original; but only for brief moments. These well articulated
percepts seem to change even as she is looking at the card. Her representations, while intact on one level, lack stability and constancy, and she is
vulnerable to momentary intrusions by internal and external stimuli. Her
associations are loose, she finds it difficult to maintain focus and direction,
and she can be flooded by transient impressions and experiences and extreme affects. There are strong preoccupations with merging and fusing and
frequent retreats to grandiose ideation. Her representational world is filled
with creatures which are strange blends of animal, human, and inanimate
objects. While these boundary disturbances are expressed in the unstable
responses, the human–animal–inanimate blends, and her ambivalent wish

for fusion, there is a basic intactness to B's perceptual processes. She also appears to have the capacity to reflect on her experiences, and she seems to be struggling to achieve some understanding of what has been happening to her. This patient has considerable resources which could enable her to benefit from psychotherapy. While there is evidence of psychotic features in the protocols, there is also evidence of active struggle with her difficulties and of considerable resources, which have remained relatively intact, so that, with adequate therapy, she should be able to develop more adaptive ways of achieving separation and of coping with her intense experiences of estrangement and loneliness.

After several years of inpatient treatment, B was discharged from the hospital and continued therapy as an outpatient. At last report, she had terminated therapy, graduated from college and was applying to graduate school.

Case III—Patient C: Confabulations that Indicate Difficulty in Distinguishing between External Reality and Internal Reactions.

C, a 20-year-old single female, was hospitalized after a number of years of increasing loneliness, isolation, school difficulties, and suicide attempts. Eventually she became very withdrawn and mute and was then hospitalized.

C's mother was ill during the time she was pregnant with C, and it was recommended that the pregnancy be terminated because of the mother's ill health. Despite pressure from her family physician and her husband, the mother refused to have an abortion. Apparently, C did not know this story, but she was aware that her mother could not have any more children after her birth.

According to reports from the parents, C's developmental landmarks were essentially normal, although she was somewhat slow in walking. C stated that she was kept in a "pen" because she was a very active child and ran around a great deal. She discovered a way to escape from the pen and finally "my parents just gave up, and let me out, and watched me more." When C was 3-years old, she had the first of a series of major accidents; she fell down a long flight of stairs and suffered a concussion. Later that year she began nursery school. Apparently, she demanded to go to school and would often try to follow her older siblings on to the school bus. Finally the family gave in to her demands and placed her in nursery school, which she enjoyed. She recalled little from the ages of 5 to 10 years. During these years she was involved in many accidents; in addition to numerous cuts and bruises, she broke her right arm when she fell from a tree. When she was 10, she was hit by a motorcycle and her leg was broken. C recalled little of the interaction between herself and her family during the time of these accidents, except that her mother was always quite calm. She felt that it was good that her mother could function this way in a crisis. C had few thoughts about the accidents, but she recalled thinking "It is all my fault. Maybe God is punishing me."

Beginning at age 11 when she was entering sixth grade, C began attending the first of a series of boarding schools. This was a very difficult time for her and she often felt quite lonely. Since C's father often had to be in the area of the boarding school on business trips, he would visit C and keep her company.

C described her difficulties as beginning when she was 13-years old, when she became acutely aware of "a triangular relationship with me and my parents." C attempted to achieve some distance from her father by spending less time with him and by doing poorly in school, knowing that both of these things would disappoint him. She would become angry with her mother whenever she felt her mother was ignoring her father. But these actions did not solve her problem of feeling too close to him. At the same time, C was becoming increasingly concerned about her relationship with her mother. She stopped playing tennis with her mother because she wanted to "avoid the competition."

C began menstruating at age 13. "It was no big thing. My mother had prepared me for it and we had quite a few talks about sex. She didn't get uptight about something like that at all." C began going on group dates at age 13, and she recalled enjoying them. It was during this year that C began to experience a moderately severe pain in the back of her neck and a numbness in her left side. She was hospitalized, but all the tests were negative. C recalled that she experienced this pain when she was also aware of feeling very lonely and empty. These feelings of loneliness and emptiness persisted and became more severe.

C was 14 when she entered her freshman year in high school, and she was elected editor of the class paper. While enjoying the attention that she received, she did not enjoy the responsibility of a leadership role. During the summer after her freshman year, her brother fell from a motorcycle and suffered a broken back. The family went to visit him in the hospital in a distant city. C and her father returned home after a few weeks, but the mother remained to care for the brother. C enjoyed that summer at home, taking care of the house and her father. Despite the added work and responsibility, she felt free having her mother away from home.

Early in high school, C developed a relationship with another girl, the only sustained close relationship that C had in her adolescence. Unfortunately, her friend moved to another city. In addition to the intermittent pain that C was having in her neck and legs, she began to experience what sounded like obsessional thoughts and fantasies, primarily when trying to go to sleep. These fantasies were "weird," but C could not elaborate them. The ones that she did discuss involved masochistic violence, such as having her arms and legs slashed with a knife. It was also during this time that C began to have overt suicidal thoughts. She said that she thought about killing herself because she was so bad. The suicidal thoughts involved either jumping from a tall building or shutting herself in a garage and killing herself with the exhaust from a car. C stated that one of the main deterrents to attempting suicide was her fear that she would not succeed in killing herself but would only permanently injure herself in some way. C did very poorly in her studies that year, and, apparently because of her increasing difficulties in school and her growing physical complaints, the family doctor recommended that she see a psychiatrist. C began seeing Dr. Z, a psychiatrist whom the family knew slightly through social contacts. Partly because of his vague connection with the family, C felt that she could not trust him and never mentioned her suicidal thoughts.

C returned to school in her junior year and continued seeing Dr. Z. She did not do well in school, withdrew after several months, and was tutored during the rest of the year. She returned to school for her senior year, which was an important year because she had a regular boyfriend for the first time. C felt that her family initially approved of him, but, when they became aware that the couple were serious about each other, they began to dislike him. Despite this, C's parents did not seriously interfere with the relationship. C was to some extent sexually involved with her boyfriend but never engaged in sexual intercourse with him.

When C was 18, she entered a small liberal arts college with the intention of majoring in English. C did not recall having any special feelings about leaving home, since she had done this many times before. After 2 months, she dropped out of college because of the severe pain and numbness she was experiencing. In addition, she was lethargic and disinterested in her studies. Her parents were quite concerned about her and arranged for her to come home on a medical leave of absence. C was hospitalized after an extensive medical checkup, and she and her parents were told that she had a "neurological disorder." C asked nothing about her diagnosis but went home and looked it up. After reading that the disease was "sometimes fatal," she cried for a short time and then went out for a walk. She continually maintained an attitude of indifference toward her illness and symptoms. C stated that she did not understand what was wrong with her and did not inquire further about it. At the same time, she was aware that her parents seemed rather upset, but she asked them nothing about it. She and her parents then went on an extended vacation. When they returned home, she began college again. But after about 2 months, she dropped out because of increasingly severe pain, returned home, and often remained in bed because of pain and weakness. She remembered feeling at that time that her mother "liked me to be sick. She would spend a great deal of time taking care of me, and I think that was important to her." In the fall of that year her boyfriend, whom she had been seeing intermittently for the past few years, told her that he loved her. She was pleased but also quite confused. A few days later, they stopped seeing each other, and C had little to do with him after that.

It was also at this time that C recalled an upsetting scene with her father, when he told her that she was more important to him than anyone else in the family. On hearing this, she burst into tears and began crying and screaming hysterically. She did not remember what she said to her father but in recalling the incident stated, "It was horrible. He had just thrown everything that I was fighting against back into my lap." During that summer, C's neurological symptomatology increased and she had a brief period of muteness. In discussing her inability to talk, C was quite blasé. She felt that she could have talked if she had wanted to and recalled hiding in a corner and singing at one point. She did not remember what enabled her to start talking again, just that she began screaming and crying and after a few minutes stopped, went to the phone, and called a number of her friends.

That winter she was hospitalized for a lengthy neurological and psychological evaluation. After her discharge, she was seen weekly by a psychiatrist. She started to work, but after a few weeks she experienced an exacerbation of the weakness and other physical symptoms and was rehospitalized. Apparently, at this point, the physicians concluded that although she had a neurological disorder, she also had marked psychological problems, and hospitalization was recommended. C herself did not believe that she had a neurological disorder, but rather, that her symptoms were psychological. Subsequent medical evaluations indicated that C was probably in the early stages of a deteriorative neurological disorder, but that most of her symptoms seemed "psychogenic in origin."

When first admitted to the hospital, C wore no makeup and always dressed in slacks and some type of sweater, even on the warmest days. She usually spoke in a low tone, but occasionally became rather animated. There was no loosening of associations or tangential thinking. At times, especially when attempting to discuss herself, she had a great deal of difficulty and would "drift." She denied hallucinations, delusions, and homicidal ideation but admitted to suicidal ideation. Diagnostically, C appeared to have a long-standing schizoid character disorder. While she could be witty, playful, intelligent, creative, and articulate, her thinking at times revealed a fluid and shifting sense of self and objects. She was frequently able to control her disturbed thinking and dysphoric sense of doom and disaster by assuming a humorous, somewhat clownish attitude, but often this facade failed and she was left vulnerable to intense feelings of rage and despair.

RORSCHACH--PATIENT C

Card I.   [9 sec]

1. Oh! It looks like a prophet and mountains and valleys, but it ain't got people. (Anything else?) (Makes faces) Not really.

1. (?) Kind of like Moses. (?) I don't know, it just does. (?) He has his hands up and he's alone, but he's not really--kind of looks like he should be talking to people, but there's not any people there-- maybe he's practicing. (?) Talk- ing to people. (Mountains and valleys?) The mountains are behind him and on the side and then they go down. (Valleys?) I don't really know--I just kind of . . . maybe the empty part is part of the valley (indicates white area below the blot), but it's not really part of the blot.

C's opening Rorschach response to Card I is a confabulation, indicating her difficulty in distinguishing between an external event and her internal experience. Her extensive elaborations are based much more on her internal experiences and associations than on the perceptual aspects of the card. After her initial response of a prophet and mountains and valleys, she comments that "it ain't got people." The grandiose and exaggerated image of the prophet Moses, who might be "practicing" since he is talking without an audience, has both an absurd and confabulatory quality. The confabula- tory thinking may be an aspect of C's way of relating to people; her exag- gerations may help her to compensate for feelings of despair and depreciation. The absence of other people also suggests intense feelings of estrangement, alienation, and isolation.

Card II.   [14 sec]

1. The first thing it looks like is a medical textbook--two lungs.

1. (?) The top part--kind of looks like it. (?) The shape. (Anything else?) The color too. (?) Lungs are usually red in textbooks.

2. And then it looks like two calves--no, what would they be?

2. (?) Or playing (usual large detail). (Calves or bulls?)

Two kinds of calves or bulls--
kissing (laughs). Yeah, they're
calves--they're young.

Their faces are young--cute, kind
of cuddly.

3. The red part on the top
also looks like a hookah from
Alice in Wonderland--no, a hookah--
the hookah-smoking caterpillar.

3. (?) The caterpillar--the
shape. (?) My favorite part--
I don't know why.

4. A butterfly.

4. (?) The shape and the mixture of color. (Mixture?) The
top is kind of black and red and
the body is kind of formed like
the butterfly.

On Card II, there is a mild boundary disturbance between animal and human when C attributes humanlike qualities to animals in the response of two calves "kissing." She comments about their being calves or bulls, which is paradoxical, since in the inquiry she describes them as "young, cute, and kind of cuddly." She juxtaposes the strength, power, and aggression of bulls with the cuteness and softness of calves. The response of calves could also serve to defend against aggressive and destructive impulses. In the third response of a hookah-smoking caterpillar from *Alice in Wonderland,* there is a more extreme human–animal blend than the calves kissing. While the *Alice in Wonderland* context and the humorous aspects give the response a somewhat appropriate and acceptable quality, there is still a blending of human with animal features.

Card III. (Laughs) These are the same ones. (Subject had taken the
test 5 years previously.) [6 sec]

1. This looks like Mike Nichols
and the reflection of Mike Nichols.

1. (?) The face kind of has
his outlines. (?) The face and
then the rest of it goes along
with it.

2. It looks like two guys
pulling at the same chair and
the red things just don't do
anything for me.

2. (Chair?) It doesn't really
that much, but this is kind of
the back--a chair with arms.

On Card III, C laughs and comments about seeing Mike Nichols and his reflection. Both in her behavior (laughing) and in the content of her response, she indicates that humor means a lot to her, and it will be important to assess the degree to which she can use it constructively. There is a possible suggestion in this response, however, that she may not be able to distinguish Mike Nichols from his reflection. But reflections are not an uncommon way of dealing with the symmetry of the Rorschach card.

Card IV.   (Laughs)   [9 sec]

1. *I still see my drunken penguin leaning on a lamppost-- come to think of it, two drunken penguins leaning on a lamppost.*

1.   (?)   The shape and the black and white too and they're definitely sloshed (laughs).   (?) Just the attitude of them--penguins are funny enough, but these are extra funny because they're drunk.

On Card IV, there is once again a loss of boundaries between animal and human. In a humorous, cartoon-like response, C attributes human qualities to an animal. Her drunken penguins leaning on a lamppost are certainly funny, but also suggest some difficulty in maintaining—or unwillingness to maintain—the distinction between humans and animals. It is interesting that she is able to give a humorous response to what is often experienced as a massive and even frightening card. However, the fact that this response does not accurately conform to the contours of the blot suggests that her humor is not completely successful in coping with this card.

Card V.   [28 sec]

1. *Kind of looks like a butterfly that didn't make it.*

1.   (?)   Like a cross between an insect and butterfly--it doesn't have the fullness of a butterfly, but is too full for an insect--is a butterfly an insect?   It looks like a creature unto itself.   (?) One that is not in the annals of biology.

2. *I see the damn caterpillar at the top again (sights along edge of card).*

2.   (?)   Just his head.

On Card V, there is a tendency toward a contaminatory response where, on a relatively clear and well defined card, she sees a "cross between an insect and a butterfly." She seems unable to resolve what she feels is a contradiction—namely, that it is not full enough for a butterfly but too full for an insect—and talks about "a creature unto itself, one that is not in the annals of biology." This unique blend, this strange creature, is a response showing a contamination tendency, as well as mild confabulatory qualities. It also suggests a self-image of being strange and weird. In her second response, she comments about the "damn caterpillar" she sees again at the top of the card. Thus, the formerly humorous caterpillar is now suddenly greeted with annoyance. The humor and grandiosity of her responses, juxtaposed with annoyance, suggest extreme alternations in mood and self-image.

Card VI.   [18 sec]

1. It looks like a tiger rug.	1. (?) The kind that has the whole tiger with the head.
2. It looks like two otters. I guess that's all.	2. (?) (Laughs) Facing each other. (?) The faces. (?) The shape and expression. (?) The eyes kind of--I don't know how to describe it.

As on Card IV, C deals with the phallic implications of this card by giving a humorous response. But like the drunken penguins on Card IV, otters laughing at each other is a human–animal blend, and the form is not accurately perceived.

Card VII.   [16 sec]

1. They look like two old ladies at their last cotillion (laughs).	1. (?) They are shaped like the faces of old ladies and they look like they have garb on, and their hair fixed up. (Garb?) Headdress and necklaces on--that's why they're leaning over--and the low-cut bust that old ladies have sometimes.
2. And they also remind me of Abigail and Prudence which were two busts that used to be in our town's art museum and they're very noisy and nosy and they talk a lot and I don't think they really hear what anyone says.	

On Card VII, C's first response of "two old ladies at their last cotillion" is well articulated, and there is a high degree of specification. She elaborates on the ladies' appearance in great detail, referring to their "low-cut bust," and gives them specific names. The extreme degree of specification raises the question as to whether it serves a defensive function. As she elaborates further and gives her personal associations to the ladies, subtle manifestations of boundary disturbance appear. She talks about two figures which were "busts" in the local art museum and then attributes human qualities to these inanimate objects: "They're very noisy and nosy and they talk a lot and I don't think they really hear what anyone says." These types of manifestations of boundary disturbance occur in these elaborations. There is a loose association in the apparent connection between the women with the "low-cut bust" and "busts" in the local art museum. Then, in commenting about these busts, she attributes human characteristics to them. While this may have been a local joke, her presentation of the human–inanimate blend is consistent with the human–animal blends seen earlier in her Rorschach. However, her use of humor and appropriate contexts (e.g., *Alice in Wonderland,* busts at a museum) indicate a degree of modulation of and control over these disturbances.

Card VIII.   [7 sec]

1. (Frowns) Napoleon (laughs).   1. (?) (Top two center areas) The hat's there and his shoulders were always kind of hunched because he wore those padded things and he didn't have much of a neck and he wore the collar up and his face is kind of powerful and wistful. (?) The eyes. (?) More wistful and the face is powerful. (?) It could be because I never saw Napoleon. I thought he had a powerful face, but it just commands your attention--that's what I was talking about.

2. The two pinkish things on the side look like two bears-- what they're doing on Napoleon's shoulders, I don't know.   2. (?) Well (laughs), their shape. (On N's shoulders?) That's just where they are in the picture.

3. The face that was Napoleon also reminds me of someone else, but I can't place it--maybe like a witch doctor or something like that.   3. (?) The headdress and like when you look at it a little longer it takes on animal-like features like the masks a witch doctor would wear.

4. And this one down here kind of makes the face of a cat-- kind of an abstract cat.   4. (?) The form of the face and the eyes--the colors and everything else sort of abstract it.

On Card VIII, C gives a confabulatory response of Napoleon with a "powerful face" which "just commands your attention." However, in the third response, the face of Napoleon changes and reminds her of someone else she "can't place," "maybe like a witch doctor or something like that." Then, in the inquiry, she comments that as she looks at the face longer, it begins to take "on animal–like features, like the masks a witch doctor would wear." This fluidity indicates a lack of stability in her object representations and a potential for regression to more primitive levels of functioning with more serious types of boundary disturbance. Again, she finds a cultural context for the blending of human (the face), animal (the features), and inanimate (the mask) characteristics in this response. While she struggles to maintain a humorous attitude toward her responses, the content becomes more ominous and frightening. The grandiose, powerful response of Napoleon becomes more primitive both in content and in structure. Her second response of two bears on Napoleon's shoulders is a fabulized combination. She is unable to keep the two responses of Napoleon and bears separate and independent, but, rather, because they are spatially contiguous, they must be interrelated. Several indications of boundary disturbance emerge on this card, and while there are attempts to maintain humor and an appropriate cultural context, these defenses seem more strained than in earlier responses.

Card IX.   (Sighs--smiles) Hmm.   [28 sec]

1. *The two things at the top*   1. (?) They've got fat bellies
look like kind of comical harpies   (laughs) and not too frightening
(sighs).   looking. (Harpies?) Monsters--
                                         mythical monster that used to
                                         haunt you and come and get you.

On Card IX, once again there are comical cartoon figures. But here C indicates how her defensive use of humor serves to deny things that are frightening. The comical harpies with fat bellies become mythical monsters "that used to haunt you and come and get you." The use of humor as denial and reversal has only limited effectiveness, and the animal–human blends can become terrifying and frightening. The humorous and grandiose confabulations can shift into confabulations of monsters that threaten and frighten her. Her experiences of her world and of herself seem to alternate markedly from feeling that everything is grand, powerful, and fun to feeling weak, lonely, isolated, and terrified.

Card X.   You saved a goodie for last!   [13 sec]

1. *I don't know what this has*   1. (?) Just kind of the mood
to do with Alice in Wonderland,   of the whole picture like a bunch
but this reminds me of that poem   of sea things.

about the oysters--what was it
called? And they were all danc-
ing on the beach.

2. Two lobsters coming out of a saloon.	2. (?) That there looks like a door in the western saloon and they kind of have their arms around one another.
3. These two blue things look like they're angry, but they're separated by the two very peaceful things, I can't put a name on them--they're kind of peaceful.	3. (?) I don't know--I just see two angry eyes--maybe it's one thing that's been separated, because they don't usually have just one eye. (Peaceful things?) The shape--kind of flowing. (Anything else?) There is, but I can't really say.

On Card X, again there is a human–animal blend in an *Alice in Wonderland* context in C's response of oysters and other sea things "dancing on the beach." She elaborates this theme with another human–animal blend: "Two lobsters coming out of a saloon" with "their arms around one another." There are confabulatory tendencies in her last response to Card X, involving a struggle between anger and peace. Two things that look angry are separated by "two very peaceful things" which she "can't put a name on." The only aspects of this response that she can articulate are "angry eyes" and a "kind of flowing shape" that is peaceful. Again there is an attribution of intense feelings based on only a very limited segment of reality. She juxtaposes peaceful, comical, humorous, delightful fantasies with frightening, angry, terrifying ones. Both of these extremes are confabulatory; her fantasies of both defensive, grandiose images and frightening ones disrupt her reality contact. When under stress, she can have difficulty in differentiating what is happening in reality from her personal reactions. Her behavior can be highly volatile and her experiences can alternate from one extreme to the other, from elation to fears of depletion, destruction, and abandonment.

TAT--PATIENT C

1. (Card 1). *His name is Alfred and it's about 5:30 and he's at*
school and he got hit in the mouth with the violin bow. He's sitting
there looking at the thing, wondering why it hit him cause it was always--
you know--kind of like his friend in a way, and he was wondering if
coming home from school at 3:30 was worth it. He wondered if it would-
n't be better to be out playing with the kids. He got a lot of teasing
about playing the violin. So he went home anyway and smelled dinner
cooking--and I lost the train of thought--he decided to--he throws a
decision--he doesn't know whether to take it outside and play ball with

> *it, but he decides to give it another chance (laughs). And he picks it up and it eats him (laughs). No, no (laughs). That's the end of that.*

One of the unique features of this TAT story is C's utilization of overspecification in attributing both names and specific times and places in order to anchor her fantasies and to establish some degree of control and definition. So she begins her story to Card 1 by giving the boy the name Alfred and specifying the time as 5:30. But this defensive posture is unintegrated and ineffective. She also says he is at school, which seems inconsistent with the time being 5:30. At the end of that sentence, there is the first indication of boundary disturbance, a disruption of the distinction between animate and inanimate. In a joking way she comments that the boy got hit in the mouth with the violin bow. He was "sitting there looking at the thing, wondering why it hit him cause it was always—you know—kind of like his friend in a way." Behind the humor of this TAT story, as behind the cartoon characters on the Rorschach, are indications of severe boundary disturbance and difficulty in keeping animate and inanimate attributes separate. In this amalgam of animate and inanimate, there lies a great deal of terror and danger for her. Things can take on wild, fantastic, threatening, dangerous dimensions. It is difficult for her to predict and control what is likely to act against her and hurt her, because even inanimate objects have the potential for action and danger.

In the middle of this first story, she abruptly comments that the boy had come home from school at 3:30; and again the specification of time and place seems to be an attempt to achieve some stability and control. She proceeds to tell a fairly conventional story for a while about a boy who would rather be out playing with the kids and who gets teased about playing the violin. But then, after saying that he went home anyway and smelled dinner cooking, she comments that she has lost her train of thought. It is as if the theme of coming home distracted her from the story, and she becomes unable to contain her associations. She then comments that the boy "throws a decision" and "doesn't know whether to take it outside and play ball with it." "Throwing a decision" is a peculiar phrase, and may be an intrusion from the concept of playing ball into the concept of decision making, suggesting a boundary disturbance in which a concept from one domain inappropriately intrudes into another. She then comments that the boy decides to "give it another chance" and "He picks it up and it eats him." She laughs about this. Again humor is used as a defense. But behind the humor, the terrifying world in which she lives, a world in which inanimate objects like violin bows can be devouring, emerges. The numerous indications of boundary disturbance in this story and C's loss of her train of thought shortly after the character smells dinner cooking at home suggest that some of her disruptions may be related to themes of home and her mother.

> 2. (Card 5). She's a landlady and she runs a rooming house and the person that rents this room hasn't been out of it in three weeks--hasn't come down for any meals--hasn't picked up his mail. And her neighbor is Mr. Moskowitz and he is a rather quiet man anyway, and she liked him. She left things outside his door, and they've been taken in. She left the flowers outside the door this morning, and there they are. But she's concerned and doesn't know what to expect and she thinks it's rather bold of her to go right in, and she hears water running, and she goes to the bathroom and shuts off the water, and there's no one there and the window closes and then the door closes and locks and she left the key in the door and she's locked in.

In this story there is again an overspecification of detail in C's attributing a name, a very unusual name, to one of the figures. Though the story is a fairly conventional one, it shows themes of isolation and alienation. But there is a relative containment of thought disorder and boundary disturbance until the last few lines of the story. Just as the woman enters the room, water turns on by itself, windows and doors close and lock, even though no one is there. Again, inanimate objects mysteriously acquire animation. The animation of inanimate objects such as water, doors, and windows again is associated with danger and potential destruction. Thus her confabulatory thinking, expressed on both the TAT and the Rorschach, shows both her grandiose and her humorous defenses as well as her underlying fears and apprehensions of being destroyed and devoured.

> 3. (Card 15). (Laughs) Mmmm--this is going to take me a minute. (long pause) This is hard because it's overpowering me. (long pause) Got it! He just woke up and he remembers his name is Frederick Thompson and he's a scholar--and he's not anywhere that he recognizes. He looks for his books and they're not there and he looks around and he calls for his servant--his name is Saul (laughs). All of a sudden, he's cold, very, very cold, and he goes over to close the window, but there's no window, and he realizes he's in a cemetery and he looks down and sees a tombstone, and his name's on it.

In her opening comments to this card, C states that "this is hard because it's overpowering me." Here again the card begins to take on animate characteristics and has a disruptive impact on her. She is then overly specific in giving the man a full name, possibly as a way of controlling her thoughts and associations. The man looks for his books, but they are not there. He calls for his servant, again by a specific name, but he is not there. He feels very, very cold, and goes to close the window, but the window is not there. The sense of failure, the unavailability and lack of constancy of objects, both animate and inanimate, are very clearly expressed in this story. In the end, the man looks down and sees a tombstone with his name on it, and he realizes that he is dead. Not only does this story contain blends of animate with inanimate but there are also themes of merging in feeling both alive and dead.

---

4. (Card 14). Hmmmm. (long pause) This man who lives on a beach-- and he went to sleep the night before and he's just woken up and he looks out his window--and he's realizing it wasn't a dream and that it's floating in water and he sees no land anywhere. (Thinking and feeling?) His first reaction is that he should go back to bed and maybe when he woke up again it would be all right. (Ending?) He floats onto a mountain and after a period of time (smiling), he sees land around and he has to start all over again--he's kind of like a new Noah.

Disturbances in object constancy are expressed in this story about a man who is unsure whether he is awake or dreaming. The grandiose and confabulatory theme of the man being a "new Noah" offers her some temporary relief from the terrible uncertainty about whether he is awake or dreaming, alive or dead. As discussed earlier, confabulatory thinking often indicates difficulties in distinguishing between inside and outside, between real and unreal; and in this story with a confabulatory figure (Noah), C describes a man who is confused about whether he is dreaming or whether the events are really happening to him. It is important to note that these themes may be stimulated by the lonely and isolated quality of the figure depicted on this TAT card.

---

5. (Line drawing). (long pause, much sighing) It's Cain and Abel, but it's not like you read about--like it happened. It's like somewhere else. I don't know where, and the tree is their parents rooted into the soil--like we all are, and Cain and Abel are also rooted into the soil, but they have bodies. And they just have to stay there and look at one another and get old, but never die, and they're feeling what? (laughs) Abel is--always--forgiving Cain--I mean like Cain tries to kill him every day--I mean like it was done, but Abel's soul is not really there, so Abel is OK--somewhere else. (?) I kind of mean his body is really there to frustrate Abel, I mean Cain--I'm getting them mixed up.

The story told to the line drawing shows the clearest indications of serious boundary disturbance in this patient. Boundary disturbances have been noted in her blending of human–animal and animate–inanimate features.

But in this story about Cain and Abel, she comments directly that the tree is their "parents rooted into the soil, like we all are, and Cain and Abel are also rooted into the soil, but they have bodies," Then there is a fusion of trees and people, and a fusion of parents in the image of a tree. She tries to articulate the aggression between Cain and Abel, but Abel is safe because his soul is not there. His body is really there to frustrate Cain, whom she mistakenly calls Abel, but she is aware that she is "getting them mixed up." This confusion between Cain and Abel indicates the vulnerability of her boundaries, but her recognition that she is getting them mixed up is a constructive and adaptive feature. Even though she has a tendency toward contamination and merging, she has the capacity to be reflectively aware of her confusion.

---

6.   (Card 7GF).   The girl's name is Helen--and she's blind and mute. She can hear--touch.   The lady that's reading is the woman that's been working in the hospital for years where Helen was born and she reads very badly, but it's the only voice Helen really knows.   Helen cherishes it.   And the doll is new and it's from her parents who she doesn't know. I mean they live in the house, but she doesn't know them.   They are noises and they are touches, but--and Helen is sitting there not really listening to Agnes, and she has the two things to contend with--she has the old familiar friendly voice, and this new doll, and Helen would like to know what's really hers, and she doesn't feel like the doll is hers--that's why she's kind of holding it at a distance.   And Agnes is struggling with the book and she starts getting confused about the word or something and she kind of giggles and then gets kind of upset because she thinks she reads badly and Helen reaches over to touch her and the doll drops and breaks and the doll just is left there and for a moment, Helen knows where she belongs.

C's fantasies about her ultimate fate may be expressed in this story, where she talks about a girl named Helen who is blind and mute. She comments that a lady is reading to her, a woman whom Helen has known for years, because she has been working for years in the hospital where Helen was born. Though the woman reads very badly, "It's the only voice Helen really knows," and she "cherishes it." She does not know her parents, even though they live in the house, since they are only "noises" and "touches." Here, she poignantly expresses her difficulties in distinguishing among people. There is a failure of object constancy, for the parents really do not exist as separate individuals apart from their noises and touches. It is possible that her reference to the physical disabilities of being blind and mute may be an expression of her fears about her neurological difficulties. However, she indicates that both the young girl and the woman reading her a story are confused, but for different reasons. The girl is confused because she is trying to understand what is really hers, to distinguish between the old, familiar, friendly voice of the woman reading the book and the new doll which was given to her by her parents. But, as with her parents, she feels that the doll is not really hers. Likewise, the woman "is struggling with the book and is starting to get confused about the word or something," and then she giggles and gets upset. The confusion and giggling that she attributes to the woman are like her own confusion and use of laughter as a defense. The young girl, seeking to comfort the woman, reaches over to touch her, and the doll drops and breaks. The doll is just left there. It is at this moment, when the doll is dropped, broken, and abandoned, that the girl for the first time "knows where she belongs." While the woman may represent some important figure from C's early life, such as a nurse or a maid or a current figure such as her therapist, it seems clear that she feels she needs some dependable constant object to replace her parents. She wants a figure who will provide her with some stability, who will protect her, allow her to find a place where she belongs, and enable her to establish a sense of herself.

> 7. (Picasso "La Vie"). (Frowns) Hmm--the pictures on the wall were done by a man--his name was Horace Stuart. Art was his life, and he didn't really get along with people--people he created were his life, and the people in the paintings are the people that are standing there, and they're in a museum which is a hell of a place to come to live! (laughs) And they don't know exactly where they are--it's during the daytime and people are coming through the museum and they're being stared at and they're frightened and the lady on my right is just trying to protect the baby and they knew they've been created by someone and they knew he must not have really cared for them and all the museum guards are trying to get the people out of the way and get to them, and are shouting obscene names and calling them freaks and telling them to go back where they came from and they try to get back into the frame, but they can't and they're carted out into the sunshine and melt--and leave a picture on the sidewalk. (How did they know their creator doesn't care?) Because he didn't teach them anything. He just left them alone.

The story C tells to this card is a classic illustration of difficulty with boundary articulation. Again she begins the story by overspecifying, and, from her prior stories, a fuller understanding of this overspecification has been gained. She has difficulty with object constancy; objects lack substance and continuity. She attempts to cope with this difficulty by giving very precise attributes to objects in order to enliven and enrich them and give them some definition, substance and stability.

In the story told to the Picasso "La Vie" card, she talks about a man being defined by his work; art and the people he created were his life. He did not get along with people, but those he created in his art were the people he was involved with. In this story, C expresses her loneliness and isolation and her difficulty in defining herself and her life. There is meaning and vitality only in fantasies. Again there is a confusion between alive and dead, between real and unreal; fantasy productions may give so much more comfort that sometimes they may not only replace real interactions but also be difficult to distinguish from them.

The difficulty in distinguishing between fantasy and reality and the confusion between real and unreal are expressed by the people in the painting becoming real people who have come to the museum to find a place to live. Again she uses humor as a defense, but the impact of the statement nevertheless stands. She expresses her degree of confusion by indicating that the people do not know where they are and are frightened. She comments about the "lady on my right," as if using an egocentric position to define the world. She seems to react as if the lady on the TAT card were real and to be struggling to keep the relation between herself and the lady clear and stable.

She comments further that the people in the picture know they were created by someone who must not have cared for them and that the people who come to the museum to see them are "shouting obscene names and calling them freaks and telling them to go back to where they came from"—to get back into their picture frames. Here, she expresses her feeling that as people venture out into the world, they realize that they are unwanted by their creators and are scoffed at and abused by the people they meet. She then says that the people cannot get back into their frames, are carted out into the sunshine, melt, and leave a picture on the sidewalk. This statement is an indication of the instability of her self and object representations, with tendencies toward experiences of fusion and dissolution. She says that the only thing the people leave behind is an inanimate picture.

---

8. (Card 13MF). Hmmmmm. (long pause) OK. The lady in bed's name is Grace, and this fellow's name is Thomas, and this is his room, and he was at the New York Public Library getting some books, and he was supposed to meet Grace at 8:00 and he got carried away with studying and stuff. Then he picked her up a book of poetry of her own. He bought it for her and he came to his apartment and was kind of happy that he found this book--it was something special, because Grace was something special and he didn't think he had really told her that, and he got kind of panicky because he began to remember some of the things Grace had been saying, and he was afraid he wouldn't find her there, and he comes in and she's not in the living room or the kitchen, so he runs to the bedroom and sees her in bed, and he's very glad and relieved and goes to the living room and takes off his jacket and starts to get something to drink and he panics because something's wrong, and he doesn't know exactly what it is and he runs back to Grace and touches her and finds she's dead, and he blames himself. And he's angry in a way-- I have to end this. Some more? (Just tell me how she died.) She killed herself.

This story told to 13MF is very similar in structure and content to earlier stories. There is a concrete specification of the objects in both time and space, but this concretization does little to contain C's intense anxiety and panic. As indicated in the story, the panic is around object constancy—will the woman be there when he seeks her. The sight of the woman does little to soothe and diminish his panic; he has to touch her, and then he finds out that she is dead. The intense experience of panic around the instability and unavailability of people, particularly a woman, is vividly communicated in this story.

---

9.   (Card 3BM).   (Sighs, frowns)   Hmmm, OK--it's a (sigh) a woman and she's thirty-three and she's in a cell and in the cell there's noises coming in and voices--constant voices--constant noise, a very intensi-fied thing, and she doesn't know what she's doing there and she doesn't know who she is really. I mean she does, but she doesn't know what she would be doing here and the only thing she's thinking about is getting out, and she has to get out and she's checking every way and then she looks around at the walls and they start to move and come closer and closer and she looks down at her feet and there's a knife and she grabs for it, but it was covered with glass--I mean, it wasn't there, it was covered, and she tried to get through the glass and she didn't--and she starts to scream, but she can't even hear her own voice--the walls keep moving and she grabs for the knife again and the glass breaks and she grabs the knife and kills herself--or she runs the knife into her chest and just at that moment the door opens and a person she recognizes--lover, husband--puts his hand out and she thinks maybe it really didn't happen, but she feels the pain and realizes it did, and she cries out and dies.

In this story there is a careful specification of the age of the woman, but C omits giving her a name. In describing isolation and possible auditory hallucinations, she comments that the woman "doesn't know who she is really," and without a name, the woman has no identity. The intense loneli-ness and isolation lead to suicide. Though a man finally enters to save her, it is too late. A sense of utter isolation and uncertainty about whether people are really there or not, or whether she is simply hallucinating, per-vades her response. Human representations are unstable, lack substance, and exist only because of their perceptual and sensory features. In this story there is once again a disturbance of the boundary between animate and inanimate. The walls of the cell begin to move and come closer and closer. The walls keep moving in on her, and as she tries to reach for a knife, it is covered with glass. Just as she reaches the knife to kill herself, she recogniz-es her lover, or husband; and it is only through the experience of pain that she realizes what has happened to her. The instability of people, the uncertainty of reality, and the feeling that the only real things are pain and death are poignantly expressed in this story.

---

10. (Card 18GF). Hmmm--OK. These are two sisters that live in a house which their parents owned--it was a family house--the mother died when they were young and the father lived a rather long time. Carol's thirty-five and Winifred's forty-three, and Winifred had been taking care of the father--all her life and Carol had gotten married at about the age of 22, and that didn't work out, and she got married again at the age of 28, and that didn't work out, and Winifred always made up excuses for her, that she was just young, etc., and the father died about a few days ago and Winifred doesn't know quite what to do because all of a sudden she feels quite relieved--it kind of makes her feel strange, like she wasted her whole life and she doesn't know what for-- and then she thinks for Carol--"I have to take care of Carol now that father's gone." And she goes down the stairs and Carol comes in and she's been out and she's kind of drunk and Winifred all of a sudden thinks, "My God, she's drunk." And she doesn't know exactly what to do, so she sees herself in the hall mirror and there's really no reflection (sighs), so she grabs at Carol yelling, "What do you see?! What do you see?!" and, she panicked, I guess when she grabbed her and all the feel- ing of waste and stuff came out and she lost herself for a few minutes and she looked down at Carol, and Carol was dead and she realized that she also was dead, and she set fire to the house with herself, Carol, and the father who was upstairs in a kind of wake-type thing.

This story portrays the chronic lifelong struggle of a family, the unavaila- bility of the mother, and the search for her replacement. It also expresses a lifelong struggle to achieve some separation from the family, only to find oneself still enmeshed in the family pathology. The outcome of these strug- gles is an initial awareness that one does not exist, followed by suicide and murder. In addition to the content, the story contains indications of the unavailability of objects, the instability of self and object representations, and boundary disturbances in which a person can be both alive and dead.

Summary

While the case history suggests that C's problems are primarily related to oedipal issues and sexual identity, the psychological test data indicate that the basic issues are at a much earlier level. C can maintain an impressive defensive facade in which she uses humor, grandiose thinking, and counter- phobic defense mechanisms to ward off frightening and primitive concerns about the reliability and stability of people and fundamental concerns and doubts about her own existence. Her defenses can be effective at times, but when they are ineffective, she is flooded by intense feelings of isolation, loneliness, emptiness, depletion, and death. There are clear indications of thought disorder in the psychological test material, primarily confabulatory in nature. She has difficulty in maintaining a clear differentiation between external reality and her intense emotional reactions. She experiences affects in extremes—from feeling powerful, humorous, and comfortable, to feeling utterly depleted and nonexistent. There are psychotic features in both her defensive grandiosity and her underlying fears and apprehensions. These fears are compounded by her concerns about her neurological disorder, but they extend beyond that. She uses humor both to gain distance from and to express her fears and apprehensions, but it soon becomes apparent that the humor is hollow. She has serious impairments in her capacity to represent objects and herself, and often her representations lack stability and substance. She attempts to give her representations stability and constancy by being overly specific and concrete, but these attempts are only partially effective. There are numerous indications of boundary disturbance, such as her blending of human, animal, and inanimate features. There are also some indications of a more regressive wish for and fear of merging and fusion. This suggests a potential for further regression, but at the present time these indications occur relatively infrequently. However, C also shows impressive adaptive capacities; particularly the capacities to take distance from her experience and to use humor as a defense. These capacities would be an asset in therapy. However, she feels hopeless about interpersonal relationships since there are few, if any, positive interactions in her TAT stories. Therefore, while she has some resources to respond positively to therapeutic endeavors, it would probably take a long time for her to establish a trusting therapeutic relationship.

C was discharged from the hospital after several years of therapy. She continued in psychotherapy as an outpatient and later was married. She also returned to college and when last heard from, was doing reasonably well.

Case IV—Patient D: Fabulized Combinations that Suggest Only Minimal Difficulty in Maintaining Boundaries

D, a 19-year-old single female, was a sophomore at an Eastern university at the time she was hospitalized. Her family indicated that the difficulties they experienced with her began the summer before she started college, when she shocked them by announcing that she was going to live with a boyfriend. Despite considerable disagreement, argument, and turmoil at home, she followed through on her plans, even though she was not particularly romantically involved with this boy. She entered college as a freshman feeling "miserable" because she missed her boyfriend so much. Within a few months, however, she met another boy, whom she described as her first real romance. By spring, the relationship had blossomed and they began sleeping together. That summer she returned home but again felt miserable and depressed without her new boyfriend. She lived in an apartment with some friends and tried several jobs but continued to feel unhappy and lonely. One night when she was at home with her parents, she took an overdose of pills because of her loneliness and misery. She immediately told her parents what she had done and was taken to a hospital for observation, even though she had not taken a lethal dose. She had seen a psychiatrist on occasion during the previous 2 years, but following this incident, she began seeing him more frequently. Toward the end of the summer, her parents left for an extended vacation, her boyfriend came to town, and they lived together.

D returned to college that fall and continued to live with her boyfriend. She described how wonderful these months were, and how kind, understanding, warm, and sensitive her boyfriend was. She described their relationship as one in which they always understood one another and could talk about anything. They spent every moment together and were "deeply in love."

D and her boyfriend began to smoke marijuana frequently and took LSD several times. Generally, their trips together were pleasant for both of them. Once, a few hours after taking LSD, they decided to go for a ride and were involved in an accident. The boyfriend was seriously hurt, but D received only minor injuries. With her boyfriend on the critical list, D continually spoke of wanting to commit suicide because she felt responsible for the decision to go for a ride. She continued to feel suicidal for several days, until it was clear that her boyfriend would survive his injuries. During her 2 weeks in the hospital, D spoke at length about her unhappiness, her feeling that she was to blame for her boyfriend's accident, and her fear that she would never be allowed to see him again. It was at this point that her parents decided to place her in a psychiatric hospital.

There were no apparent major disruptions in D's developmental history. Her mother's pregnancy was essentially normal, except that her mother had to undergo some surgery late in the pregnancy. But there were no apparent effects on the pregnancy. Her mother tried to nurse D, but felt that she lacked sufficient milk so switched to bottle-feeding after the first few days. D was reported to have been "a very easy and happy infant," who slept with a smile. She began walking at about 10 months. At about 18 months, D showed the first signs of constipation, which became an ongoing problem for her. Shortly after her second birthday, she was toilet trained, which she accomplished essentially by herself. It was at this time that the family made the first of several moves. D's constipation continued, and at times she was in considerable pain. Other than the problem with constipation, D seemed to be a happy child and enjoyed starting nursery school. The following year the family moved once again and D began kindergarten. Her constipation persisted, and when she was 6 she was taken to see a child psychiatrist and her mother consulted a social worker. Within a few weeks the constipation cleared up.

D did very well in grammar school and was always in advanced classes. The family went on frequent vacations and D was reported to have complained frequently of missing her friends and to be generally negativistic and uninterested, so that the family found traveling with her unpleasant. This negativism continued even during D's high school years. She was often scornful and critical of her peers and had difficulty keeping friends. Though she was a physically attractive girl, she rarely went on dates. She frequently alienated not only her peers, but also her teachers. Despite her difficult interpersonal relationships, the schools she had attended described her as a richly endowed, alert, creative child, with a penetrating mind and a capacity for being thorough and attending to details. She achieved honors in high school, winning several awards, and was active in extracurricular activities. She was described as an ideal and outstanding student who was concerned about problems in society.

D's older and younger brothers were described as handsome, charming, popular, and successful. Her older brother was reported to be sensitive, affectionate, and eventempered. D remained closest to him, and he continued to be her champion even when she was at odds with the rest of her family. However, her younger brother was described as antagonistic to his sister, always ready to criticize and attack her. He was hostile toward her during all the years that they were growing up.

During D's second and third years of high school, her parents became more and more concerned about her depressed state and what appeared to be her increased alienation and her difficulty in establishing peer relationships. They took her to see a psychiatrist who reported that her father was never really able to accept her as a girl and often insisted that she behave and think like a boy. The psychiatrist also reported that D continually depreciated her femininity and sought relationships that were demeaning to her. These contacts with the psychiatrist were only occasional, but they continued through her last 2 years of high school and terminated when she left home for college. While D continually used threats of suicide to put pressure on her family, the psychiatrist felt that her symptoms were not serious enough to warrant hospitalization, and he did not increase the frequency of the contacts because he felt her motivation for treatment was poor. She saw the psychiatrist more often during the summer after taking the overdose, and he felt that sufficient improvement had taken place so that she could leave home for college. Following the automobile accident with her boyfriend and the increase in D's suicidal ideation, he recommended psychiatric hospitalization, and the parents complied with the recommendation.

When D was admitted to the hospital, she seemed like a frightened, very sad girl, with quiet, distraught eyes. Almost immediately, she burst into tears and continued to sob plaintively and despairingly. Once this initial period of crying had subsided, she was able to say that it was all a mistake and she could not believe that her parents would actually leave her in a mental hospital. She was shocked at her surroundings, horrified at the locked doors, and frightened of the "crazy people" around her. She seemed distraught, distracted, and very depressed. The day following her admission, her behavior was strikingly different. She seemed much less frightened, depressed, and tearful. She put on makeup, and the patients and staff saw her as a very attractive girl. Initially she did not eat and had some difficulty sleeping, but she spoke with many other patients. During the first several weeks of her hospitalization, she began to wear flattering clothes and to look increasingly attractive and appealing. After the first few weeks, however, her therapist was scheduled to go on vacation and she became angry and insisted on another therapist because she was going to "be in the hospital for only a very short time." Despite her anger about her therapist's vacation, she was able to become increasingly involved in therapy after her therapist returned. She seemed to anxiously await therapy hours and worked hard during the sessions. She presented dreams and details of her early life and spoke extensively about her feelings and apprehensions. She disclosed her anxiety about her sexuality and her chronic difficulties in this area. There had been considerable tension between her boyfriend and herself about their sexual relationship. She never achieved orgasm, and she worried that she might be an "asexual person." She was puzzled by the fact that others often commented on her sexy appearance and behavior, but she was concerned because she did not feel that way. Also, she disclosed deep concerns about the degree of her psychological disturbance and was quite anxious to "get the results" of her psychological testing. Her therapy hours were filled with material, and she often felt that she did not have enough time to reveal everything that was on her mind.

During the first weeks of her hospitalization, D became the center of the patient ward meetings. The first time this occurred, she was protesting her hospitalization and how it was disrupting her relationship with her boyfriend. She said that she would tolerate hospitalization only if it meant that she could get out and rejoin her boyfriend. Once, during a ward meeting, another patient began to criticize D and she broke into tears. She then revealed to the group her fear of this patient and how she had tried to maintain an image of strength so that she could be discharged. While she was frequently the center of the group's attention, she remained isolated from other patients and related only to a very disturbed and withdrawn girl. During ward meetings, D usually knitted or crocheted and rarely spoke about herself, only commenting on issues that she felt confident about. She was helpful at times in facilitating discussion or helping the group arrive at decisions.

Diagnostically, D was eventually considered to have a mixed neurotic character structure with chronic and strong depressive tendencies. She was in the midst of an acute depressive episode when hospitalized, but the depression rapidly lifted. Staff were concerned about her long-term difficulty with personal relations; she usually seemed to have been either lonely and "friendless" or involved in a near symbiotic relationship. Suicidal ruminations had been intermittent for several years; although the question of a borderline state had been raised, there was little evidence of psychotic features. She appeared to be in the midst of a fairly acute adolescent crisis. Her pseudo-delinquency and defiant and cynical behavior seemed to be an active attempt to deny intense passive feelings of depression, neediness, and dependency. Major issues appeared to be her primarily unconscious feelings of rejection and her need to control others, specifically her father. She seemed to need to guard against potentially intense feelings of despair. Her desperate attachment to her boyfriend seemed to be a displacement of her feelings of rejection by her father and, probably more basically, by her mother. Her image of herself as physically "beautiful" seemed to be in part a reaction formation against other less positive self-images. She became rapidly involved in psychotherapy and everyone on the hospital staff was impressed by her capacity to gain from intensive individual psychotherapy. After being in the hospital for 6 months, she was transferred to an outside therapist and began a job. Toward the end of her hospital stay, she became increasingly angry and bitter toward her therapist and spoke with great warmth about her new therapist. In part, it seemed as if she was struggling with a feeling of rejection, having to criticize and attack an earlier relationship in order to facilitate her move to a new therapist. During the hospitalization, she changed from a depressed, defensive, and restive patient to an involved and interested person who impressed many members of the hospital staff. At last evaluation, she was continuing to progress quite well in outpatient therapy.

RORSCHACH--PATIENT D

Card I. What am I supposed to be looking at--the whole thing or what?
[20 sec]

1. It looks like sort of a moth
or a butterfly that's been in a
fight--more? Can I turn it over
and stuff?

1. (?) Here's the middle and
wings. All this stuff (side areas)
makes it look damaged--these here
(white spaces)could be holes, but
look more like designs on butterfly
wings.

2. Looks like it could be sort
of a Japanese landscape or something, except that these little
things here sort of ruin it. I
don't see anything else (still
looking).

2. (?) Mountains (top, side
projections) and the symmetry makes
it look Japanese--then there's sort
of a marsh and field with lakes in
it--these things (top center
"hands") don't look like trees--
they don't fit--I like the perspective with the mountains and fields.
(Japanese?) Things in Japan are
usually symmetrical. (?) Silk
screens and paintings and such.

3. This thing here could be
lips over on the side (still
looking).

3. (?) (top "humps") (?)
The slope of the lines.

4. I suppose it could very,
very vaguely be a face upside
down of an old man--with wisps
of hair on the side.

4. (?) Eyes, moustache (in
white spaces), nose (small gray
spot), hair (side area). (Old?)
The shape of the head. (?) Sort
of like he's bald with wisps of
hair and his eyes slant down
tiredly.

5. It could be sort of a face
this way--a cartoon cat--sort of
an evil type of cat like they
have in cartoons.

5. (?) Cartoons are in favor
of mice--cats with fat cheeks,
ears, whiskers, and eyes slanting
up to indicate how evil they are.

On this first card, there are no indications of boundary disturbance. Each
response is well articulated and delineated, and its integrity and definition
are maintained. Her responses are consistently well articulated, even
though she criticizes them and struggles to consider alternatives. Thus a
moth or a butterfly can either be "damaged" or have "designs" on it, depending on how it is viewed. She sees a picture of a "Japanese landscape,"
which she describes in detail, but it is "ruined" by some small irregularity.

On this opening card, there are features that could be interpreted as
suggestions of amorphous experiences. Her comment on the fourth re-

sponse as being "very, very vaguely" a face of an old man could indicate amorphousness, but in the inquiry she articulates and elaborates this response in great detail. This vagueness may be related more to the content of an elderly man than a description of her perceptual experience. Another response that might be interpreted as suggesting possible boundary disturbances at the confabulatory level is her fifth response of an "evil type of cat." But she does not lose distance from the response and uses the idea of it being "a cartoon cat" to successfully modulate and contain the confabulatory tendency. It is tempting to discuss some of the dynamic issues in her self and object representations, such as a damaged butterfly, the slanted and tired eyes of an old man, an evil cat, or a ruined Japanese landscape. But in terms of boundaries, there are no indications of disruptions in this series of responses. On the contrary, her responses are well articulated and accurate, and they have substance and vitality, even though there is often a depressive disparagement of them.

```
Card II.  (Shrugs)  [15 sec]

 1.  Another insect again.           1.  (?)  A fat butterfly.  (?)
                                     Wings (side detail).  Antennae
                                     (red projections)--I don't know
                                     if this could also be part of a
                                     butterfly or not (connecting area).
                                     I don't know if butterflies have
                                     a thing going all the way through--
                                     I think they do.  (Fat?)  So short
                                     compared to how wide it is.

 2.  And this red thing here
would be a horseshoe crab.

 3.  When I first looked at it,       3.  (?)  Entranceway (top section
it looked like this was some sort    of white space) with a stone wall
of a temple with an entranceway.     on the side with a path in the
                                     middle.  This could be part of it
                                     too (large white space) a garden
                                     surrounded by walls.  (Temple?)  I
                                     don't know--it's a different color
                                     than the stuff surrounding and the
                                     pointed top makes it look like a
                                     building--actually it has a cross
                                     on it, but I don't think I noticed
                                     that before.

 4.  I suppose this looks             4.  (?)  Do I have to go into
vaguely like a penis.                that?  There's not much to say--
                                     just the head of a penis.

 5.  Hmm, there's two heads of        5.  (?)  They're pretty good,
giraffes right there.                too (top, red).  The right size
```

	neck, looking out from behind this thing (side area). You could imagine it could go on and on and on--ears--the nose is a little long.
6. *This all by itself could be a mountain with the sun rising-- I think that's all--it feels like you could go on forever and pick out teeny things that look like something.*	
7. *This white thing in the middle here looks like sort of a person, actually.*	7. (?) Sort of strange though-- the top of the body is sort of heavy and her legs are real, real teeny--sort of a girl with a cape or standing on her toes.

Again, on Card II, D's responses are accurate, well articulated and stable. She again uses the phrase "vaguely" to introduce a response that has masculine content (fourth response). Her description of something as vague does not seem to express difficulty in her representational processes but rather to be a defensive reaction, probably on a neurotic level, to masculine figures. Her third response of a temple with an entranceway, with a stone wall on the side, a path in the middle, and a garden surrounded by walls, suggests a degree of differentiation with articulated and stable boundaries. Her concerns about her self representations, particularly her body, seem to be more around beauty and attractiveness (response seven) than around any issue of basic definition and intactness. Her concerns about her body are intense and seem to involve issues about the relative size of parts of her body. These concerns can result in disruptions of reality testing. But thus far there is little evidence to suggest that the disruptions are of psychotic proportions, involving manifestations of boundary disturbance.

Card III. [8 sec]	
1. *That could be a face.*	1. (?) The shape of the head-- either these are ears (heads) or these red things are ears. It sort of looks like a cat--the eyes are close together (middle red) and the whiskers and mouth (lower middle gray). Cats really do have a line in the center of their face like this (indicates).
2. *And two people.*	2. (?) Their clothes are sort of tight so it looks like a Spanish dancer--men (points out clothing)

leaning backwards very precarious-
ly--forward actually--asses out--
they look like they're bowing to
each other. (Tight?) Their legs
are so that their pants would have
to be tight and when they lean
down their jackets go pointing
out--makes it look like a very
tight jacket.

*3. And bird shit--only it's
orange.*

3. (?) (Top red). That's what
it looks like--on the window of a
car, except it isn't orange. (Do
you see the window?) No.

*4. And some sort of a bow tie
or something.*

*5. I guess a winter scene--
sort of a closeup of it because
it's not very much. I think
that's all I feel. I ought to
be able to see something because
it's such a nice shape, but I
don't see anything--only a nice
shape.*

5. (?) It has to be pretty
little or otherwise it would have
snow all over it. (?) Snow falling this way (indicates 45° angle)
would get on all of it if it was
larger--if it wasn't black and
white it could be shading--the sun
here (?) and the rest in shadow--
this is just like it here (indicates other half of blot).

On Card III, there is continued evidence of problems with sexual identity. There is an inaccurate perception of a cat's face and a preference for
seeing the ambiguous figures on this card as men; and the center red area
(response four) is seen as a "bow tie" rather than the more feminine association of "butterfly." There are depreciating responses such as "bird shit"
and themes of coldness and warmth (response five) interspersed among the
responses with masculine content. While dynamic issues about her difficulty with sexual identity and her ambivalence about men are clear. there are
no indications of boundary disturbance on this card.

Card IV. This is really a drag! [13 sec]

*1. It looks like an animal
that I've never seen.*

1. (?) A sort of a combination
of a bear and an ape with hands
and a tail and its back is to us.
(Bear and ape?) And some other
things--sort of looks like an ape
head and it's so big--enormous
shoulders and the color. (Ape and

bear?) Dark and really big feet--
looks kind of furry--somehow it's
too ugly to be a bear--so that's
out.

2. Two of them (shrugs and
smiles).

2. (?) A real strange animal
out of Alice in Wonderland--not a
specific animal--arms, legs, tail--
arms raised--wearing a crown--he
would really have a lot of trouble
with big enormous feet and little
tiny arms--it looks like he'd have
to walk on his head and then he'd
turn into the ape and the bear.

3. (Deep in thought) Some
sort of insect there, but I can't
remember what it's called--I know!
I think it's a snail without the
shell.

3. (?) (Lower center detail)
I don't know, I guess the way the
ink is blotted that makes it look
sort of squishy. (Squishy?) Most
snails are squishy--these pointed
things also--actually a snail doesn't
have them on his body--only
on top of his head, but this (on
body) looks more like what a snail
would have than this (on head)
does.

4. Kind of looks like Piglet--
I think that's all.

4. (?) The two white spots--
leaning against a tree. (Piglet?)
The nose and its little funny body
and the way it's sitting against
the tree. (?) Just leaning there
with the top of its back.

For the first time in this Rorschach protocol, on Card IV, there are some
indications of boundary disturbance. The opening response of some "sort
of a combination of a bear and an ape" is a fabulized combination. D does
not, however, blend the features into a unified response as in a more regressed contamination response. In fact, she eventually discards the image
of the bear, so the response can be considered as only a tendency toward
fabulized combination. She continues to indicate similar difficulties, however, in the second response, but again she seems to be able to contain the
boundary disturbance by placing the response in the context of an "animal
out of Alice in Wonderland." Fabulized combinations are one of the least
serious forms of boundary disturbance, and, in addition, D seems to have
the adaptive resources to place these unrealistic percepts in appropriate
contexts. It is important to note that these responses occur on a card with
striking phallic features. It will be important to see whether boundary disturbances occur on subsequent cards or whether they are limited to this

card. Thus far, her mild boundary disturbance appears to be associated with the issue of sexual identity that she is vulnerable to—like "a snail without the shell." This issue also seems to provoke more childish and depressed modes of functioning, as seen in her response "Piglet" with its "little funny body" sitting against a tree. It suggests that her problems in sexual identity may be expressed in her view of herself as an asexual piglet with a funny body. These self representations do contain some evidence of boundary disturbance, and she tends to view herself as a childish, asexual cartoon figure. There may be some loss of reality testing around these issues, but the fact that there seems to be a reasonably successful defensive organization to cope with them suggests that the disruptions around them do not reach psychotic or even borderline proportions.

Card V.   [3 sec]

   1. *Another fucking butterfly!*
(frowns)

   2. *It's strange because somehow*   2. (?) Some sort of an animal
there's a sense of a fox or a   in here, but there's not enough of
wolf--some kind of movement, but   it. (Fox or wolf?) Just the sense
I don't see the animal very well--   of movement--I don't know why--now
a sense of movement without the   that I see the crocodile heads I
animal--can't really see him.   can't see it very well.

   3. *Wow! Looks like there's*   3. (?) (Laughs) His feet
some really strange guy standing   (lower projection)--legs--he had
behind a screen with bunny ears   a fat head with a long strange
on his head.   nose, big eyes, heavy eyebrows--
    a pervert or something. (?) Looks
    sort of strange standing behind
    that screen with bunny ears on his
    head. (Screen?) It's got to be
    a screen of some sort.

   4. *And two alligator heads*
or crocodile heads (puts card
down quickly).

There is a recovery on Card V from the mild boundary disturbance manifested in the fabulized combinations on the previous card. While the hidden figures seen in the second and third responses to this card could be interpreted as some continued disruption of object representation, these responses also reflect a capacity for object constancy—the ability to represent a figure that is not fully present in the perceptual field. The third response of a guy "with bunny ears" is a human–animal blend and a fabulized combination again involving masculine content. Despite the indications of possible disgust about her femininity (response one), and concerns about sexual perversion (response three), there are no indications of serious boundary disruption.

Card VI. They're so boring! [22 sec]

1. *Ugh! I see an owl.*

    1. (?) Just this top thing right there--nose and eyes (in shading). (Just the head?) The whole thing--tiny owl which is practically all head--a hawk owl-- very small.

2. *And the back of a cat's head.*

    2. (Usual cat's head)

3. *(long pause) I suppose there's another cat's head, but it doesn't have any eyes.*

    3. (?) The whole thing--face-- ears. All these cats are really ugly--not like real cats--like cartoon cats.

4. *And I suppose two little animals, but they're stuck way out in the middle of the air.*

    4. (?) These little guys (side area) stuck up on this pole. (What sort of animal?) I don't know--sort of like bear cubs, but not as cute.

5. *And two lips again--that's it.*

On Card VI, there is an alternation of aggressive and passive figures— from a "hawk owl" to an ugly cartoon cat to "two little animals" or "guys" stuck up on a pole. The passivity in being "stuck way out in the middle of the air" is emphasized by the oral content of the last response "lips." This passivity, however, does not seem to be an expression of any wish for or fear of symbiosis. There is a slight peculiarity to the comment "hawk owl" which might suggest some blending and merging of concepts. This response should have been inquired into more fully, but generally there appears to be little if any indication of boundary disturbance in the responses to this card.

Card VII. Hmmm (shrugs). [10 sec]

1. *Two faces.*

    1. (?) Women's faces--looking at each other. (Women?) Hair and the things sticking out of them--I think they could be feathers and then you could call them squaws, but they don't have the

	right facial features to be Indians.
2. *A house.*	2. (?) You can't see very much of it--a wall (bottom detail) and a gate (center of detail). It's back there and all you can see is one window.
3. *Some sort of very strange Dr. Seuss combination animal. That's it.*	3. (?) Just the head here with the trunk, but no ears and very alive eyes for some reason (middle detail).

D is somewhat critical of the feminine figures she initially sees on Card VII, and she distances herself from the content by making them Indians. Her distance from feminine figures is also suggested by her second response of "a house" which she "can't see very much of," only "one window." Some boundary disturbance, probably a fabulized combination, is suggested by her response of a "very strange Dr. Seuss combination animal," but again it is modulated by being placed in an appropriate childish and humorous context.

Card VIII. Hmmm, how lovely (half sarcastically)! I'm dizzy from looking at all these. [28 sec]	
1. *A couple of really beautiful animals. Wow! Hmmm.*	1. (?) This group--they sort of look almost like polar bears--getting out of water--real fine looking--except of course they're pink.
2. *And a dog's face.*	2. (?) A terrier or something--whatever tramp was in "Lady and the Tramp." This thing (white space), the ears and the eyes.
3. *And a dinosaur.*	3. (?) (Laughs) This guy--I guess this shape here and he looks like he's coming this way.
4. *And hands.*	
5. *(long pause) Woman silhouetted.*	5. (?) The white part facing this way. (?) Hair and shoulders--could be nurses--wearing nurses' caps, but it could be part of the hair--I think they're kind of nice.
6. *A goblet.*	6. (?) This little orange

	thing--right up to there.
7. And sort of another dog's ~~rjr'н нʼlᵒ ʈᵗⁱᵉ nⁱₗ ᵢᵤₗᵧ ₙₗₗₗ.~~	7. (?) This guy (~~dotail~~) ~~Ɩⁱᵏₛ,~~ ~~Uⁿᵉ öₜ~~ those little chow dogs with fat cheeks and little ears (sighs).

On Card VIII, D's use of boredom, seen on Card VI, and of playfulness to defend against the feelings emerging on the Rorschach begin to give way to sarcasm and anger. In terms of boundary articulation, the responses remain intact. Underlying oral needs are again expressed in the closing responses to the card—"nurses," "a goblet," and "chow dogs."

Card IX.   (Grabs card and frowns in a disgusted manner.) [34 sec]

1. There's some little head peeking out.	1. (?) This little thing (center) with the eyes. (What sort of head?) I don't know-- just a cute little head with big eyes.
2. This way it's a whole animal.	2. (?) (Same area as above-- inverted) Head and body. (What sort of animal?) I've never seen one like it, I don't know.
3. A couple of birds sitting in some trees.	3. (?) Orange things--head, feet, and tails--turned looking back into this thing--not looking at us.
4. A couple of very, very vague frogs. It can be turned to the side and still be frogs (sighs).	4. (?) These little green guys here--heads up here and the backs of frogs.
5. Now I want to make this pink thing into an animal or a cloud--but it doesn't look like anything at all--it starts to look like an animal, but it's too bad. I'm tired.	

When offered Card IX, D grabs it and frowns, and her anger becomes more apparent. In her fourth response of "frogs," there is another reference to something being "very, very vague." But again the experience of vagueness does not seem to refer to her representation of the objects. The frogs are reasonably well articulated and, as before, the vagueness is associated with masculine content ("these little green guys"). In her closing remarks to the card about wanting to make a part "into an animal or a cloud—but it doesn't look like anything at all," she maintains a clear separation between these two ideas. Though she avoids completing this response, her behavior seems to reflect a resistance to cooperating further rather than any indication of boundary disturbance. Her constant reference to animals as "guys" suggests at least some tendency toward human–animal blends.

Card X.   [7 sec]

1. *Spider.*

1. (?) Blue spiders--all the long little things that look like legs. (Blue?) Yes.

2. *A couple of teeny poodles or lions.*

2. (?) The orange gets in the way--it's not part of them-- it's just in front of them somehow (points out parts of animal) pretty complete. (Poodle or lion?) Both. (?) Could be either--it looks sort of like they're posing--the tails look sort of cute like poodles, but their chest is big like lions, they could be roaring instead of posing and could be lions.

3. *A rabbit head.*

3. (?) Ears, smile, and nose.

4. *Skunks.*

4. (?) These guys standing up (points out parts) big, rounded backs because they're standing on their feet--coloring like skunks. (?) Dark face and body--bottom-- gray-like fur.

5. *A wishbone.*

6. *Two little faces.*

6. (?) (in the center)

7. *Two more.*

7. (?) (under "skunks") Like sort of guys who wear hair long-- when it was established--white with a sort of tail on it. (Established?) Not sort of hippy freaks. (?) Like sort of European.

8. *A couple of combination horse and camel--a very undignified horse--scrawny.*

8. (?) (side brown area) I guess just a camel because of the coloring. (Combination?) It looks like a horse type of animal, but colored like a camel, and

	they're not dignified like horses-- they're sort of silly looking.
9. *And a skunk.*	9. (?) This guy--the two skunks behind this thing instead of in front of it.
10. *Two butterflies.*	10. (?) Two butterflies--there and there.
11. *Two ponies and I quit!*	11. Two donkeys--kind of nice- looking, and here--staring off in opposite directions.

In the second response (teeny cute poodles or lions) and the eighth response (undignified and scrawny camels or dignified horses) to Card X, she gives alternate responses somewhat similar to the fabulized combinations seen on Card IV. These responses are mild fabulized combinations, and they express her concerns about her appearance and her sexual identity. Her concerns about sexual identity—her depreciated image of the woman and the vague and unavailable male—may provide further understanding of the meaning of the fabulized combination responses that appeared previously on Cards IV and V. These responses all involved masculine figures and phallic themes. It seems that the mild boundary disturbance noted in D's fabulized combination responses reflects the intensity of her struggle around sexual identity and oedipal issues. In addition, there is ample indication that she has the resources to place these mild expressions of boundary disturbance in appropriate contexts. Thus, it seems that her difficulties are not on a psychotic level but rather are severe neurotic struggles with unresolved oedipal problems, with consequent confusion about sexual identity and strong feelings of depression. She feels unappreciated and neglected by her father, and there are suggestions of an unsatisfying relationship with mother as an identification figure but, more important, as someone she feels did not care for or love her.

TAT--PATIENT D

1. (Card 1). I can't decide which story to tell you. (How many stories do you have in mind?) Three or four (shrugs). O.K. The little kid's mother wants him to practice the violin because he's going to have a lesson the next day and he hasn't practiced all week, but he'd rather be outside playing with his friends. (long pause) (Thinking and feeling?) He's sad. (pause) (Thinking?) He's thinking about how all of his friends are having a good time outside and he has to practice his violin. (Ending?) How does what end? (pause) His mother comes into the room and sees how sad he is and tells him to practice only a few minutes and then he can go outside to play--he isn't very good, because he doesn't want to practice. The next day he goes to the lesson and the teacher is shocked that he has made so much progress in the last week.

Although D indicates that she has a number of stories in mind, she is able to select one of them and does not seem to be distracted by the other themes she was considering. There is an incongruous ending to this story, a somewhat wishful ending in which the teacher is shocked by the boy's progress, but there is no boundary disturbance apparent in this response.

> 2. (Card 5). This lady is coming into the living room to tell her husband that dinner's ready--she's a little bit worried because he's fallen to sleep reading his paper. He's worried that he's growing old. She wakes him gently so he doesn't know that she saw him asleep. Before she came in she knew he was worried about growing old and now she has a worried look on her face because she's afraid it's going to upset him. (Ending?) I already told you--she wakes him up and they go eat dinner.

There is a shared secret concern about the husband's aging in this story, but D never loses the focus of who is feeling what about whom. Shared concerns or secrets often create a complex situation in which more regressed patients confuse the various people in the story. D, however, is able to manage this type of story without any indications of boundary disturbance.

> 3. (Card 15). This is from the Edgar Allan Poe story, "Anabelle Lee"--he's an outcast from society--he was in love with a beautiful girl--passionately in love, and then she died, completely alienating him and he becomes gloomy, morbid, and totally withdrawn, and every night he goes to the cemetery and weeps in front of her grave.

Again there is no indication of boundary difficulties, but there is a repetition of the theme of loss, and feelings of alienation and severe depression.

> 4. (Card 2). This young schoolgirl here is obviously infatuated with that rugged, virile farm guy whose pregnant wife is standing there watching him work. And she is thinking all these naive thoughts about being a farm wife. And this whole thing is very romantic because she doesn't even know him. She just walks by his farm on the way to school. But her father will send her off to finishing school and she'll marry a promising young businessman and laugh at all her youthful fantasies.

In terms of boundary disturbance, it is impressive how D is able to keep the two female figures separate. There are obvious oedipal themes in the story, but no indication of boundary disturbance.

> 5. (Card 18GF). How awful! They look European--a brave young couple who have been hiding Jews from Nazi soldiers, but the soldiers just came into their house and shot the husband who is dying, and he's filled with fear and lotrism and more because he's leaving his wife alone. He's afraid for her--and that's what he's thinking about as he's dying-- along with the pain. She can't believe he's dying--they knew something like this might happen, and they prepared for it. They had saved money for her to go away. I don't know if she will make it or not--she'll try.

The themes of this story are about secret relationships leading to punishment, pain, death, and object loss. The theme of abandonment by the male is repeated in this story, with concern about whether the woman can survive this loss. The story again seems primarily oedipal and depressive in content, with no indications of boundary disturbance.

> 6. (Card 10). It's just that the husband's been away, and he's just come back and they're very happy to see each other. He hasn't been away that long, but they're very much in love, and they're glad to see each other. What will happen is that they will make love and feel wonderful--for a while at least. It could be that he hasn't been away at all and they're very happy to see each other anyway.

This appears to be a restitution of the loss communicated in the previous story. The instability and uncertainty of her relationships with men are clearly expressed and experienced in this response.

> 7. (Picasso "La Vie"). (Frowns) It looks like they might be part of some ancient culture with the drawings on the walls and stuff with this mother having a new baby and she looks sort of angry, but it being an ancient culture and their not being ashamed or anything, that it's not that she's caught them at it, but it's just like she's jealous. Maybe she feels her son should be put in the fields or whatever this culture does to get food. (Ending?) (long pause) It doesn't exactly end--I mean I suppose the way it ends is that after 70 years the two of them die after a long life. After a short time the angry expression on the mother's face will leave. (?) It's really a drag telling you stories because you're not listening. (Thinking and feeling?) They're thinking they're right and it doesn't matter what the mother thinks. She will learn that they were meant for each other. And isn't it too bad that things have to be difficult for a while, but things will turn out all right. If you think that's a projection, you're right. (Why are you angry?) I don't like telling you stories and having you find out about me and then not telling me--I don't like to tell a story and always have to be thinking what it's going to show.

D responds with intensity to the manifest sexual and oedipal themes of this card. She tells a very long story, and she is angry that the examiner is discovering embarrassing things about her. It is interesting that the resentment in the story is between the mother and her son, and there is no direct mention of the younger woman in the story. She attempts to contain the intensity of the issues by placing the story in an "ancient culture," but this defense is relatively unsuccessful. The resentment between mother and son continues for 70 years. It is of interest to note that she sees the infant as belonging to the mother rather than to the couple. While she considers the possibility of the sexual aspects of the relationship between the younger man and woman (maybe the mother "caught them at it"), she quickly returns to the mother's jealousy and dependence on her son for sustenance. After telling the story, D feels that the examiner has not been listening to her, yet, at the same time, she feels that he has invaded her privacy. D's statement of feeling toward the examiner parallels the theme in the story of the mother's resentment and jealousy of her son's involvement with the girl. D, like the mother in the story, is angry about not getting enough attention.

> 8. (Card 13MF). (Frowns and grabs a cigarette) (long pause) Maybe she just died in childbirth and he can't bear it. (Thinking?) He's not--just in anguish. (Ending?) He's just miserable for a few years and gradually as time passes he gets stronger and stronger. I don't think he ever gets remarried though. Or maybe they're not married, in which case he never falls in love again or maybe he's married to someone else in which case he lives a life full of guilt and unhappiness-- reminiscing.

Again D avoids the sexual implications of the card and instead tells a story of object loss and a man's anguish, grief, guilt, and unhappiness, and his inability ever to love anyone else.

> 9. (Card 12F). This young lady here has invited her best friend who happens to be a witch and has taken her to a fashionable salon where they have their portrait taken, and she takes it home and puts it on her mantle, and she probably has little ones made and sends them out as Christmas cards. (Thinking and feeling?) Pleased. (About what?) To have their picture taken. (sarcastically) She's thinking what a great addition that will be to her livingroom. The witch is trying to decide whether she should try to make it with the photographer because he looks kind of dumb and she thinks he would make a good specimen. She's not a with-it witch, she's sort of underhanded.

This story could easily have led to expressions of boundary concerns, such as the young girl being controlled, dominated, taken over, or consumed by the witch. Instead the story contains oedipal themes such as "little ones made" from a big one, the witch deciding if she should "make it with the photographer, and a denigration of both the witch and the photographer.

> 10. (Card 3GF). (sarcastically) Oh, she's caught her finger in the door. She's in a lot of pain and what will happen is that she will open the door and the miracles of modern medicine will rejuvenate her left hand.

This very brief story suggests possible masturbation conflicts and concern about castration and penis envy.

> 11. (Card 16). Ah ha! You're getting tricky--this is definitely the nicest picture so far--I think it's a close-up of the bottom sheet of a beautiful big double bed, or maybe it's a close-up of a blanket on that bed in which case the bed is out in the snow. Or maybe it's sleep. (Tell a story.) A new patch of snow--a couple comes along (sarcastically, then sadly) laughing hysterically--not hysterically--having a good time. They mess the snow up with their feet making all sorts of designs. A puppy then comes along and pisses on the snow. And then comes cars and smog and muck on top of the footprints. This card is dirty, you should clean it before you give it to someone--or have them wash their hands.

Her story to this blank card starts off with what seems to be a sexual theme of a couple and a "beautiful big double bed." The happy content of the story is in counterpoint to the examiner's observation that her sarcasm has changed to a tone of sadness. The content does not stay on a sexual level, but changes to more phallic and anal themes.

Summary

There are relatively few indications of boundary difficulties in D's Rorschach and TAT. D's responses are well delineated and stable. Her difficulties seem much more on a neurotic oedipal and preoedipal level. She depreciates the feminine role and image and at the same time feels rejected by men, particularly her father. There is evidence of an unsettled and confused sexual identity and longings to be a man. There is also evidence of anal preoccupations and the use of obsessive–compulsive defenses. The only evidence of boundary disturbance in the entire record occurs on Card IV of the Rorschach, a card with predominant phallic implications, and in responses with themes of masculinity and sexual identity confusion (Cards V, X). These boundary disturbances were relatively mild (fabulized combinations), and they were presented in contexts that indicated that she was able to mobilize adequate defenses to cope with these issues. Thus the test protocols do not show any psychotic processes, but rather suggest a predominantly neurotic organization centering around themes of sexual identification and depression. She feels rejected by her father and distant from men, and at the same time she sees her mother, and women generally, in a denigrated and depreciated way. She does not view her mother as an adequate figure for identification; and, in basic ways, D feels rejected by her and sees herself as ugly, damaged, evil, and misshapen.

Case V—Patient E: Few Indications of Formal Thought Disorder, but Themes of Merging in the Content Juxtaposed with Exaggerated Attempts to Maintain Boundaries

E, a 17-year-old male high school student, was admitted to the hospital subsequent to several years of outpatient therapy. E's difficulties apparently began 2 years prior to admission, when he was a junior in boarding school. As E entered his junior year, he began seeing a psychiatrist, who found him to be very anxious, depressed, and bewildered, with some fluidity of thinking, and considered him to be in a borderline schizophrenic state. His scholastic record had previously been excellent; he entered therapy shortly after he had broken up with a girlfriend. In general, E did well throughout his junior year, and he discontinued therapy at the beginning of the summer vacation. During that summer he worked in the kitchen of a summer camp and, while working at this camp, met and had an affair with a girl who was a few years older than himself. During this relationship he had sexual intercourse for the first time.

Upon returning to school that fall, he seemed to be functioning well and resumed therapy. Over the following several months, however, he felt that his behavior and manner were adolescent; so, as he began his senior year, he resolved to conduct himself in a more serious, masculine, and adult fashion. He covered the windows of his dormitory room to create a kind of monastic privacy, which he felt would help him to study hard and to become a more serious person. Whereas he had previously participated in many extracurricular activities, he now placed severe restrictions on his activities. That winter, while skiing, E sustained a broken leg and was briefly hospitalized. His leg was placed in a cast and he was discharged after 10 days.

E stated that his difficulties began at this point. Just before he was discharged from the hospital, an elderly man in the bed next to E suddenly died. E was quite upset by this and had nightmares about this man's death during the next few days. Immediately after returning to school, E wished that he was back in the hospital. He felt helpless and extremely self-concious about the cast. He could not get around well and was especially embarrassed by being waited on by fellow students. He became increasingly depressed and isolated and began to have recurrent dreams relating to death and homosexuality. Also, he began to experience feelings of depersonalization and to suffer from insomnia. He began to study more, until he was studying 7–8 hr a day for six courses. E explained that he became more and more obsessed by "accuracy of expression" and a great deal of his study time consisted of writing papers, which became an increasingly laborious task.

Just before spring vacation, his agitation became such that he was placed on a daily dose of 200 mg. of thorazine. While visiting friends during the vacation he slept with a girl, she told her parents about it, and he was asked to leave the house. E stated that he felt extremely ashamed and embarrassed about this. On his return home, his parents noted that he was rather depressed. He slept up to 20 hr each day, and they urged him to call his therapist, which he was hesitant to do. While at home, E talked to his mother about some homosexual experiences, and his mother thought that he seemed preoccupied with homosexuality.

Soon after E's return to school from vacation, he was admitted to a general hospital because of symptoms of mononucleosis that had been present for several weeks. During this period, E felt so upset emotionally that he wanted to remain in the hospital. During this hospitalization, too, a patient who occupied the bed next to E suddenly died. E felt overwhelmingly depressed and guilty about the man's death. After his discharge, he was in a panic state, preoccupied with themes of death and homosexuality, and he repeatedly told his therapist that he should be hospitalized. He had a dream in which he and his therapist were meeting for a therapy session. E stated that in this dream he wanted to talk about his depression, but his therapist's response was to make homosexual overtures toward him. Shortly after this, E announced to his therapsit that he wanted to terminate therapy, and he did not return for his next appointment.

After this interruption of therapy, E continued to stay in his room except to attend classes. He felt extremely upset and confused during this period and was preoccupied with the thought of getting admitted to a psychiatric hospital. He decided to act in such a way that neither his therapist nor the school's headmaster would have any choice but to hospitalize him. Several days later, he attacked a classmate physically and verbally in a way that was highly sadistic and erotically tinged. The boy reported the incident to the headmaster, who became alarmed and called E's therapist, insisting that E could not remain at the school and had to be hospitalized. His therapist had not seen E in several days, but he had E admitted to a general hospital. At that time, he found E extremely agitated, depressed, and openly expressing fears over homosexual involvement with the therapist. Psychological testing done at this time showed that he was markedly excited and lacking in control, and his responses on the projective tests revealed a great deal of primitive drive material. The examiner noted that E seemed to be experiencing a deeply disturbing panic reaction involving sexually threatening impulses. He showed marked regression and acute schizophrenic disorganization.

The therapist arranged for long-term hospitalization for E, who arrived at the hospital alone. When seen for admission, he was extremely agitated, his speech was rambling, and he made highly intellectualized allusions to suicide. Although he seemed anxious to be hospitalized, he was not willing to be admitted. Since his parents were out of town, he was committed to the hospital on a 30-day paper.

On admission, E was in a state of marked disorganization. However, his reality testing was fairly intact, and there was no evidence of gross delusions or hallucinations. When he met his new therapist, he talked at length in a loose, rambling fashion. He appeared to be under considerable pressure, and constantly shifted around in his chair. Sometimes he was very angry, claiming that he did not want to be at the hospital or on a locked ward. At other times, he would directly express his fright and his wish to be cared for, or he would display a warm and somewhat seductive interest in the therapist. Most often he would speak in a highly intellectualized and philosophical way about himself and his problems. He was particularly adept at using psychological language, and he pointed out that he had been in psychotherapy on and off since the age of 7. He stated that he was not convinced that he wanted to be in a hospital. Yet he said that he had wanted to be admitted to a psychiatric hospital for several months but had been unable to convince his former therapist that it was necessary. He seemed preoccupied with homosexual themes, talking at great length about a paper he was writing on the conflict between Freud's views on homosexuality versus those of Sartre. He said that he was somewhat stunned that his fantasies of becoming a mental patient had come true. He said that his knowledge was all disorganized, that he had become more and more isolated at school, and that his mind had been completely taken up by therapy. He complained of having felt very anxious and of having had difficulty sleeping for the past few months and stated that his troubles had all begun when he broke his leg the previous winter.

On the day following admission, E's parents arrived. E was extremely hostile to them and initially took the position that he would not remain in the hospital. The parents had talked with his previous therapist and very much wanted him to stay. When it became clear to E that they were firm in their position, he seemed markedly reassured and dropped all talk of not remaining in the hospital.

E was the first of four children. His parents described the pregnancy and delivery as normal. They agreed that E was a difficult baby from the start. He cried all the time, and his mother felt that her care was inadequate, although she did not elaborate on this. During the first 2 years of E's life, he and his parents lived in an apartment. The parents recalled that during this period they had quite a hard time keeping E quiet so that he would not wake up the elderly people living in the building.

The parents said that E was very difficult to toilet train. They also reported that he had been an unduly aggressive child from the earliest years and always difficult to control. At the age of 7, while the parents were vacationing, E and his infant brother stayed with a relative. E stole a substantial amount of money from a maid and went out and spent it on toys. Initially the theft was considered to be an unsolved mystery, but when the parents returned, E told them about it. E recalled that his father beat him severely for this. E stated that for the next 7 years until he was 14, his father punished him physically on many occasions; and he remembered his father as being sadistic. E stated that he recalled at times taking some pleasure in seeing his father lose his temper in this way. Earlier, E had begun to be assaultive to his younger brother in much the same way that his father was to him, and this became a chronic problem in the family.

E was referred by the parents to a psychologist, who saw him in play therapy for 1–2 years. Apparently therapy was very difficult and E was referred to a psychiatrist because of continued general rebellion, minor thefts, poor school and social progress, overagressiveness, and punitive behavior toward his siblings. When first seen, he was described as "an emotionally deprived, animal-like youngster," who was "shrewd, ingratiating, complaining, paranoid, and lost." Therapy sessions were described as a continuous and horrible testing of the limits. It seemed to the psychiatrist at that time that E consciously idolized and feared his father and was greatly disturbed by his mother's seductiveness. His sexual identity was confused, and he tried to overcompensate in athletics and body consciousness. In general, however, E responded well to treatment. The parents said that they decided to send E to boarding school at the beginning of the eighth grade because he was unmanageable at home. E recalled being very happy to go away to school, feeling very uncomfortable and unhappy at home.

E remembered that his father stopped punishing him physically when he was 14, in response to his hitting his father back for the first time. He felt a great sense of achievement about this and was very eager to tell his therapist about it. E's recollections of his adolescent experiences began with his bar mitzvah. At that time he went out and bought $100 worth of clothing with some of the money he had received as gifts. He hid the clothes, fearing that his father would not approve. However, his father discovered them. Rather than punishing E as he had expected, his father stated that E was now a man and would be expected to assume responsibilities consistent with being a man. E recalled feeling extremely uncomfortable about this and said that he had always felt somewhat uncomfortable about the idea that he was becoming a man.

During the summer when he was 13, E went to a camp for boys. During this summer, he was introduced to some sexual exploration with a girl his own age and felt very pleased about this experience. He was determined to excel at various camp activities but was not permitted to go on overnight trips because of his youth and was spurned by older boys with whom he wished to make friends. A short time later, he was seduced by an older male member of the camp staff and then had further homosexual activity with boys at the camp. When he was back with his parents, E told them about the homosexual experiences. When he was 16, E had a sexual relationship with a girl whom he described as very attractive and seductive. But E recalled feeling very embarrassed and uncomfortable about his sexual activity when he met the girl's parents.

E characterized himself, since the age of 12 or 13, as always feeling like an outsider—somewhat inferior and unmasculine in relation to other boys his own age. He said that he had always tried to appear tougher, more grown up, and more masculine with both boys and girls than he had actually ever felt. These efforts consisted of carefully choosing his words, gestures, clothing, and so on, in order to give an impression of masculine toughness.

E's father was handsome, affable, and successful in his career. He felt that his relationship with E had always been bad, which he really did not understand. During E's early years, his father was away from the home a great deal and worked long hours. In discussing E, his father emphasized the chronic difficulty he had in controlling him and dealing with his incessant demands. The father tended to deny or minimize E's difficulties, tending to ascribe them to problems with growing up. On the other hand, the mother emphasized that she had always felt that E was unstable and disturbed.

The family seemed to have a tradition of considerable candor about feelings, especially as related to sexuality. For example, E recalled a detailed question and answer session which took place between him and his mother when he was 12, which included an explanation by his mother of sexual intercourse, contraceptives, and so on. Also, E would often ask for and receive definitions of various sexual terms from his parents. When E and his parents were together, they had long discussions often consisting of their sharing intimate details of their personal experiences.

In general, E presented a picture of a psychotic reaction with a long history of poor impulse control and mild sociopathy. His mother had apparently been attached to E in a way that had not encouraged growth and separation, and his father's punitive behavior made it hard for E to identify with him. E apparently struggled with confused sexual identity throughout his adolescence, and his fears and anxieties about his heterosexual impulses were heightened by his experiences with girls during the year preceding his acute disintegration. Despite the primitiveness of E's responses on the psychological testing done before he was admitted to the hospital and the psychotic degree of his disorganization when first admitted, his reality testing was never severely impaired, nor was there much evidence of paranoid thinking. It was hard to consider his difficulties as primarily schizophrenic in light of the rapid reintegration that occurred following hospitalization. E's difficulties seemed best understood as an "identity crisis" of adolescence, more closely resembling an adolescent turmoil than a schizophrenic reaction.

```
RORSCHACH--PATIENT E

Card I.   [10 sec]
```

1. *An inkblot. Should I tell you if I'm going to turn it? A dance to the music of time.*

1. I saw in the inkblot two figures such as this and there was an implication of movement, and the movement would seem to be relatively perpetual. And since movement is a time sequence, I would call it a dance to the music of time. (Perpetual?) Nothing, I had that impression. (How come?) No, I think if one is creative, it's not necessary to have to have finite or lucid ideas of what he's creative about; even if I looked at this ink blot tomorrow, it's still going to be dancing. If you write a paper you never say the character was, oh we say is, the character is in the present. The same with the inkblot, now or a hundred years, it'll still be dancing to me. (He became quite hostile when asked to point out the dancer and said it's something the examiner should be able to see.

When asked if the dancer had any
characteristics such as arms and
legs, he responded with hostility
by asking, "Does a dancer have to
have arms and legs?" He talked
at length about the circular movement.)

2. Unification over a core.

2. I don't understand why you're
asking these questions. What does
unification over a core mean? The
words speak for themselves. (I
don't know what it means.) You
should, I don't know how to explain
it. A core is a seed, not necessarily a beginning, could be a
political platform, a rock, could
be a mass in the early 1600s or
1700s. What it is in my eye is
something similar to a foundation
from which other things are borrowed from, identified with, etc.
(How is it related to the card?)
I'm sorry if you don't see how.
I can't make something any clearer.
If you'd like to turn the card
over I can show you where the core
is. It's unified because you see
these objects tend to fuse into
the core, borrow from it, dance
on it.

*3. Coherency. I literally
don't see anything else in this
inkblot. Looks exactly like
its name, it's an inkblot.*

3. (Seems annoyed and astonished
at inquiry.) (Coherency?) Logical,
comprehensible, following a set
pattern. I see nothing in the card
to indicate errancy, the errant.
(Errant?) I saw nothing in the
card to indicate the errant. (What
does that mean?) Wandering (seems
annoyed). (Anything else about
the card?) The object tended to
fuse into it and it is a compact,
comprehensible figure. (Seems
very annoyed.)

E's opening response to the Rorschach is a highly abstract, symbolic response that suggests a great deal of intellectual pretentiousness and the use of intellectualizing defenses. While the response initially seems to have a quality of movement, the movement seems to be driven, almost like a person running in place. The movement is described as "to the music of time" and "relatively perpetual." Though he emphasizes his creativity and stresses the degree of movement, his statement that the dance is to the music of time implies that it is controlled by an external source. This response suggests that he experiences himself as compelled and driven with little control over his actions or sense of a goal he is moving toward. He offers additional support for this inference in his discussion about the ink-blot dancing not only now and tomorrow, but even for 100 years. Then he describes at length the "circular movement," reinforcing the impression that even though the object is moving, it is not going anywhere.

In his second response to this card, "unification over a core," he offers some leads to what the struggle in the movement is all about. He talks about a core as "a seed, not necessarily a beginning, could be a political platform, a rock," or a seventeenth- or eighteenth-century mass. He then says that what he has in mind is "something similar to a foundation from which other things are borrowed from, or identified with," and proceeds to discuss it as unified because "objects tend to fuse into the core, borrow from it, dance on it." These statements suggest that he feels closely tied, "fused with," and highly dependent upon some primary object, such as his mother, an interpretation that is consistent with his associations to the core as "a seed . . . a support . . . a foundation," or something you can borrow from or identify with. It seems as if the movement is an attempt to achieve some separation from this unification with a core, but that the movement is relatively unsuccessful, and he still feels controlled and static. As part of a unification with a primary object, he expects others to understand immediately what he is thinking and experiencing without his having to elaborate it. Thus, the examiner has a difficult time in getting him to elaborate his experiences; E expects the examiner to understand all his experiences and thoughts.

In his third response, "coherency," he talks about something "following a set pattern," and that there is nothing "errant" in the card. When asked what he means by errant, he says in an annoyed tone, "wandering." He finds nothing errant or wandering about the card because the "object tended to fuse into it," and it is a "compact, comprehensible figure." Thus he elaborates even further that the wandering, the movement, is an attempt to achieve separation and differentiation, but that this is difficult because he is fused with and part of "a compact" figure. He seems very annoyed at the examiner's questions, but while the annoyance and anger seem to be about being questioned and not understood, it is possible that the annoyance is also about the fusion and serves to help him keep more distant from the examiner. In some ways, he seems to find the fusion, "the unification over a core," attractive and pleasant, but also constraining, limiting and destructive. He struggles, through movement and probably through negativism and acting out, to achieve some separation and individuation.

While E's use of esoteric, highly symbolic, and overly abstract concepts and language could reflect an expectation of being automatically understood in a symbiotic relationship, it could also serve to facilitate E's experiencing himself as separate and distinct. In giving responses that most people do not understand and have to request elaboration and clarification of, he experiences a sense of individuation and separation. His thoughts are uniquely his own, no one else understands him, and people are forced to ask him for elaboration and clarification. While on one level the esoteric responses may reflect functioning characteristic of an early symbiotic relationship with the mother, on another level they may represent a defensive structure, like acting out, which reinforces and asserts his individuation and individuality.

Card II.   [5 sec]

1. Again I see an inkblot pastel and gray. Nothing else. No, an abstract form. (Does it resemble anything?) Are you serious? I've seen nothing that could resemble that. A dichotomy.

1. (Dichotomy?) To the best of my ability, I believe I use definitions that are similar to the dictionary's, and a dichotomy is two halves. How can I say what I mean by a dichotomy? Two equal halves. Everything in that inkblot is equivalent, from the pastel to the gray, to the two forms on each side. (Equivalent?) Yeah, they're equal. (What's equal?) The two sides of the picture--it's a dichotomy.

The hostile interchange with the examiner and the pretentious intellectualization continue on Card II. In his only response to this card, E confirms the inferences drawn from his responses to the previous card about his struggle around separation and individuation. He gives a very abstract and symbolic response to this card, a "dichotomy," and he defines the dichotomy as two halves, "two equal halves." Like his responses to Card I, of a unification over a core and coherency, the dichotomy seems to be another expression of the attempt to break away from an intense symbiotic relationship and possible fusion with his mother. Relating this to his opening response on Card I, of a dance to the music of time, by breaking the fusion with his mother he attempts to get time moving again.

Card III. (Picks up card.) [30 sec]

1. Segmentation of limbs.

1. (Segmentation of limbs?) I
saw two legs on two objects and
presumably living, and they were
not connected. They were segmented.
(What not connected to what?)
Torso was not connected to the
limbs. When I say limbs, I mean
legs. I don't see any arms or
anything like that.

*2. The red pastel in the
center has a contour, a contour
substance.*

2. (Contour substance?) It
would seem to mold, would seem to
fit. (Fit what?) To fit into the
two objects. (Relation between
them?) Not other than that it is
a contour and it's a contour for
the substance, for the objects.
They seem to be intrinsic to each
other. (Intrinsic?) Is that a
possibility? (Could you tell me?)
When you read a book do you become
very disconnected because you don't
understand something. I think the
words speak for themselves. Any
explanation of intrinsic has innumerable variables. All the variables have equal possibilities and
probabilities. It would take me
days to explain to you what I mean.
And I think you wouldn't know if
I answered your question. Your
interpretation is yours and my
interpretation is mine. I presented it to you in a word. (Could
you explain?) I could but I don't
think it's sensible. It would
take me days. In any abstract
interpretation there are innumerable
definitions fitting innumerable
possibilities.

*3. Again this is a diffusion
of unity.*

3. (Diffusion of unity?) Diffusion *into* unity. I said "of," should
have said "into." I explained it
the first one. Very similar (yawns)
excuse me.

*4. Something similar to a
crab.*

4. (Looks like crab?) What
makes a crab look like a crab?
Nature. It bore a resemblance to
a crab by its physical aspects.
(Lower central detail)

*5. In an abstract way there's
a hermaphrodite present.*

5. (Hermaphrodite?) I hoped
that abstract would explain it.

It does not bear a resemblance to man or woman particularly. But by process of elimination, because it did not bear resemblance to an animal, but because I believe it was alive. It bears some resemblance in an abstract form to something human. As I say, hermaphrodite because I'm giving it an equal chance, equal chance in the sense of interpretation. Most human forms seem to have a combination of man and woman. (What about card made it seem that way?) I'm describing a form to you, a form which I said by a process of elimination I believe to be human. I believe I'm referring to the form on the card and therefore the card suggested the hermaphrodite. (Features of the card?) No features on the card, I believe it's human. I'm giving it equal opportunity because I believe humans have equal opportunity for both. (Human?) Do you think you're becoming rather redundant? (How so?) You just asked me that question before. You said, or I said, that I explain to you that by a process of elimination and because I believed it was alive, I limited it to a human. It does not resemble any animal to me. (Alive?) Vitality, animacy, animation. (Animation?) Movement. (Looks like it's moving?) The figures were a capture of movement. They were not moving when I saw them, but they were captured while in movement. As a picture of a dancer, or a person working. If I took a picture of your hand now it would not be moving, it would be a capture of the movement, an inert capture.

E's first response to Card III is a "segmentation of limbs," rather than the popular human figure. This is an oligophrenic response (Do or Hdx), in which only a part of a response is seen, rather than the more usual integrated complete figure. This type of response is characteristic of mentally retarded patients who are unable to achieve the closure of the total gestalt, and it is strikingly inconsistent with E's intellectual capacities and strivings. In this case, the fragmented response seems determined more by E's need to maintain separateness than by intellectual restriction or impoverishment. He comments several times in this response that the various parts are not connected.

In the next response to this card, he again emphasizes fusion, as he did in the responses to Card I. In an abstract, almost contentless response, he talks about a "contour substance" that was molded to "fit into the two objects." The objects are "intrinsic to each other." However, in the inquiry, he asks if the examiner is "disconnected" and draws a sharp distinction between his own thoughts and interpretations and those of the examiner. Thus once again there is an alternation of fusion, of things being intertwined and "intrinsic to each other," with their being "disconnected" and independent.

The following response, a "diffusion of unity," also includes both sides of E's struggle. The examiner was quite certain that E said diffusion *of* unity, but in the inquiry he changed the response to a "diffusion *into* unity." The sense of diffusion that occurs with breaking the union, the coherency, the unification over a core, is both desirable and frightening. Likewise, a diffusion into unity is both attractive and overwhelming. The expression of unity represents E's symbiosis and fusion with his mother.

In his fifth response to Card III, E comments that "in an abstract way, there's a hermaphrodite present." There is a peculiar phrasing to this response that leaves open the possibility that he is referring to himself, as well as to his perception on the card. His comments also clarify his second response to this card, where he describes all the variables as having equal possibility and probability. He applies this same notion to the fifth response, where he gives his percept an "equal chance" of being a man or a woman. He comments on the "vitality, animacy, and animation" of the figures, which "were a capture of movement"; they were not moving, but were captured while in movement. Like a picture of a dancer or of a person working, this is an "inert capture" of movement. As discussed about his responses to Card I, the emphasis on movement seems to be an ineffective struggle to achieve separation, and the movement is really only suspended animation.

Again, in this respose of a hermaphrodite, he elaborates the feeling of captured movement, his feeling of being locked in and frozen. The issue of homosexuality, of being either male or female, may be another expression both of his sense of fusion, being part of a unity with his mother in his feminine identification, and of his selection of males as love objects, as a defensive maneuver to break the symbiotic fusion with his mother. As discussed earlier, homosexuality in males can be one way in which male patients seek to separate from the symbiotic fusion with their mothers by selecting alternate objects for affection, objects as distinct and different as possible from the maternal object. E also seems fearful of committing himself in any way and wants to leave all possibilities open.

Card IV.   [45 sec]

1. An inkblot impaled.

1. (Impaled?) I was being funny. I'll tell you, why don't you tell me what you don't understand about it and then I can explain it to you. (Not sure what you have in mind.) Why are you not sure about it? (?) Something in the picture should suggest to me impaled. Because I cannot relate whatever it is to anything in the picture at all I'd say it is an ink blot and the ink blot is impaled upon an object in the picture. (One object impaled upon another?) I have never heard of reciprocal impaling, so I suppose yes. (Rest of card is impaled on lower middle detail?)

2. It's very difficult for me to tell you what this suggests because I don't even see that this bears a distorted resemblance to anything I've ever come across, or thought about, even a distorted resemblance. Looks like something they sell in Times Square.

2. (Times Square?) Some of the very gaudy shops in Times Square sell very strange little objects sometimes. It's an eye-catcher, whatever it is. I told you, I don't know. (General idea of what it looks like?) I've just told you I don't know. There's no resemblance to anything I've ever seen, or ever thought about. Of course it could bear a resemblance to something, but if so, I don't know what to. (Ever seen an object like this in Times Square?) I just explained it to you. Well, I'd say they sell very strange little things in that area and that's what it appeared as. You know they sell little gnomes, dwarfs, funny dolls, strange magazines, something gaudy, eye-catching, comes from a gaudy, eye-catching area. That inkblot is an eye-catcher though. (How so?) It's an eye-catcher. (Tell me more?) Has qualities which are very blatant and different. It's a continuity of color, the grays and blacks, the shape.

On the fourth card, E's opening response is an "inkblot impaled." By impaled he means the entire card placed upon the lower middle detail. He does not specify any details of the upper portion of the card, but he merely focuses on the impaling detail, the lower central phallic area. Considering that the upper part of the card is frequently seen as a monster and generally masculine, this response may have homosexual in addition to aggressive implications.

The second response to this card is little "gnomes, dwarfs, funny dolls" that are sold in the shops in Times Square. E stresses that both the inkblot and the objects sold in Times Square are "eye catchers." Here he may be referring to his own experience of finding the phallic area an "eye catcher." Boundary disturbances are suggested both in his relating the concept of "eye catching" to the little dolls and to the card as well, and in his blend of human and innimate features. The figures in this response, gnomes or dwarfs, are quasi-human. In addition, there are suggestions of aggressive, and possibly homosexual, responses, which alternate with themes of unity, coherence, and fusion.

```
Card V.   [3 sec]

  1.  Bat.                         1.  (Whizzing along?)  The es-
                                   sence of the inkblot was captured
                                   it seemed, capture of movement.
                                   The angulation of the bat's wings.

  2.  Bat and a rabbit.  Whizzing    2.  (Rabbit?)  Just the head of
along to a Bach harpsichord       a rabbit.  (You see just the head?)
fugue.  That's it.                Maybe these could be legs.  I don't
                                  see a torso, though maybe could
                                  assume torso between head and legs.
```

On Card V, in addition to the popular bat response, E sees a rabbit in the central area, and both the bat and the rabbit are "whizzing along to a Bach harpsichord fugue." He comments that this "whizzing along" is again a "capture of movement." The "whizzing along to a Bach harpsichord fugue" is an amusing image, certainly for an image of a rabbit. It also implies that the movement is not experienced as actively self-directed, but as externally modulated and controlled. Again, human are blended with animal characteristics, and there is also a contamination tendency, since the rabbit is seen in part of the same area of the blot in which the bat is perceived, and both are whizzing along.

Card VI. [30 sec]

1. If I were to mix some pan-
cake batter very well, and then
pour it on a table, and take out
some gray paint and pour it on
the pancake batter, and then take
a glass shield and press it, I
would say it would come out some-
thing like that. I honestly
can't tell you anything it resem-
bles.

The response to Card VI is most peculiar. The response of pancake batter poured on a table and mixed with grey paint seems to be a depreciation of food and possibly also of his mother. The shading response to this card as well as to Card IV suggest an underlying dysphoric tone that may be associated with the depreciation of his mother. As he separates from his mother and achieves some individuation and self-definition, there may be intense feelings of loss, depression, and even suicidal ideation.

Card VII. [15 sec]

1. Felicity, balance, and a
seesaw.

1. (Seesaw?) We're talking about an object in the card, you seesaw on rocks back and forth. This figure has curves which if they were pushed could rock back and forth. The card does not look like a seesaw, only the object. (Felicity?) Felicity is being a happiness that is grace and telling and there seemed to be a quality of happiness about the card. That's why I would call it felicity. Balanced because again these cards are all balanced, not liable to teeter or totter. Within my definition of felicity there seems to be a certain happiness in felicity, seems to be a way of expressing happiness. It was a passing thought. But in all my elucidation to you I seem to be quite aware of the universal interpretation of the card and therefore I'm not able to put it down exactly.

2. A metamorphosis of an ugly
duckling.

2. (Metamorphosis of a duckling?) Because it seems to be the quali-

ties of a duck and it's progressively changing for the better. (Changing?) I haven't asked it (What
does it seem like to you?) Pure
conjecture. (What does it look
like on the card?) It looks like
it was undergoing a metamorphosis.
(What gave you the impression?)
I don't know I did not see it
going through the different stages.
A capture of progression. That's
all I saw.

3. And possibly two Indian
squaws, that's about it.

3. (Indian squaws?) Resemblance
of Indian squaws. A feather. That
was part of that inkblot that
resembled a feather. On top of
their heads. As one thinks about
it, maybe squaws don't wear feathers. More accurately there is a
quality to the face when I saw the
face, to be gentle and feminine.
I'm talking about the face on the
card, on this card, it's the essence, its grace. Of course, you
could ask the same question about
grace. What makes something
graceful? Its movement, its essence, its existence, its softness.

On Card VII, E's opening response is highly abstract: "felicity, balance, and a seesaw." He talks about things rocking back and forth, even though he does not actually see a seesaw. The sense of balance and of a figure having "curves which if they were pushed could rock back and forth" gives him a feeling of felicity and grace. The rocking back and forth has a sooth-ing quality, possibly an expression of longing for fusion with his mother. This response is followed by a "metamorphosis of an ugly duckling" which is "progressively changing for the better," but there is a "capture of progres-sion," and he "did not see it going through the different stages." It is inter-esting to note a sequence similar to that seen on earlier cards—a theme of fusion, union, and peace followed by some experience, often disruptive, that represents growth and change. On this card too, the second response concerns growth and change, but there seems to be a static quality to this process, as if it were suspended in time.

The final response on this card is two Indian squaws. But in the inquiry he comments that he based his response on the presence of a feather, and maybe "squaws don't wear feathers." He says that the faces seem "gentle and feminine" and that they are the "essence" of this card, its "grace," its "movement," its "existence," its "softness." In many ways, E is caught on a seesaw, hoping to find closeness with a soothing, gentle, soft mother and then struggling to move toward progression, change, and individuation, continually moving back and forth between these two positions and going nowhere.

Card VIII.   (Looks at back of card.)   [10 sec]

  1. Pastel.

  2. An animal climbing. That's about it.

Card IX.   [15 sec]

  1. Again pastels and a quality of diffusion. That's it. [40 sec] (Look at it a little longer.) I don't see anything else.

  1. (Quality of diffusion?) Colors seem to fuse into each other in certain parts of the inkblot.

E gives the popular response of an animal to Card VIII with little elaboration. On Card IX he again returns to his concerns about "fusion" and "diffusion." It is interesting that he uses the word "diffusion" when he is really talking about a fusion of colors on the inkblot. This seems to be one more manifestation of his intensely ambivalent longing for fusion and merging, which results in a loss of self-definition, and his search for separation and individuation, which results in experiences of disorganization and of a loss of "coherence."

Card X.   This is my favorite.   [12 sec]

  1. It has leaps, a quality of climbing, it's got a vitality to it, that's about it. If I were these objects and someone asked me what are you doing I would say, "equitibus cano."

  1. (equitibus cano?) I speak only for knights. There's a contempt in their vitality which cannot be disturbed. Their mood should not be captured. (Contempt?) Did I say contempt? You misunderstood. There's nothing at all contemptful about that. Did you hear me say contempt? (Vitality?) Movement, its freedom, it's almost a dramaticism. (What about the card made it seem that way?) Its essence, no it's what the card is. (Climbing?) There were some figures going up and some figures going across as one would climb. (Leaps?) I'm not quite sure what

```
                         you're asking me.  Leap is a pretty
                         simple word.  I don't see how it
                         could be clearer.  I don't see why
                         you're not sure, but I'll be glad
                         to make it any clearer to you if
                         I can.  (Something leaping?)  Oh
                         yes.  If you would have asked that
                         before, I could have explained it
                         to you.  This picture, another
                         thing about it, is it seems to
                         have an imaginative quality, being,
                         not being, yes, being as being
                         there.  And one would say they're
                         imaginative, therefore they belong
                         and they're free.  (What gave it
                         an imaginative quality?)  It's not
                         real.  (What isn't real?)  This
                         ink blot.  (Not real?)  Not actual.
                         Looking at this inkblot as a
                         complete substance, I would not
                         separate any of the parts.  If I
                         want to say it resembles something,
                         I would have to say it resembled
                         it in its completion.  And I find
                         nothing in actuality which resem-
                         bles it.  Kind of an imaginative
                         Lewis Carroll quality, The Hunting
                         of the Snark, Through The Looking
                         Glass.
```

The closing response given to Card X of the Rorschach summarizes many of the issues expressed on the previous cards. In this response he emphasizes climbing, leaping, and vitality. He comments that the objects on the cards "speak only for knights" and that there is "a contempt in their vitality which cannot be disturbed." In the inquiry he denies having used the word "contempt" and comments that their "mood should not be captured." He then seems to say that the vitality of the card comes from its movement and freedom. The card also has an "imaginative quality," or "being," and "one would say they're imaginative, therefore they belong and they're free." Thus, action, movement, contempt, and imagination are associated with freedom. In his use of peculiar, esoteric, and pretentious phrases, he seems to be seeking to define himself as unique and separate, since no one else can understand his thoughts. In fact, the very process of experiencing himself as thinking and imagining seems to bring him a sense of "being" and freedom, but also of belonging. Then, after all the emphasis on action and freedom in this response, he returns in his closing statements to talking about looking at the inkblot as a "complete substance," saying that he would not "separate any of the parts." Only in its "completion" does it resemble anything. Thus, he moves back and forth from actively seeking independence, freedom, and individuation to seeking union and symbiosis, unable to fully accept or reject either position but suspended between them.

TAT--PATIENT E

1. (Card 1). A sensitive young boy. Let's see what we can assume. He's sensitive because of his attraction to the instrument. But that's not necessarily true. He seems to possess a mixture of curiosity and inquisitiveness. That's all I can say. Do you want me to go further? (Tell the story.) Let's say that hopefully the boy will play the violin but for now we leave him in the hands of competent professional care. (Thinking?) He's peering into his instrument, which is seemingly a new attraction for him and he's curious. (Curious about?) About whatever one is curious about with a new object, trying to look into it, into its nooks and crannies. (Feel?) I think the action of his thinking is congruent. I think he feels interested, curious, but not in an objective way. There is no way he can anticipate what will happen. He's just peering into it, curious. Perhaps, what I'm going to say now is analytical, perhaps the exploration of the finite, and of course the finite has great depth to it, too. (Finite?) I think that's about it, finite being the limits known, but of course the possibility within these limits that the violin would be a finite object. It's important that this be an analytical statement and not that the boy is feeling this. There's an interesting relationship between this violin and the boy. They both seem to, and I'm not speaking in terms of the personification of the violin, but in a way they both can get to know each other. This all falls within the realm of exploration of the finite, curiosity.

E's first TAT story is about a very curious and inquisitive young boy who is attracted to "the instrument," and the degree of curiosity and attraction seems intense for the relatively quiet tone of the picture. There is an intrusion in the opening few lines of his story when he comments, possibly playfully, about how "hopefully the boy will play the violin but for now we leave him in the hands of competent professional care." He seems to identify the curiosity and inquisitiveness, like the struggle for separation and individuation, as one part of his potential for growth. On inquiry, he elaborates that the boy is peering into the instrument and that it is a new attraction for him. He clearly states that this intense curiosity is not an "objective" curiosity, but an exploration that "has great depth to it." The intensity of the curiosity is reminiscent of his response to Card IV of the Rorschach, where he talks about something being an "eye catcher."

In this story there is a suggestion of boundary disturbance when he begins talking about an interesting relationship between the violin and the boy. He denies that he is personifying the violin, but then goes on to elaborate that "in a way they both can get to know each other." Thus, in this story there is some degree of loss of the boundary between animate and inanimate, and he tries to control it through denial. He seems to be aware of his tendency toward personification and he tries to take distance from it. Also, as on the Rorschach, in this story there is a tendency toward stilted, symbolic functioning, which suggests the use of paranoid maneuvers.

2. (Card 5). I'm not quite sure how to begin these. The look on the woman's face implies incomprehension, possibly worry. She leaves to the viewer the task of understanding upon which her facial expression is applied. The room itself adds nothing, it is simple, early 1900s. The woman's feelings border on the intensely curious and obviously what she is curious about would seem to affect her in some way. (Story?) The reason I'm having difficulty is because, obviously it's made so you don't see what she's staring at. There's actually nothing that occurs to my mind that she could be. I assume that it's something--like it's not the dog eating his bone after dinner, and it's not the cat on the sofa. It's something that this woman wants to look at very intensely, something that can affect her in some way. I'd prefer to say this woman would not go out of this room until she can understand whatever is there or at least feel satisfaction over the object of her curiosity. The mother in Long Day's Journey into Night, peering into the room, while her husband and her son talk about her drug addiction. Looks like a scene from that script. Is that any better?
   I think her facial expression is quite representative of how she feels. Curious, expressive curiosity could certainly lead to fright. To be honest with you, I don't know how this woman feels. I'm not this woman. (Make up a story.) You know me. I can't even draw pictures of people. Let's say she's anticipating and feeling the worry of antici-pating. (Anticipating what?) Do we, if we go back to the O'Neill script, say she's anticipating that her husband and son feel she's gone back to drug addiction. (Outcome?) That remains to be seen. (Try to make up a story.) Let's say that I believe that this woman is not going to leave until she has her curiosity satisfied. Whatever case it will be, whatever the O'Neill script, whatever something from that play, The Weavers, whatever from Brecht's Mother Courage, whatever this woman is thinking about is very important to her and the outcome will be either remaining there or understanding. (Which?) I think it's both, either she remains, or she understands, but in a sense, it's pretty much the same. You do remain. You understand. (Examiner sneezes. E explains how the expression, "God bless you," came about. He asks if the examiner knows Latin--wants to know if the examiner knows the mean-ing of Latin phrase on a cigarette pack. He thinks it means "wherever people gather.")

It is impressive that in this second TAT story the feelings, actions, and thoughts attributed to the woman are very similar to the feelings, thoughts, and actions attributed to the boy in the previous story. The "woman's feel-ings border on the intensely curious," but "you don't see what she's staring at." The similarity between the feelings of the boy on Card I and the wom-an in this story suggests that he may not be able to clearly differentiate the characters in his stories from each other or to separate his own feelings from theirs. Such difficulties suggest the possibility of a symbiotic relationship involving the assumption that mother and son share identical feelings and thoughts.

E's difficulty with object constancy is also seen in this story. He is unable or unwilling to go beyond the immediate perceptual aspects of the stimulus to make up a story. When encouraged, he says that the woman is not curious about a dog eating his bone after dinner or the cat on the sofa, but cannot say what she is curious about. The things she is not curious about have a peaceful, benign, and possibly regressive tone, in that both are animals rather than people and have an eating or sleeping quality. Then E falls back on the plot of *Long Day's Journey into Night* to develop his story further.

Based on the sequences observed in the Rorschach, it would be expected that, subsequent to manifestations of fusion, the story should contain themes indicating a struggle to become more separate and independent. After he identifies the woman in this story as the mother in *Long Day's Journey into Night,* he says that her husband and son are talking about her drug addiction. When asked how the woman feels, he asserts that he is not this woman and says to the examiner, "You know me." By telling a story in which a son forms an alliance with his father against his mother, and by his assertion of not being the woman and his statement that the examiner knows him, he seems to be struggling to differentiate himself from the woman. In a somewhat ambiguous ending to the story, the woman either "remains" there or she "understands," but these outcomes are "pretty much the same. You do remain. You understand." Curiosity and understanding, like imagination on Card X of the Rorschach, seem to be associated with achieving freedom and separation. When he ends his story by saying that the woman both remains and understands, it could be speculated that he is expressing a resolve to continue struggling with his dilemma until he reaches understanding and freedom.

It should also be noted that on the more structured TAT cards, as compared to the more ambiguous Rorschach stimuli, these themes are presented in a more coherent, integrated, and socially appropriate form.

---

   3.   (Card 15).   Who makes these up? Don't write that down. Well, stylistically you have the overbearing effect in the employment of angulation, squares, acute graphic structures, which is present, for example, the squares. The angulation, the harshness of geometrical figures and the grave, grave sites, and especially the acute delineation of the man's face, the employment of shadow to disguise and much more important to emphasize the subject. Then you have a series of contrasts in this figure, for example, the hands seem to pray while there is an

omnipresent sign of death and the graves and yet this man seems so ter-
ribly powerful. He has the strength to rise above this desolate scene.
Before one can start discussing remorse or the graves, this man is here
and it would seem unnecessary to me to say the scene does not exist in
actuality. It's quite obvious that no such graveyard exists and that
no such man exists. I mean by this in the physical structure, the
graveyard's cluttered, the man is a drawing, yet what is more important
is that the feelings and the image of life and death do exist in actu-
ality. The man and the graveyard, the tombstones seem to be a static
reminder of the sterility of death and the vitality of life even in
remorse. This man is terribly sad and yet I think he fully understands.
He's going to remain here, or there, until he can come to grips with
his, whatever he's praying to or sobbing over, and it doesn't necessarily
have to be a person, it could be the very institution of death. When
he wants to he will leave.
      (At the end of this story, he began to ask the examiner about his
response to the card and to say how fascinated he was by its very many
possibilities.) Trying hard but can't choose because of the large number
of possibilities, could be about the death of his mother or children,
or just the institution of death. Trying to describe common features
of it all. (Doesn't exist?) I would not expect to walk down the street
and see a man who physically looked like this or a graveyard so cluttered
with graves. This is a form of art which is representative of feelings
which do not exist in actuality; I think many people think that death
is overwhelming. You would not see a man like this walking down the
street, but the stylistic features express what the artist feels about
death. (Sad about?) I think he's sad about the institution of death.
(Understands?) I think he understands the institution of death as best
as one can.

In this third story, E again uses overly symbolic abstraction as a way of distancing himself from the impact of threatening material. Thus, he talks about the angulation, the harshness of geometric figures, the use of shadows to disguise and emphasize the subject, and so on. He then indicates that there are a series of "contrasts" in this figure; although there is "an omnipresent sign of death," the man "seems so terribly powerful." He stresses the man's strength and ability to defend himself against threat. He has "the strength to rise above this desolate scene." The sense of hypermasculinity, the sense of strength—which he must establish by his acting out and assertiveness—seem to be ways in which E deals with loss and death.

He attempts to distance himself further from his story by saying that the scene does not exist in actuality and that no such man really exists. While his abstract and symbolic functioning seems to distance him from threat, it also leads to confusion about what is real and what is unreal. In his description of the "static reminder of the sterility of death and the vitality of life," he uses what he called "dichotomies" on the Rorschach. The sterility of death is a lack of movement, and the vitality of life is energy, action, and movement. Again, as in the previous story, the man remains there until he can get control over the situation and understand it. It is interesting that a patient who, both in his responses and in his case history, has a great deal of emphasis on movement and acting out presents stories that end with the person remaining in a conflict situation. His intense reaction to the deaths of the two men during his two hospitalizations may partly stem from the fact that he was immobilized during these traumatic episodes and could not run away or act out. His being restrained in the hospital may have forced him to remain and face the painful issues of loss and death. After finishing his story, he goes on to elaborate, in an aside, his preoccupations with death, which underlie his abstract and overintellectualized concerns about the "institution of death." These preoccupations are about the death of a man's "mother or children." It is not surprising that his psychotic episodes followed shortly after his unfortunate experience of having a patient die in his hospital room during each of his two successive periods of hospitalization.

> 4.   (Card 14).   Looks like a scene from Vertigo in Alfred Hitchcock--
> looks awfully mysterious in there and I think he wants to get some air,
> some light.   Interesting thing is this man in the silhouette, but he's
> coming from a blackness.   This room or attic or whatever it is, is
> totally black.   The man has come upstairs to open a trunk, opens the
> windows and looks out at the sun.   (Thinking?)   He's thinking it's aw-
> fully dark in here, I'd like to look out, get some light in here.
> (Outcome?)   He'll leave the room.   This is tiring me, it must be for
> you.

This story seems relatively free of any boundary disturbance, though there is a peculiar intrusion in the story about a man coming up to open a trunk, but   E talks, instead, about the man opening the windows and looking out at the sun. There is one subtle indication of possible boundary disturbance in his closing comment, where he talks about this story being tiring and then says that it must be tiring for the examiner as well. He seems to assume that his feelings are shared by those he is with.

> 5.   (Line drawing).   If I looked at that Degas (a picture on the wall
> of the office) or up there I wouldn't want to make up a story I would
> try to appreciate them and that's the way I'm going about these things.
> One has the feelings of the supernatural, the delineation of lightning,
> of charges, the very acute lines.   More important these two men are one.
> You know they grow out of each other.   I would tend to see it as a con-
> flict, a struggle one feels in himself, of ambivalence, of trying to
> understand.   But to make up a story!   I'd get mental indigestion if I
> tried to make up a story about this.   There seems to be a violence in
> this picture, an explosive tendency, a digging sort of thing.   But I
> can't tell you anything about it, absolutely nothing.

(Two men are one?)   The picture of one, the beard grew into one of the men's arms and they seem to be merging into each other almost as if one had created the other.   (Ambivalence?)   Whatever the ambivalence is over, but I think this picture is vague enough so that the ambivalence is over anything.   You see, one can't say because you're ambivalent about going to the movies.   That's it, not a strong conflict.   Whatever it is, it is a potent ambivalence bordering on violence.   (Violence?)   I say there's an implication of violence.   These objects seem to border on violence.   The hands with the long fingernails may express tearing, but not tearing at the moment.   His hands are on the man's head, but I don't see any anguish.   There's not yet violence taking place, but it's certainly very likely to become violent.   (What would bring about the violence?)   An excess, an excess of anything.   (For example?)   I don't feel this is the right way to look upon this picture. I think it's supernatural.   Could be a battle among the gods.   Lucifer rebelling from God.   Some may reach the violence by aspiring too hard, to too great a degree to be united.   (E asked to take a break at this point.)

(During the break, he got a drink of water and began to discuss the testing for quite a while.   It is tiring because he has to do what he is not used to doing; he used to appreciate things, not seek motives. There is a complexity of human motives, and you cannot do justice by superficially choosing one over the other, that is too easy, and he noted that understanding seems to be the main theme.   Some pictures are easier because they are abstract, some of them remind him of his conflicts, particularly death, the death of his grandmother he is close to and who, at the time of the testing, was very sick, possibly dying.   He also talked of having been in the hospital twice during the last three months and each time the man in the bed next to him died.   The examiner noted that he seemed much friendlier, especially during the talk and was very grateful for the break.)

This story is told to a card (line drawing) which frequently stimulates themes of fusing. On this card, E initially attempts to distance himself by looking at a picture on the office wall and, in an intellectualized way, stresses that he tries to appreciate the card as an art form. After some description of the angles and lines, he comments that "more important, these two men are one. You know they grow out of each other." Though he tries to place his story in a supernatural context, he clearly indicates the intensity of his concerns around merging and fusing. He elaborates quite clearly the formulations derived from prior responses to the TAT and the Rorschach; he sees this "as a conflict, a struggle one feels in himself, of ambivalence, of trying to understand. . . . " He makes clear not only that themes of merging and fusing are very much on his mind but also that he experiences this as a conflict in which he struggles to find himself, and that the theme of understanding is a way of asserting himself. He explains even further that if he made up a story he would "get mental indigestion" and that "there seems to be a violence in this picture, an explosive tendency, a digging sort of thing."

This adds support to the formulation that his explosive anger, rage, and acting out, along with his abstract intellectualizing, are ways of asserting his autonomy and independence. But the danger of assertion and individuation is that he will get "indigestion," and be unable to function.

The examiner in inquiry encourages him to elaborate what he means by "the two men are one." He comments that "the picture of one, the beard grew into one of the men's arms, and they seem to be merging into each other, almost as if one had created the other." When the examiner inquires "What is the ambivalence over?" E responds that it could be over almost anything, but "It is a potent ambivalence bordering on violence," and this violence is one man tearing at the other. Though violence has not yet taken place, "It's certainly very likely to become violent." He elaborates even further that it is "Lucifer rebelling from God." In his fantasies he may see himself as Lucifer in his excessive acting out and rebellion from his parents, particularly his mother. In a further elaboration of this violence he states that it may be because of "aspiring too hard, to too great a degree to be united." Thus in this story again union is associated with violence.

Shortly after telling this story he asks to take a break from the testing because of it being stressful. He then talks of his conflict about death and the impending death of his grandmother. He associates this with the deaths of the two men who were next to him during his periods of hospitalization. The death of his grandmother may be related to the loss of his mother, and his fear of death probably partly represents his fear of losing his mother. While violence may lead to separation, it also arouses feelings of being unable to function and stand alone, and fears of becoming ill, of having "mental indigestion" and dying.

---

6. (Card 10). These two people had been brought together through some instance. Could be the institution of marriage but more important it seems to me is a reaching out. I wouldn't care if it were mockery or deceit whatever it is, two people are being brought together. The common denominator is this togetherness, this bringing together. I don't see any mockery in the picture or any deceit . . . There seems again in this scene to be a blending, diffusion into each other, the dominant theme or figure is the two heads and hand. There's eyes and nose and this sort of thing because this is all part of the head, and there's the woman's head and I would assume a compassionate element and both these people want to be together, they are together, and they express a mode of union that seems to perpetuate a way of thinking about each other, of living with each other, of living in each other's minds, which is quite, quite nice. The two people are brought together by the common denominator, need. My ending is that togetherness is perpetuating, a nice sort of feeling of living in each other's minds and feelings. I think that the end of the story would be the act of needing each other. Is that any better?

In this sixth story E describes two people who are brought together by the institution of marriage, which is a "reaching out." The thing about care if it is mockery or deceit, or whatever; it is just that two people are being brought together, and that the common denominator is their togetherness. Again, in this scene, there seems to him to be a "blending, a diffusion into each other." "Both these people want to be together, and they express a mode of union that seems to perpetuate a way of thinking about each other, of living with each other, of living in each other's minds, which is quite, quite nice. The two people are brought together by the common denominator, need. My ending is that togetherness is perpetuating, a nice sort of feeling of living in each other's minds and feelings." And so, after discussing death on the previous card, he now returns to the other side of the ambivalence and elaborates in greater detail the deep attraction of merging, which brings a sense of life, fulfillment, and eternity. The word "perpetuating" suggests that in fusion he does not have to face life, and eventually death. But, as we have seen earlier, his feelings about closeness with his mother are fraught with great ambivalence because, while comforting, they involve the loss of his sense of being a separate person.

7. (Picasso "La Vie"). I'd be tempted to say late 19th or early 20th century movement in art, perhaps Picasso . . . You have two people in nudeness, a state of naturalness. This is further emphasized by the pictures on the wall, yet there's an air of lugubriousness on the people's faces. Now the question on my mind is concerned with the newborn baby and the woman who's holding this child, infant, and the question of all those people: one, Are these people aware of the presence of this person with the child? and, two, Why would this woman be holding the infant? This is a very beautiful picture. The man and the woman are very pleasant to look at each other. One wants to almost clasp them. For lack of a better word I'd say it's beautiful, beautiful is too general, they're very beautiful together. You see, there's also another dimension to this, you look at the naked woman's face and there's a quality of ruminating, pondering, of an almost dejected disbelief. She's a mixture of being very aware and very stunned. The man, on the other hand, is gesturing to the woman with the newborn babe, and I would assume that rite which is beyond me. She's going to take this child from them which is almost representative of some blundering world, some blundering arbitration stepping in. You have a complete lack of embarrassment in this picture, these people just being together, just two naked people, and the naturalness of the sexual act, the naturalness of being together, the need of people for each other, and the naturalness of a child being born, the results of their sexual activity. And this woman, the clothed woman, seemed to blunder in. (Turns the card over.) The theme could be about the arbitrary laws of society which are contradictory to human passions. The clothed woman is harsh in contrast with the two lovers. I believe she wants to take the baby away. There's good possibility

that she will. Probably my main concern though is the delineation of human conflict. You know, you say the woman is arbitrary in wanting to take the child away, that's very human, too. I think the outcome of this picture is a common denominator, human, you could put quotes around human, in all situations, which could be further subtitled into the conflicts of the human will and passion.

E's story to the "La Vie" card is lengthy and involved. It is impressive that in this complex story told to a complex stimulus that tends to stimulate boundary disturbance, there seems to be relatively little expression of themes of merging; rather, the struggle is around the beauty of sexuality as a natural act. He tells about the child being taken away from his parents by a woman whom he sees as harsh and arbitrary, but he is willing to accept the woman who has taken the child as "human" also. He sees this scene as a conflict between human will and passion. Though this story could be a derivative of his struggle around symbiosis and separation, it is impressive that the story is relatively intact, without any intrusion of themes of merging in its content or disruptions of its form.

8. (Card 6BM). The faces of the old woman and man seem to be a definite contrast, woman has something which implies stunned appearance, as if she is looking out. Her mind has either been overwhelmed in a situation at hand, or isn't even aware of the situation. There's a troubled look in this man's face. Whatever he's about to do or has done, implies it is in his mind. But not too sure. One notes the stylistic idea of the painting, in this picture, that he's dressed for the outside and she's not. I'd assume he's leaving or just came in. What I am driving at is that there is some connection between the woman's and his objective, whatever that may be. (Story?) The German occupation of France. This man had a choice of either staying with his mother or going into the underground. He chooses the underground--fine. (Thinking and feeling?) The conflict and the trouble in his mind could be summed up as such: If stayed with mother, certainly feel ambivalent about not being with the French underground. And yet with the French underground certainly feel ambivalent about not being with his mother. It comes down to a conscious decision with him, the subject, as the roles of importance of each of his acts. What seems to be the most important facet here is he seems to be making a conscious choice. He has chosen France and the underground because he feels his mother can subsist without him--yes, can subsist without him. (Her thoughts and feelings?) Well, this woman is certainly, as I say, stunned. I will assume she is possibly afraid for her son's life, possibly afraid son is leaving her. Just the act of leaving itself is somewhat frightening. Almost oblivious appearance to her face, and she seems somewhat detached--that's it. (Outcome?) The son's going into the underground. (Elaborate--outcome?) No, there are no ultimates.

This story is initially overly abstract and symbolic, devoid of content. E comments on the stylistic idea of the picture, the way the people are dressed, and makes some general statement about the stituation. This highly distant and overly intellectualized posture suggests that the theme of the card may be of particular relevance for him, The card depicts an interaction between an older woman and a younger man, certainly a theme that one would expect to have importance for him. He goes on to elaborate that the story he would like to tell is about the German occupation of France and a man who has a choice of either staying with his mother or going into the underground. His concern is whether she "can subsist without him." This story places the earlier themes of merging and fusing in more mature form as an adolescent struggle for independence and autonomy. While he presents the alternatives, staying home with mother and taking care of her or getting involved in the underground and violent activities, in a reasonable way he concludes by commenting that what is important and what is difficult is the very act of leaving itself. But it is impressive that he can place his intense concern about the basic struggle over fusing in more appropriate adolescent form.

Summary

Though E's test material is replete with themes of unification, merging, and coherence, there is relatively little formal thought disorder. Symbiotic content is juxtaposed with themes of a desperate but ambivalent struggle against experiences of merging, and E seems to be actively contending with these issues. Especially on the Rorschach, his thinking is often overly abstract and symbolic, serving to keep him excessively distant and detached from reality and his own feelings. His responses also have an extremely pretentious, condescending, and "put on" quality, so that it is hard to tell how much control he has over them and how seriously to take them. His thinking seems to serve a primarily defensive function and shows relatively few obvious manifestations of formal thought disorder. At times on the Rorschach and often on the more structured TAT, he demonstrates that his cognitive and perceptual functions are intact and that he has achieved a fairly high level of object permanence. The discrepancy between extreme emphasis in the content on themes of fusion and the relative absence of formal cognitive difficulties suggests that he is in an acute adolescent turmoil around issues of separation, rather than that he is schizophrenic.

Also impressive in this record are the illustrations of how a young adolescent boy struggles to deal with problems of symbiosis. E illustrates the use of aggression, antisocial behavior, assault, homosexuality, and hypersexuality as alternative ways of attempting to separate from a symbiotic relationship. While E has problems around fusion which are characteristic of psychotic states, he seems to be at a much higher level of organization than many other patients with similar concerns. Problems around fusion are present in the content but do not seem to be expressed in the formal aspects of his thinking. Because there is relatively little formal evidence of boundary disturbance, E would be expected to appear relatively more paranoid and less severely psychotic and to have had reasonably adequate object relationships early in his life. Treatment should lead to further growth and development, in comparison to more chronic and diffuse patients with poor object relations early in life, who require much longer hospitalization and treatment and for whom the prognosis is less hopeful.

After 7 months, E was discharged from the hospital and continued therapy as an outpatient. He completed his high school credits while in the hospital so that on discharge he was able to enter college. He graduated from college, and at last report, he had begun to develop a meaningful career.

5 / Retrospective and Prospective Consideration of Boundary Disturbances in Schizophrenia

In this chapter we shall summarize the findings suggesting that a wide range of disturbances frequently noted in schizophrenia can be understood as later manifestations of early developmental disturbances in the capacity to experience, perceive, and represent boundaries. We shall also consider the limitations of this concept, and we shall propose a series of procedures for the systematic investigation of this formulation. These considerations about future research on the concept of boundary impairments in schizophrenia, however, raise a number of important issues for research on psychopathology more generally. Thus, while we shall discuss issues relevant to the systematic investigation of boundary disturbances in schizophrenia, we shall consider these in the context of their more general implications for research design and research methodology in the study of psychopathology.

Observations about the importance of boundary disturbances in schizophrenia are certainly not new. For many years now, and from many different vantage points, clinicians and theoreticians have commented on boundary disturbances in schizophrenia. Tausk (1919) first introduced the concept in his paper on the influencing machine, where he ascribed the formation of this delusion to a projection of the patient's body, with an accompanying loss of the boundary between self and objects. Freud (1930) commented on the role of boundaries in psychopathology, and Federn (1952) made an extensive theoretical contribution to the understanding of boundary disturbances in psychosis. In contrast to Freud, Federn viewed psychosis as a withdrawal of cathexis from the ego boundary, rather than as a withdrawal of cathexis from object relationships. Fisher and Cleveland

225

(1958) and Landis (1970) noted boundary disturbances in schizophrenia in Rorschach images of the penetrability and permeability of the body surface. E. Bleuler (1911) referred to a vagueness of conceptual boundaries in schizophrenia, and Cameron (1944) discussed boundary disturbances at length in describing the cognitive processes of schizophrenic patients. Cameron noted an interpenetration of themes and overinclusive thinking in the concept formation and language of schizophrenics. Cameron's observations of overinclusive thinking in schizophrenia have been confirmed by numerous investigators; and there have been many attempts to relate overinclusive thinking to other phenomena such as the tendency to respond to the "strongest meaning of a word" (Chapman, Chapman, & Miller, 1964) or deficits in attention and information processing attributed to defects in a hypothetical filter mechanism (Lang & Buss, 1965; McGhie, 1966; Payne, 1966; Yates, 1966). But overinclusive thinking can also be seen as reflecting boundary disturbances, since it involves fluidity and instability of the limits of a task set or definition of a concept.

In addition to the impairments in cognitive functioning that can be interpreted as manifestations of boundary disturbance, there have been numerous recent observations of boundary disturbances in the interpersonal relationships of schizophrenic patients (e.g., Burnham, Gladstone, & Gibson, 1969; Lidz et al., 1965; Lidz & Lidz, 1952; Rosenfeld & Sprince, 1963, 1965; Searles, 1965; Thomas, 1966). There are reports of an inordinate need for and fear of merging with human objects, with both fusion and separation resulting in experiences of annihilation and dissolution. These intense longings for and fears of fusion have been understood as expressions of the schizophrenic's impaired differentiation of the boundary between self and nonself.

At the same time as an increasing number of reports in the literature consistently suggests that some degree of boundary disturbance is central to schizophrenia, evidence has been accumulating that boundary differentiation is a very early and fundamental achievement in normal development. Both Piaget (1954) and Werner (1948) discuss the first perceptual–cognitive differentiation as involving the perception of a boundary in an initially undifferentiated perceptual field. Roth and Blatt (1974), on the basis of clinical evidence, and Kagan (1971), summarizing the development of the neonate's visual orientation, conclude that the earliest visual orientation occurs at the boundary between highly contrasting contour edges. Initially, boundary differentiation appears to be between independent objects. Later boundary distinctions include the differentiation between an object and one's actions upon the object (Piaget, 1954) and between the object and its mental representation and verbal signifier (Werner, 1948; Werner & Kaplan, 1963).

Psychoanalytic theorists also have emphasized the importance of boundary differentiation in normal development. The infant is seen as initially unable to differentiate self from nonself and inside from outside (Décarie, 1965; Escalona, 1953; Jacobson, 1964; Mahler, 1968; Schafer, 1968). Mahler discusses an early autistic phase of development in which the child does not differentiate animate and inanimate objects from each other or from the self; and she sees the child's eventual capacity to differentiate self from nonself and inside from outside as resulting from the ability to form and subsequently to break a symbiotic fusion with the mother. Freud (1915), Mahler (1968), and Bettelheim (1967) discuss how locomotion, action, normal negativism, and aggression (Roth & Blatt, 1961) facilitate the child's emerging differentiation of boundaries. Freud (1911) and Loewald (1951) also emphasize the father's role as an alternate object to the mother in facilitating the child's evolving separation from the symbiotic relationship with the mother. Mahler views disruptions of these very early developmental differentiations as a central issue in some of the most severe forms of psychopathology.

For some time now there have been frequent references to boundary disturbances in schizophrenia and considerable agreement in both developmental psychology and psychoanalytic theory that early developmental processes involve the articulation of boundaries. But there has been relatively little systematic investigation of this concept as it relates to schizophrenia. Thus, in Chapters 2 and 3 we reviewed a large segment of research on schizophrenia to see whether an integrated conceptualization of boundary disturbances was useful in understanding the diverse, and at times contradictory, clinical and experimental literature on schizophrenia. In Chapter 4 we also sought to examine whether these formulations were helpful in understanding the experiences and modes of functioning of a range of hospitalized psychotic patients. Levels of boundary differentiation were defined as the capacity to maintain separations between independent objects, including the self and nonself, between objects and their mental representations, and between objects and their verbal signifiers. We considered the capacity to articulate boundaries as a continuum proceeding from rudimentary distinctions between separate objects and between self and nonself to the various stages in the development of the concept of the object as discussed by Piaget, resulting in the attainment of the capacity for stable mental representations of the self and of human and nonhuman objects. Later boundary differentiations include the capacity to maintain the discrimination between the actual object and its mental representations and verbal signifiers, and between representations of the self and others. This definition was differentiated from the broader use of the concept of boundaries in the work of Fisher and Cleveland (1958) and Landis (1970).

We sought to explore the hypothesis that boundary disturbances have a central role in schizophrenia by reviewing a wide range of research and clinical reports on a variety of aspects of schizophrenia, including reality testing, perception, attention, concept formation, language, thinking and thought disorder, sense of self, and interpersonal relationships, including relationships within the family. Cognitive and perceptual dysfunctioning in schizophrenia has been studied extensively, and, while there are contradictory and inconclusive results, many findings reviewed in Chapter 2 are consistent with the formulation that schizophrenic patients have difficulty in maintaining boundaries between independent events, between self and nonself, and between inside and outside. Hallucinations and delusions, as examples of disrupted reality testing, illustrate the loss of a differentiation between inside and outside in psychosis. Amorphous and global perception, difficulty with figure–ground articulation, a tendency toward perceptual fusion, higher thresholds for the separation of independent stimuli in the phi phenomenon and flicker fusion, and a tendency to underestimate the size of objects in studies of perceptual constancy all suggest that chronic, undifferentiated, process schizophrenic patients have difficulty in experiencing objects as distinct and unique. This inability to respond to, and articulate, objects as separate and independent appears to be at least partly a function of impairment in the capacity to differentiate between objects and between an object and its context. It is important to note, however, that there seems to be a marked difference between the perceptual functioning of nonparanoid and paranoid patients. While the perception of nonparanoid patients is global and diffuse, with difficulty in articulating objects, there is evidence that perception in paranoid patients is highly articulated, with even greater than normal capacity to maintain a separation between independent stimuli. In comparison to nonparanoid patients as well as normals, paranoid patients also have significantly less tendency toward perceptual fusion and are overconstant rather than underconstant; that is, they tend to overestimate the size of objects.

Marked differences between paranoid and nonparanoid schizophrenic patients have also been observed in studies of attention. Nonparanoid patients have global attention. They have difficulty in distinguishing salient from irrelevant aspects of a stimulus configuration, they show interpenetration of themes in their concept formation and language, and their thinking is overinclusive and may show contaminations, in which independent and separate images and concepts merge and fuse. In contrast, attention in paranoid patients is more focused and organized, and there is relatively little interpenetration of themes and contaminatory thinking. Thus it seems that nonparanoid and amorphous schizophrenic patients have an impaired capacity to maintain focused attention and directed thought. Objects are often perceived and experienced as merged and fused. On the other hand, paranoid and fragmented patients seem to struggle in an exaggerated way to maintain object articulation and focused attention.

This formulation of schizophrenia as, at least partly, an expression of disturbances in the development of the most fundamental boundary differentiations provides a framework for integrating a diverse literature on schizophrenia and for understanding aspects of paranoid psychosis. The paranoid's hyperalertness, overly focused attention and perception, fragmented thinking, extreme constriction, excessive autonomy and interpersonal distance, preoccupation with power and control, and guarded and suspicious behavior can all be understood, in part, as exaggerated defensive efforts to prevent the dissolution of boundaries and accompanying experiences of merging and fusing. This formulation of paranoid psychosis highlights the possible restitutive aspects of some paranoid functioning. Likewise, homosexuality in schizophrenic males and promiscuity in schizophrenic females may represent efforts to select objects as different as possible from the mother in an attempt to achieve separation from her. The conceptualization of boundary disturbances in schizophrenia makes possible a fuller appreciation of the desperate struggle of some patients to deal with threats of merging and fusing. In some cases, paranoid functioning and "antisocial" and aberrant sexual behavior may be part of this struggle for individuation.

The recent findings in the literature showing important differences between paranoid and nonparanoid schizophrenics are consistent with the interpretation that there are marked differences in boundary articulation between these two groups. But beyond that, research using different types of thought disorder as measures of degree of boundary disturbance (e.g., Blatt & Ritzler, 1974; Jortner, 1966; Zucker, 1958) indicates that severity of psychosis may be evaluated by a careful consideration of the extent of impairment of boundary articulation. For example, Jortner measured impairment of boundaries as expressed in the confusion of different levels of abstraction (e.g., concrete and abstract, animate and inanimate) and found that these measures significantly differentiated schizophrenic from nonschizophrenic psychiatric patients. Jortner found significant interrelationships between measures of body image boundaries and the ability to make essential cognitive and conceptual distinctions. He found that these measures also correlated significantly with interviewer evaluations of poor reality testing and thought disorder. Zucker (1958) measured "boundary fluidity" on the Rorschach, Mosaic, and Figure Drawing tests and found significantly more fluidity in hospitalized than in nonhospitalized paranoid schizophrenic patients. Blatt and Ritzler (1974) conceptualized three major types of thought disorder on the Rorschach as indicating different degrees of boundary disruption and they compared six groups of patients who showed different types of thought disorder. Consistent and significant differences were obtained among the groups on degree of impairment of complex cognitive functions and reality testing, indications of difficulty with affect modulation, distorted human representations expressed in human–inanimate blends in Rorschach responses, impaired involvement in interpersonal relationships, and lack of positive response to therapeutic intervention. The increased number of distorted human representations, particularly human–inanimate blends, in patients with types of thought disorder indicating greater boundary disturbance is consistent with Jortner's (1966) findings and the formulations of Mahler (1968) and Searles (1960, 1965) that schizophrenics, as part of their failure to achieve the distinction of "whole and separate objects" (Searles, 1965), have difficulty maintaining the separation between animate and inanimate and between human and nonhuman.

In general, this research on boundary disturbance in schizophrenia (Blatt & Ritzler, 1974; Jortner, 1966; Zucker, 1958) indicates that poorly articulated boundaries occur primarily in more disturbed chronic patients who have impoverished object relationships, impaired ego functioning, and guarded prognosis. Somewhat more articulated and stable boundaries occur primarily in less disturbed, reactive psychotic patients who are more responsive to therapeutic intervention. Degrees of boundary disruption seem to provide a quantifiable variable for differentiating a variety of levels of disturbance within the extensive range of patients considered to be schizophrenic and may serve as a way of evaluating a patient's response to therapy.

In our review of the research and clinical literature on schizophrenia in Chapter 3, we considered issues related to the sense of self and interpersonal relationships, particularly within the families of schizophrenic patients. There is evidence (e.g., Ainsworth, 1967; S. Bell, 1970; Décarie, 1965) that in normal babies, cognitive capacities (object permanence) and interpersonal relationships (person permanence) develop in parallel; and it has been postulated (e.g., Freeman et al. 1966) that levels of impairment in cognitive and perceptual functioning in schizophrenia are paralleled by similar degrees of impairment in interpersonal relationships. Schizophrenic patients show varying degrees of difficulty with maintaining a stable representation of the self clearly separated from representations of other people. There is an intense wish to merge with the symbiotic partner and an equally intense fear that such merging will lead to psychological annihilation. Both fusion and separation involve the threat of psychological death either through merging with or total loss of the symbiotic figure. The schizophrenic is caught in a "need–fear dilemma" (Burnham, Gladstone, & Gibson, 1969) in which he yearns for fusion and separation, yet is unable to tolerate either because both lead to experiences of annihilation (Rosenfeld & Sprince, 1963, 1965). Studies of the families of schizophrenic patients (e.g., Lidz et al., 1965; Wynne & Singer, 1963a,b) suggest that the parents of these patients often have boundary disturbances of their own, and that the role relationships and patterns of interacting and communicating within the family contribute to the maintenance of the schizophrenic patient's difficulty with establishing himself as an independent person.

Our consideration of clinical cases in Chapter 4 suggested that the level of boundary disturbance was related to the degree of disruption of early object relationships. A relatively greater degree of disturbance in boundary articulation occurred in those patients with a lifelong history of disrupted relationships. The patients with the most impaired boundary articulation seemed to have experienced disrupted interpersonal relationships from very early in life, and they seemed unable to form meaningful ties with anyone in the present. Patients with relatively more intact, but nevertheless somewhat disturbed, boundary articulation seemed to have had reasonably stable relationships in childhood, but subsequently their modes of relating became distorted. In the case of these patients, there always seemed to be some people with whom they could maintain ties, even though at times the relationships were destructive and painful. Often these relationships bore the brunt of the patients' struggles to achieve separation and individuation from consuming relationships with parents. In contrast, for patients with minimal boundary disturbance, earlier as well as current interpersonal relationships seemed reasonably adequate, even though immature. Despite the fact that these patients had problems serious enough to warrant hospitalization, their interpersonal relationships seemed less disrupted than those of patients with more serious manifestations of boundary disturbance.

In the more disturbed group, there were frequent indications in the case histories and psychological test protocols that the mother was seen from very early on as either aloof and unavailable or intrusive and consuming or both. Frequently, these patients felt intense hostility toward younger siblings for demanding the mother's attention, and they also expressed dismay about the father's unavailability as an alternate figure to the mother. In female patients, there were frequent indications of a flight into heterosexual activity to cope with symbiotic ties to the mother. Other patients used flight (patient B) or hostility and defiance (patient E) as modes of attempting to establish some distance, separation, and individuation from a consuming relationship with the mother. The struggle to establish separation and individuation can be expressed in many forms. While some of these forms may be considered "antisocial" and "acting out" behaviors, more active and successful struggles for separation occur most often in the more integrated patients. These struggles for separation can be easily confused with "adolescent rebellion." But one of the distinguishing features of the more primitive type of struggle is a lack of differentiation between parent and child, with the suggestion of an underlying wish not for dependence, but rather, for fusion and merging. In normal adolescence there is a struggle around dependence–independence; in schizophrenia the struggle is more around merging.

The patients presented in the clinical examples in Chapter 4 manifested boundary disturbance in a variety of ways. There were significant expressions of a wish for fusion. For example, patient A seemed at peace in those therapy hours when he and his therapist were doing the same thing (e.g., smoking cigarettes), and he reported a dream in which he looked at himself in a mirror and saw the face of another patient; and patient B seemed to be engaged in a desperate search for intimacy, going from person to person and from place to place. But to varying degrees and in different ways, the patients also struggled for separation and individuation. They seemed to be involved in an intense conflict over symbiotic longings. The alternating longings for fusion and desperate struggles for separation support the formulation of a need–fear dilemma (Burnham et al., 1969), in which there is a simultaneous wish for and a dread of merging.

There were numerous expressions of boundary disturbance in the psychological test protocols of the clinical examples. Foremost among these was the blending of human and inanimate features. Other indications were feelings of nothingness, emptiness, or dissolution, confusion between aspects of the testing situation and features from the patient's life or from the current environment (e.g., a picture on the wall), confusion of generation and sex roles, and extreme shifts in affect from humor and grandiosity to weakness, isolation, and terror. These additional indications of boundary disturbance were most marked in those patients who on the Rorschach revealed thought disorders with the greatest degree of disruption of boundaries—the contamination response.

The clinical cases show that boundary disturbances can be manifested in a number of different aspects of functioning. The disturbances can be expressed in the early developmental history as well as in current cognitive–perceptual processes, interpersonal relationships, fantasy life, and overt behavior. While we have considered cognitive processes and interpersonal relations separately in our review of the literature, it is apparent that this division is an artificial one. Even within our review of the literature on cognitive processes, a variety of interdependent and overlapping functions (e.g., attention, perception, and reality testing) were considered in isolation, because research is usually focused on one or another specific function. Rarely do studies consider the interrelationships among disturbances in these various functions. But it seems clear that all these processes, cognitive as well as interpersonal, are intertwined developmentally. The nature and quality of interpersonal relationships affect the capacity for cognitive differentiation, and cognitive capacities affect the degree of interpersonal differentiation and the quality of interpersonal interaction.

The developmental formulation of boundary disturbances in schizophrenia assumes that these disturbances are a result of profound disruptions in early transactions with human objects, leading to distortions in a host of psychological functions and processes. This formulation does not necessarily assume that the effects of impairment in the concept of the object consistently appear in the functioning of schizophrenic patients. Rather, it assumes that this is a basic weakness or vulnerability that can be provoked by stress and conflict, particularly in an interpersonal situation that is intense and threatening. There may be particular vulnerability to situations that contain threats of rebuff, rejection or abandonment or that create fears of being dominated, inundated, or overwhelmed. Certainly, there are individual and subgroup differences in the degree of vulnerability. But in schizophrenic patients these types of situations are most likely to disrupt the tentative levels of organization that have been established. There is a regression in levels of functioning, and the experience of objects, including the self, becomes unstable and inaccurate. These boundary disruptions may be brief and transitory or they may continue for extended periods. In borderline patients, they may occur only in highly ambiguous and intense interpersonal situations and be relatively brief. In more seriously disturbed patients, these disruptions may be more easily provoked, appear in a wider range of psychological functions, and persist for some time. But the formulation assumes that all schizophrenic patients have some degree of vulnerability in the fundamental stability and articulation of the object. With progress in therapy, there is increasing differentiation and stability of self and object representations (Blatt, Wild, & Ritzler, 1975).

One of our basic assumptions is that the establishment of boundaries is a fundamental sequence in the development of the concept of the object, which can be considered from the vantage points of development of cognitive functions, intrapsychic structures, or sense of self and relatedness to significant others. Cognitive functions, intrapsychic structures, and interpersonal relationships develop in a complex and reciprocal fashion; the quality of the transactions with significant figures (e.g., the consistency of the mother) affects cognitive development, which, in turn, influences the emerging capacities to appreciate and understand important dimensions of the environment. Disruptions in the development of boundaries will be expressed in a lack of differentiation in the cognitive, intrapsychic, and interpersonal spheres.

The inherent value, and at the same time the inherent limitation, of the developmental formulation of boundary disturbances in schizophrenia is that these disturbances can be expressed in a host of different functions, processes, and contexts. They are not limited to a particular dimension, such as thought disorder, or to a particular context, such as family relationships. Rather, boundary disturbances are expressed in these areas as well as in many others.

The formulation of boundary disturbances in schizophrenia is basically a theoretical or hypothetical construct about a fundamental issue underlying a number of symptomatic features and disruptions in functioning observed in schizophrenia. Boundary disturbances are not a direct and unitary variable that can be assessed by a specific or single procedure. It is possible for the formulation of boundary disturbances to be overused and applied indiscriminately. But if boundary disturbances are carefully defined and limited to expressions and consequences of a fundamental lack of articulation of objects, the formulation can have important heuristic value. The formulation implies that the experience of objects, including the self, is not well articulated; objects lack definition, are experienced as unstable, and are easily confused with other objects or events. Boundary problems are expressed in perceptual functioning, in thinking, in interpersonal interactions, in thoughts and feelings about the self, and in many other areas. This formulation seems to be helpful in organizing a large number of observations made about the symptomatic behavior, functioning, and experiences of schizophrenic patients. In addition, it seems to lead to a number of potentially fruitful hypotheses about aspects of schizophrenia. It highlights the possible underlying similarity in such diverse phenomena as disturbances in attention, disordered thinking, amorphous and poorly articulated perception, disordered familial communication patterns, and the need–fear dilemma frequently observed in schizophrenic patients. It suggests that there are important relationships among many of these variables, and that disruptions in different functions are associated with each other.

Most research on psychopathology has investigated impairments of very specific and limited functions, in isolation. While some of these studies have made important contributions to the understanding of psychopathology, there is also a need for large-scale, configurational research that examines a wide range of functions in various types of psychopathology. There is a need for careful consideration of possible interrelationships among the many impairments in functioning observed in schizophrenia. A configurational research design would examine the interrelationships between cognitive–perceptual, intrapsychic, and interpersonal functions, and investigate how different configurations of impaired functions are related to etiology, prognosis, and type of psychopathology. We are at a point in research on psychopathology that we need not only focused studies that examine isolated functions and factors; we must also design multivariate studies to investigate the relationships among complex patterns, or constellations, of variables.

In studying complex patterns of variables, we must distinguish among levels of observation and degrees of inference. There is a need to distinguish data based to a greater degree on manifest behavior from primarily inferential data about such intrapsychic phenomena as the nature of fantasies, defenses, conflicts, and ego organization. Data can range from observations of overt behavior to laboratory and clinical assessments of cognitive and perceptual processes to evaluations of such intrapsychic dimensions as defenses, conflicts, and fantasies. While there is a need to investigate relationships among variables within a given domain, such as perception or cognition, there is also a need to consider relationships among variables in different domains and at different levels of observation. It would be of considerable value, for example, to examine the relationships of individual cognitive and perceptual functions to patterns of family interaction (e.g., Singer & Wynne, 1965a, b) and how these in turn relate to aspects of the treatment process. Further understanding of schizophrenia requires an examination of the relationships among variables at different levels of observation. We need to understand how these variables at different levels interact and are organized into consistent modes of adaptation in the various types of patients we consider to be schizophrenic. We also need to specify how these consistent modes of adaptation in schizophrenia are different from the organization of the same functions in patients with other forms of psychopathology and in normals.

In studying the relationships among a variety of functions at different observational levels, it is important to keep in mind that data derived from similar levels of observation or at similar inferential levels have a higher probability of intercorrelating than data gathered at different levels of observation and inference. There will probably be higher intercorrelations among measures of cognitive processes or among assessments of family communication than for intercorrelations between these two different domains. Comparison within observational or inferential levels is partly a test of internal consistency, while comparison between levels is more often a test of theoretical hypotheses (Blatt, 1975). While it is often difficult to find consistent relationships between disparate observational or inferential levels, there is a need for large-scale, long-term studies that investigate a wide range of functions across a number of levels in several diagnostic groups, in a complex, multivariate, configurational research design.

A recent example of this type of research is the work of Bellak, Hurvich, and Gediman (1973), who studied 50 schizophrenic, 25 neurotic, and 25 normal subjects, using interviews and a battery of psychological tests. This study is an impressive effort to evaluate schizophrenia on a number of dimensions. A major portion of this group's presentation is devoted to an exposition of their theoretical model of 11 ego functions, including object relations. Ratings of these ego functions, based on clinical interviews and psychological tests, consistently and significantly differentiated the schizophrenic patients from the other two groups (neurotics and normals).

Bellak and his colleagues also present a factor analysis of the interview ratings that revealed four interesting, independent factors which they labeled as Integrative Capacity, Reality Orientation, Socialization, and Adaptive Thinking. These four factors differentiated the schizophrenic patients from the neurotic and normal samples. In further research, with larger samples, it would be useful to test whether these four factors or different types of configurations differentiate among subgroups of schizophrenic patients. The specification of several different configurations among schizophrenic patients could contribute to a fuller understanding of the nature and phenomenology of schizophrenia.

Bellak and his colleagues did divide the schizophrenic group into three subgroups on the basis of degree of variation among factor scores—omitting 10 borderline patients. Paranoid patients tended ($p < .10$) to show more variation in their factor scores than did undifferentiated schizophrenic patients. Bellak et al. (1973) also briefly compared hospitalized schizophrenic patients with hospitalized nonschizophrenic patients; but this was only as a test for the possible effects of hospitalization, not as an exploration of different types of psychosis.

While it is important to compare schizophrenic patients with neurotic and normal control groups, it would also be valuable to explore differences among groups within the psychotic range (e.g., schizophrenia, hypomania, paranoia, psychotic depression, and toxic psychosis). This exploration could provide important insights into the specific nature of impairment in each type of psychosis, as compared to an evaluation of impairment in psychosis more generally.

Many of the recent clinical and research findings that demonstrate the importance of distinguishing between types of schizophrenic patients (e.g., process–reactive, nonparanoid–paranoid, amorphous–fragmented, and nondifferentiated–nonintegrated) suggest that there is much to be gained by further careful consideration of subgroups within schizophrenia. The degree of impairment of boundary articulation seems to provide one important dimension for making these differentiations. Patients in the process, nonparanoid, amorphous, and nondifferentiated subgroups can be seen as having a lesser capacity for boundary articulation, while those in the reactive, paranoid, fragmented, and nonintegrated subgroups appear to have a greater capacity for boundary differentiation.

In order to refine research on psychological disturbances, we must begin to specify with greater precision the criteria used in differentiating types of psychopathology. As Wynne has commented (cited by Rosenthal, 1968) we frequently neglect "sufficient consideration of principles and methods for describing, classifying and differentiating schizophrenics [p. 415]." There is "considerable ambiguity and vagueness" about what is meant by schizophrenia. Not only would this more precise definition permit more effective integration of research findings; it would also contribute to further refinements of criteria for subsequent research. In the present state of affairs, nosological distinctions are often based on unspecified and vague definitions, making it difficult to integrate the results of various studies or to increase the precision of definitions of types of psychological disorders. What is needed is a series of well-specified, qualitative and quantitative criteria to differentiate types of psychopathology. The degree of disturbance of boundary articulation may provide a meaningful dimension that can be used in establishing further criteria for distinguishing degrees of psychopathology, particularly within the psychotic range.

The developmental approach to schizophrenia—and other types of psychopathology—may foster a view of psychotic disturbances that will help to integrate analysis of the disruptions in functioning with an understanding of their etiology. The utility of the conceptualization of levels of disturbance in boundary articulation in integrating a diversity of observations on the functioning of schizophrenic patients suggests the value of considering other types of psychopathology within a model that emphasizes interrelationships in the development of cognitive functions, interpersonal relationships, and the representation of self and objects. Such a developmental approach would investigate systematic relationships between types of psychopathology and the nature and degree of impairment in these spheres. Developmental disturbances need not necessarily be serious and pervasive or immediately manifest; depending on their nature and severity, they may appear only later in life when stresses congruent with the developmental impairment reach a certain intensity (Blatt, 1974). Developmental impairments do not have to be considered only in psychological terms. Such a model of psychopathology would allow for the possibility that significant genetic and biological factors (e.g., stimulus thresholds) interact with environmental influences to bring about the disruption of developmental processes.

The formulation of the role of boundary disturbances in schizophrenia has the advantage of relating disturbances in psychopathology to issues observed in normal development. Development of the capacity to experience, perceive, and represent boundaries is one of the earliest and most basic steps in the complex development of the concept of the object. This developmental sequence proceeds from rudimentary boundary differentiation through the sensorimotor, preoperational, and operational stages, in which the object concept becomes increasingly accurate, differentiated, integrated, conceptual, and stable (Blatt, 1974). The level of development of the concept of the object indicates the general level of psychological development and capacity for adaptation. The concept of the object is a basic cognitive structure that guides and directs behavior. It is a basic step in the development of cognitive and perceptual processes, and it has a major role in determining the nature of interpersonal interactions. Recent research indicates that the quality of the mother–child transaction influences the development of cognitive capacities, including the concept of the object and object permanence (Décarie, 1965). Findings show that mothers who are generally more available have infants who develop object and person permanence more rapidly (Bell, 1970). The amount of auditory and visual stimulation provided by the mother has also been found to correlate significantly with the child's overall cognitive development and the development of specific cognitive–perceptual modalities (Clarke-Stewart, 1973). Clinical research by Spitz (1951), Provence and Lipton (1962), and Mahler (1968) indicates that disturbances in the early development of the mother–infant relationship can disrupt the development of many ego functions.

One of the basic assumptions in the formulation of boundary disturbances in schizophrenia is that a vulnerability to experiences of separation and loss results from profound difficulties in early object relations. Based on the complex transaction between the infant's biological and psychological predispositions and early experiences in being taken care of, there can be an impairment in the early development of the concept of the object and of object constancy. This impairment serves to compound even further the difficult interpersonal relationships that are evolving between the child and his caring agents. The child attempts to struggle with the difficult caring relationship in a variety of ways, alternately seeking safety, by merging with the need gratifying object, and maintaining excessive distance from it, to avoid experiences of highly inconsistent patterns of gratification and profoundly painful moments of frustration and deprivation. Given severe disturbances of the basic caring relationship, the infant subsequently becomes especially vulnerable to stressful interpersonal situations, particularly those that involve separation and loss. These are reacted to as profound dangers that threaten the tenuous balance of the object concept. There are strong wishes for fusion alternating with desperate attempts to maintain distance.

These formulations suggest the importance of investigating the development of the concept of the object and its impairment in psychopathology. Recently, Blatt, Brenneis, Schimek & Glick (1975) studied the normal development and pathological impairment of the concept of the object in adolescents and young adults. They examined the level of differentiation, articulation, and integration of human responses on the Rorschach in a normal longitudinal sample and in a hospitalized sample of disturbed adolescents and young adults. In normal development, they found a marked increase in the number of accurately perceived, well articulated, full human responses seen in appropriate, integrated, positive, and meaningful interactions. Patients, in contrast to the normal sample, consistently gave a significantly greater number of human responses at lower developmental levels (e.g., quasi–human, distorted, unmotivated, incongruent, nonspecific, malevolent and passive) on accurately perceived responses and a significantly greater number of developmentally more advanced human responses (e.g., full human, functionally articulated, benevolent and reactive) on inaccurately perceived responses. These data suggest that the levels of the concept of the object on the Rorschach can be assessed with a high degree of reliability and that properties of Rorschach responses of human figures show consistent developmental changes and differential impairment in psychopathology. Even further, they conclude that the systematic analysis of the concept of the object on the Rorschach provides data that elaborate important dimensions of psychotic experiences. They suggest that there are at least two dimensions in the representation of objects in psychosis. When contact with conventional reality is maintained, the concept of the object of psychotic patients is at lower developmental levels and people are portrayed as destructive and malevolent. When psychotic patients do not maintain contact with conventional reality, they function at higher developmental levels and portray people as kind and benevolent. "For psychotic patients, adequate interpretations of reality seem to be a painful and disruptive experience, and they retreat and withdraw to find comfort and peace. Psychotic patients appear more disorganized when they are struggling to deal with and integrate a painful reality and less disorganized when absorbed in unrealistic experiences. It is only in the most seriously disturbed patients, those with severe boundary disturbances, that both accurately and inaccurately perceived responses are at lower developmental levels [p. 14]." These findings suggest that important aspects of psychotic experiences are expressed in the representation of objects. There is a need for further systematic investigation of object representations in psychosis and of the development of the concept of the object in early stages of normal development.

In both the theoretical and clinical literature, much attention has been given to the impact of faulty caretaking patterns of the mother of the schizophrenic patient and her failure to provide consistent and stable patterns of need gratification for her infant. And in a significant number of schizophrenic patients, particularly those with mothers who have a history of severe emotional disturbance (e.g., psychosis or severe depression), highly disorganized and chaotic caretaking patterns may play a major role in the etiology of schizophrenia. The more severe the mother's disturbance, the more seriously disturbed the child (Gardner, 1967; Rutter, 1966). There is a much less significant relationship, however, between the severity of the father's pathology and that of the child (Gardner, 1967; Nameche, 1965). But it is important to consider all of the caretaking agents and their transactions with the infant. The role of the father, both as providing caretaking in his own right and as an alternate object to the mother, is important in the infant's early development. The father can contribute additional stress and distraction, support and facilitate the caretaking of the infant, or remain aloof. The role of other alternate objects such as a grandparent, sibling, or maid also needs to be considered.

Ricks & Berry (1970) reported a series of studies that examined the clinical files of children seen at the Judge Baker Guidance Center who later were hospitalized in Massachusetts and diagnosed as schizophrenic. They found that there were many disrupted marriages among the parents of these children; while the parents often did not seek divorce, the marriages were characterized by "covert hostility, estrangement, and distrust [p. 36]." Ricks and Nameche (1966) found that the early home environments, particularly of "chronic schizophrenic" patients, had an atmosphere of symbiotic union between mother and child. The mothers usually infantilized their adolescent children, who, if they struggled to break out of the family, were overwhelmed by anxiety and decompensated into a schizophrenic state (Fleming & Ricks, 1970; Ricks & Nameche, 1966). Less severely ill schizophrenic patients who had been discharged from the hospital tended to have been rejected and excluded from the family when they were children, and they were also more rebellious—often involved in stealing, running away, truancy, and promiscuity. Sameroff and Zax (1973a), based on an unpublished dissertation by Kelly (1974), report that schizophrenic mothers tended to be more physically distant from their infants and to touch and play with them less. Sameroff and Zax (1973a) also report that Anagnostopolou (1974), using the same sample, found that while there were no differences among 4-month-old infants from mothers of four different diagnostic groups, by 12 months, the children of schizophrenic mothers were different from the other children, particularly in being less disturbed when their mothers left the room and when they were approached by strangers (Garmezy, 1974a). Lewis and Rosenbaum (1974) point out that research in child development has "neglected the significance of the interaction between mother and infant and . . . the subtle contributions that each makes to the other in shaping their ongoing dyadic behavior [p. ix]." Brazelton, Koslowski, and Main (1974) discuss an interdependency of rhythms between the infant and his caregiver as a basic dimension of attachment and communication. There are subtle, transient as well as major developmental changes in the infant's activity patterns that require continued readjustment of caretaking patterns. The ease with which the infant–caregiver dyad adjusts to these changes in rhythms reflects the depth of the attachment. Some mothers have difficulty in maintaining a differentiated responsiveness to their infant's rhythms (reciprocal patterns) and some of these infants may decrease their overall responsiveness to their mothers. R. Bell (1974) stresses the complexity of the infant–caregiver interaction and how it must be considered from a developmental perspective; specific behavior of the infant in one period of development may have different meanings and effects on parents than in a subsequent period.

At times, the factors that disrupt the early caretaking of the infant may be more subtle than the parents' general capacities to respond to and manage the demands and stresses of caring for an infant. As illustrated by Searles (1965), an infant may have some very special meaning for a parent because the birth, for example, coincided with the death of an important family figure or occurred at a particularly stressful time for the parents. These factors might make it difficult for the parents to respond to this infant, but not necessarily to children born either earlier or later.

There is a need for more extensive research on the impact of disturbances in early relationships between the infant and his caring agents to test the hypothesis that difficulties in attaining the concept of the object result from serious disruptions in these early relationships. But it is necessary to consider all the participants in that interpersonal transaction—child, parents, and other caretaking figures—and to evaluate their relative contributions to disruptions of the early need–gratifying relationship. The severe disruption of the caring relationship, which is at issue in schizophrenia, is not necessarily the contribution of any one particular member of the transaction. It is also important to consider the role of the child and his responsiveness in the caretaking relationship. There is evidence, for example, that a monozygotic twin who develops schizophrenia has a lower birth weight and more respiratory, sleep, and eating difficulties, colic, cyanosis at birth, and such medical complications as infectious diseases than his nonschizophrenic co-twin (Pollin & Stabenau, 1968). Pollin and Stabenau found that the nonschizophrenic monozygotic twin is "born at a different and higher state of physiological and biological maturation and competence [p. 325]." Sameroff and Zax (1973b) found a relatively higher incidence of birth complications in women with severe psychopathology, who lacked adequate concern about their physical health and nutrition. Mednick (1970) found a relatively higher incidence of pregnancy and birth complications in schizophrenic mothers of children who later became mentally ill. Infants with unfortunate biological and psychological predispositions at birth, whether caused by genetic factors, prenatal deficiencies, or birth defects and injuries, may be unusually difficult to care for. An unresponsive child, a hyperkinetic child, or a child who can be soothed and comforted only with great difficulty, may place tremendous stress on parents who under other circumstances might be able to provide adequate and consistent care and nurturance. Schaffer and Emerson (1964), for example, found that "social attachment" (cuddling behavior) in normal infants was not a function of the mother's behavior but rather seemed to be an innate response tendency of the infant. The responses and characteristics of an infant have an important impact on the behavior of the mother (Thomas, Chess, & Birch, 1968; Clarke-Stewart, 1973). Dealing with an unusually difficult infant can place excessive stress on one or both parents, resulting in their distancing themselves from the infant. This disengagement would further compound the infant's already existing problems in finding satisfaction and gratification; and subsequently these parents might appear similar, at least in some respects, to more disturbed parents who had problems coping with a relatively less difficult infant. Wender, Rosenthal, and Kety (1968), for example, note that many adoptive parents of schizophrenics present "pictures of depression, apathy, social withdrawal, preoccupation, anxiety, feelings of futility, and guilt." These problems "seemed clearly related to the onset of severe problems in the offspring," frequently leading to marital difficulties and problems in each parent [p. 245]. The evidence of a significantly greater number of prenatal and birth difficulties and injuries in schizophrenic patients suggests that the state of the infant may be an important factor in determining the disruptions of the basic caretaking relationship. A defective child may require more consistent attention and care and more capable, sensitive, and responsive parents in order to develop adequately. Thus, many different factors may contribute to the disruption of the caretaking relationship.

Our understanding of schizophrenia would be greatly enhanced by longitudinal research examining the interaction of biological, psychological, and sociological factors that influence the normal development of complex human behavior. There is a need for more research on sequences in the development of the concept of the object and on the nature and effect of events that disrupt these sequences. It would be of value, for example, to study the subsequent development of children like those in Bell's study (1970), who developed the concept of the inanimate object before they developed the concept of the person. These children developed the general concept of the object more slowly and were less responsive to their mothers. It would be of considerable interest to study the later consequences of this atypical early development. We need to consider the complex transaction of genetic, biological, and environmental factors, and how these influence developmental sequences.

Studies of children at risk for schizophrenia can make valuable contributions to understanding the etiology of this disorder. Recently, Garmezy (1974a,b) has provided an excellent review and critique of this rapidly increasing area of research. Garmezy believes that:

> Risk studies are meaningful because they represent a legitimate stage in the evolution of psychiatric research—one exemplified by a growing commitment to the study of the *development* of schizophrenia following a prolonged but necessary immersion by researchers in the *structural* properties of the disorder. The sequence of structural concerns followed by developmental study is a predictable one, as is the initial effort to delineate development by focusing exclusively on manifestly schizophrenic adults. The progression is rooted in psychiatry's history, but whereas the adult patient is the legitimate source for inquiry into the structure of schizophrenic pathology, this is not true for the study of its genesis. Thus the turn to the child at risk [1974b, p. 92].

Garmezy (1974a) discusses several different types of studies of children at risk. The "retrospective" type of study utilizes material gained from personal accounts or from prior clinical or public records of current patients, with the goal of identifying early indications and factors that may have contributed to the current psychopathology. Differences in reliability, accuracy, sensitivity, and precision of these retrospective accounts, however, place limits on the potential contribution of this type of research. There are also "followup" studies, in which children previously identified as being "at risk" are sought out as adults in an attempt to understand how the earlier "risk" factors contributed to subsequent development. Robins (1966), for example, studied a large sample of adults who, as children, had been seen in a psychiatric clinic. Though Robins was primarily interested in the development of sociopathic patients, there were a substantial number ($n = 23$) of boys who subsequently, as adults, were diagnosed as schizophrenic. The developmental histories of those boys who became schizophrenic, as compared to a matched control group, showed a greater incidence of "somatic symptoms, nailbiting, depression, being overdependent, and ruminative [p. 239]." There was also more truancy and running away from home. In terms of the parents of these boys who became schizophrenic as adults, there was a significantly greater incidence of divorce and separation and a greater rate of unemployment. Clinical research by Fish and her colleagues (Fish et al, 1962, 1965, 1966, 1973) is another example of followup research; infants who showed disorganized patterns of activity, alertness, autonomic stability, and proprioception were followed through adolescence. The findings of Fish and her colleagues suggest that there is a complex interaction of very early biological and environmental events that have an important relationship to the subsequent development of psychopathology.

Garmezy (1974a) also discusses another type of research design, which he calls a "follow-through" strategy, involving longitudinal or cross-sectional prospective studies of children identified to be potentially at risk, such as children of mentally ill parents (e.g., Mednick & Schulsinger, 1968, 1970). Such studies have the important advantage of enabling the investigator to select his own variables and measures rather than relying on retrospective reports or on data gathered by others, often for a different purpose. A number of these studies are currently being conducted, most of which have selected the children at risk on the basis of one or both parents' psychiatric status. Garmezy (1974b) calls attention to many complex problems and methodological issues in this kind of research, including formidable logistical difficulties, selection of the risk group, selection of appropriate controls, and selection of variables that are applicable to adult schizophrenics as well as vulnerable children. The formulation of schizophrenia as a developmental disturbance in the capacity to establish boundaries has the advantage of suggesting links between early vulnerabilities and later manifestations of boundary problems in adult schizophrenics. The formulation suggests that it would be very important to include assessments of the attainment of the object concept in studies of children at high risk. Grunebaum et al. (1974) included such an assessment in a study comparing 15 one-year-old children of psychotic mothers with a control group of 15 children of normal mothers. The high risk children had more difficulty with the Escalona scale of object permanence, in which the child has to locate "lures" hidden in progressively more complicated patterns; but it was difficult to distinguish whether this was a failure in object permanence or in attending to the task. In research on infants at risk and their families, relationships between many variables, such as maternal caretaking patterns, the role of the father, and attainment of the concept of the object could be investigated.

The longitudinal study of children with atypical developmental patterns may provide important insights into the etiology of psychopathology. Much of our current research on and understanding of the development of psychopathology is reconstructive; we infer the etiological processes from reconstructive observations based on current memories, records of past events, or analyses of current behavior. Long-range longitudinal study of normal and atypical developmental processes is an important step for further and fuller understanding of the etiology of psychopathology. Longitudinal research is obviously difficult and complex. The possibility of self-selection in determining participation may result in a sample of "normal" families who covertly are seeking advice, counsel, and therapy. The selection of families "at risk" is a complex matter and can also result in a distorted sample. Schizophrenic mothers who have children, especially those who are currently living with the children's father, could be an atypical sample. These families could create a sampling bias in favor of studying more reactive schizophrenic parent(s) and organized families. In addition, contact with a research team may provide advice and direction and even a form of supportive therapy that could influence the results.

One of the important developments in the study of children at risk has been the investigation of adopted children of schizophrenic parents. These studies offer considerable promise for separating out the respective contributions of genetic and environmental factors in the etiology of schizophrenia. An important factor to be controlled in these studies is that the adoptive families do not have any knowledge about the possible atypical nature of their adopted child or the history of mental illness in the child's biological parents. While genetic studies (Gottesman & Shields, 1972; Heston, 1966; Kety et al., 1968; Kidd & Cavalli-Sforza, 1973) show that there is a higher probability of schizophrenia in the offspring if one or both parents is schizophrenic, most of these children at high risk never become schizophrenic (M. Bleuler, 1974). Garmezy (1974b) argues for broadening the criteria for the selection of children at risk, such as identifying families in which the parents show communication disturbances in sharing focal attention. Problems with attainment of the concept of the object could also be used as a criterion for selecting children at high risk for longitudinal studies. For example, the babies in Bell's (1970) study who had higher scores on object than on person permanence showed more problems with attachment behavior than those babies who had higher scores on person permanence. This finding suggests that the former group of babies may be more at risk for future difficulties than the latter group.

Since most of the children of high risk parents never become schizophrenic, it is important to investigate both the high risk children who become schizophrenic and those who do not become mentally ill. In addition to focusing on maladaptive behavior and psychopathology, it is crucial to learn more about the factors that enable children at risk to cope with unusual stress. Garmezy (1974b) has recently emphasized the need for more studies of competence and adaptation in the "invulnerable" children who do not develop schizophrenia despite genetic and environmental disadvantages. While Heston's investigations (Heston, 1966; Heston & Denny, 1968), like other genetic studies, found a significant concordance rate in children of schizophrenic mothers, his data point to another important, and unfortunately often overlooked, finding. He noted that 21 of his sample of 47 children born to but separated from schizophrenic mothers at an early age became "notably successful adults" and "possessed artistic talents and demonstrated imaginative adaptations to life which were uncommon in the control group [Heston, 1966, p. 825]." These 21 index subjects, when compared to the control group, "were more spontaneous when interviewed and had more colorful life histories. They held the more creative jobs: musician, teacher, home-designer; and followed the more imaginative hobbies: oil painting, music, antique aircraft [p. 824]." Karlsson (1968) also noted a sizable number of "gifted" people who had psychotic relatives. Subsequent to Heston's original observations, the genetic factors in schizophrenia have been extensively explored, but curiously, relatively little attention has been given to Heston's observations about the "successful" half of his sample. Schizophrenia, like psychological development more generally, is the end result of complex transactions of genetic, biological, psychological, and sociological factors in an interpersonal context. These factors must be examined to see how they can sometimes result in such profoundly painful and agonizing experiences as schizophrenia and yet at other times can result in unusual capacities for imagination, creativity, and pleasure.

While it is beyond the scope of this book to discuss treatment in any detail, the formulation of boundary disturbances in schizophrenia also has obvious implications for therapy. For example, evaluation of the capacity for individuation can be an important factor in deciding whether and when a patient should confront the family as a way of working through separation. Consideration of struggles with boundary differentiation also provides fuller understanding of "acting out" in schizophrenia. Assaultive behavior, exaggerated autonomy and independence, sexual promiscuity in females and homosexuality in males can be viewed, in part, as attempts to establish differentiation from the primary object. In attempts to foster the process of individuation, the patient's experiences of fusion and of intensely ambivalent symbiotic ties can be considered and interpreted, with appreciation for the experienced threat of annihilation entailed in either fusion or separation.

In summary, we have attempted to conceptualize schizophrenia as a developmental impairment in the capacity to experience, perceive, and represent boundaries. While this impairment varies in degree and intensity, both within and between patients, many of the disruptions in cognitive processes and interpersonal relationships in schizophrenia can be considered as manifestations of developmental impairment in the fundamental establishment of boundaries. In some patients, this impairment may be apparent only under conditions of stress, but our review of the research and clinical literature suggests that it is one of the fundamental issues in schizophrenia.

This conceptual model also has significant research implications for the study of schizophrenics and their families, for the study of normal development, and for longitudinal studies of children at risk for schizophrenia and other types of psychopathology. The model suggests the value of studying extensive samples of schizophrenics and of comparing performance within individuals on a wide variety of tasks measuring various cognitive functions. Future investigations might systematically examine relationships between various levels of boundary disturbance and disruption in such ego functions as attention, concept formation, perceptual processes, language, thinking, and interpersonal relationships. In this way, consistencies in styles and levels of functioning could be identified. Pollak (1970) and his colleagues (1973) have been following such an approach in their recent studies of schizophrenia. The model suggests investigation of associations between styles and levels of cognitive functioning and styles and levels of interpersonal relationships. Another avenue of research stemming from the model would be a comparison of individual patients' styles and levels of cognitive functioning and interpersonal relationships with individual and transactional analysis of parental styles and levels of those factors. There is also need for studies of normal development that are longitudinal in nature, to investigate the general developmental linkages between cognitive capacities and interpersonal relations. Finally, longitudinal studies investigating these linkages in children at risk could make substantial contributions to our understanding of the etiology of schizophrenia.

In our clinical work and in the many clinical accounts cited by others, schizophrenic patients continually communicate difficulties in maintaining a separation between themselves and significant figures in their lives. Careful consideration and conceptualization of these experiences should lead to a fuller understanding of their complex and baffling aspects, to more effective treatment, and to more meaningful research.

References

Ainsworth, M. D. *Infancy in Uganda: Infant care and the growth of love.* Baltimore: Johns Hopkins Univ. Press, 1967.

Ainsworth, M. D., Bell, S. M., Blehar, M. P., & Main, M. B. *Physical contact: A study of infant responsiveness and its relation to maternal handling.* Paper presented at the biennial meeting of the Society for Research in Child Development, Minneapolis, Minnesota, April, 1971.

Allison, J. Adaptive regression and intense religious experiences. *Journal of Nervous and Mental Disease,* 1967, **145,** 452–463.

Allison, J., Blatt, S. J., & Zimet, C. *The interpretation of psychological tests.* New York: Harper & Row, 1968.

Alpert, M., & Silvers, K. N. Perceptual characteristics distinguishing auditory hallucinations in schizophrenia and acute alcoholic psychoses. *American Journal of Psychiatry,* 1970, **127,** 298–302.

Anagnostopolou, R. *Mother–infant interaction, attachment, and mother's psychopathology.* Doctoral dissertation, University of Rochester, 1974.

Arieti, S. *Interpretation of schizophrenia.* New York: Robert Brunner, 1955.

Arieti, S. The loss of reality. *Psychoanalysis and Psychoanalytic Review,* 1961, **48,** 3–24.

Bannister, D. & Salmon, P. Schizophrenic thought disorder: Specific or diffuse? *British Journal of Medical Psychology,* 1966, **39,** 215–219.

Bateson, G. Cultural problems posed by a study of schizophrenic process. In A. Auerback (Ed.), (Symposium on schizophrenia), *Schizophrenia: An integrated approach.* New York: Ronald Press, 1959. Pp. 125–146.

Bateson, G., Jackson, D., Haley, J., & Weakland, J. Toward a theory of schizophrenia. *Behavioral Science,* 1956, **1,** 251–264.

Baxter, J. C., Becker, J., & Hooks, W. Defensive style in the families of schizophrenics and controls. *Journal of Abnormal and Social Psychology,* 1963, **66,** 512–518.

Behrens, M. I., Rosenthal, A. J., & Chodoff, P. Communication in lower class families of schizophrenics: II. Observations and findings. *Archives of General Psychiatry,* 1968, **18,** 689–696.

Bell, R. Q. Contributions of human infants to caretaking and social interaction. In M. Lewis and L. A. Rosenblum (Eds.) *The effect of the infant on its caregiver.* New York: Wiley, 1974. Pp. 1–20.

Bell, S. M. *The relationship of infant-mother attachment to the development of the concept of object permanence.* Doctoral dissertation, Johns Hopkins Univ., 1968.

Bell, S. M. The development of the concept of object as related to infant–mother attachment. *Child Development,* 1970, **41,** 292–311.

Bellak, L. (Ed.) *Schizophrenia: A review of the syndrome.* New York: Logos Press, 1958.

Bellak, L. The validity and usefulness of the concept of the schizophrenic syndrome. In R. Cancro (Ed.), *The schizophrenic reactions.* New York: Brunner/Mazel, 1970. Pp. 41–58.

Bellak, L., Hurvich, M., & Gediman, H. K. *Ego functions in schizophrenics, neurotics and normals.* New York: Wiley, 1973.

Benjamin, J. D. A method for distinguishing and evaluating formal thinking disorders in schizophrenia. In J. S. Kasanin (Ed.), *Language and thought in schizophrenia.* Berkeley: Univ. of California Press, 1944. Pp. 65–88.

Bergman, P., & Escalona, S. K. Unusual sensitivities in very young children. *Psychoanalytic Study of the Child,* 1949, **3–4,** 333–352.

Bergmann, M. S. The place of Paul Federn's ego psychology in psychoanalytic metapsychology. *Journal of the American Psychoanalytic Association,* 1963, **11,** 97–116.

Berlyne, D. E. The influence of the albedo and complexity of stimuli on visual fixation in the human infant. *British Journal of Psychology,* 1958, **49,** 315–318.

Bettelheim, B. *The empty fortress.* New York: Free Press, 1967.

Blatt, S. J. *Recall versus recognition memory of deteriorated schizophrenics.* Unpublished Master's Thesis, Pennsylvania State Univ., 1952.

Blatt, S. J. Recall and recognition vocabulary: Implications for intellectual deterioration. *Archives of General Psychiatry,* 1959, **1,** 473–476.

Blatt, S. J. Levels of object representation in anaclitic and introjective depression. *Psychoanalytic Study of the Child,* 1974, **29,** 107–157.

Blatt, S. J. The validity of projective techniques and their research and clinical contribution. *Journal of Personality Assessment,* 1975, **39,** 327–343.

Blatt, S. J. & Allison, J. The intelligence test in personality assessment. In A. Rabin (Ed.), *Projective techniques in personality assessment.* New York: Springer, 1968.

Blatt, S. J., Brenneis, C. B., Schimek, J. G., & Glick, M. The normal development and psychopathological impairment of the concept of the object on the Rorschach. Unpublished paper, Yale Univ., 1975.

Blatt, S. J. & Ritzler, B. A. Thought disorder and boundary disturbances in psychosis. *Journal of Consulting and Clinical Psychology,* 1974, **42,** 370–381.

Blatt, S. J., Wild, C. M., & Ritzler, B. A. Disturbances of object representation in schizophrenia. *Psychoanalysis and Contemporary Science,* 1975.

Bleuler, E. *Dementia praecox or the group of schizophrenias.* [1911]. New York: International Universities Press, 1950

Bleuler, E. The basic symptoms of schizophrenia. In D. Rapaport (Ed.), *Organization and Pathology of Thought.* New York: Columbia Univ. Press, 1951. Pp. 581–649.

Bleuler, M. The offspring of schizophrenics. *Schizophrenia Bulletin,* 1974, **8,** 93–107.

Bloom, L. *Language development: Form and function in emerging grammars.* Cambridge, Mass: MIT Press, 1970.

Boardman, W. K., Goldstone, S., Reiner, M. L., & Himmel, S. Constancy of absolute judgments of size by normals and schizophrenics. *Journal of Abnormal and Social Psychology,* 1964, **68,** 346–349.

Brazelton, T., Koslowski, B., & Main, M. The origin of reciprocity: The early mother–infant interaction. In M. Lewis and L. A. Rosenbaum (Eds.), *The effect of the infant on its caregiver.* New York: Wiley, 1974. Pp. 49–76.

Brenneis, C. B. Features of the manifest dream in schizophrenia. *Journal of Nervous and Mental Disease,* 1971, **153,** 81–91.

Brown, R. W. *A first language, the early stages.* Cambridge, Massachusetts: Harvard Univ. Press, 1973.

Bruch, H. Falsification of bodily needs and body concept in schizophrenia. *Archives of General Psychiatry,* 1962, **6,** 18–24.

Bruner, J. Personality dynamics and the process of perceiving. In R. R. Blake & G. V. Ramsey (Eds.), *Perception: An approach to personality.* New York: Ronald Press, 1951. Pp. 121–147.

Burnham, D., Gladstone, A., & Gibson, R. *Schizophrenia and the need-fear dilemma.* New York: International Universities Press, 1969.

Cameron, N. The development of paranoic thinking. *Psychological Review,* 1943, **50,** 219–233.

Cameron, N. Experimental analysis of schizophrenic thinking. In J. Kasanin (Ed.), *Language and thought in schizophrenia.* Berkeley: Univ. of California Press, 1944. Pp. 50–63.

Cameron, N. Perceptual organization and behavior pathology. In R. R. Blake & G. V. Ramsey (Eds.), *Perception: An approach to personality.* New York: Ronald Press, 1951. Pp. 283–306.

Cameron, N. Paranoid conditions and paranoia. In S. Arieti (Ed.), *American handbook of psychiatry, Vol. 1.* New York: Basic Books, 1959. Pp. 508–539.

Cameron, N., & Magaret, A. *Behavior pathology.* Boston: Houghton & Mifflin, 1951.

Carpenter, G. C., Tecce, J. J., Stechler, G., & Friedman, S. Differential visual behavior to human and humanoid faces in early infancy. *Merrill–Palmer Quarterly,* 1970, **16,** 91–108.

Chapman, J., & McGhie, A. A comparative study of disordered attention in schizophrenia. *Journal of Mental Science,* 1962, **108,** 487–500.

Chapman, L. J., & Chapman, J. P. Atmosphere effect re-examined. *Journal of Experimental Psychology,* 1959, **58,** 220–226.

Chapman, L. J., Chapman, J. P., & Miller, G. A. A theory of verbal behavior in schizophrenia. In B. A. Maher (Ed.), *Progress in experimental personality research, Vol. 1.* New York: Academic Press, 1964. Pp. 49–77.

Clarke-Stewart, K. A. Interactions between mothers and their young children: characteristics and consequences. *Society of Research in Child Development Monograph, 1973,* **38.**

Cleveland, S. E. Body image changes associated with personality reorganization. *Journal of Consulting Psychology,* 1960, **24,** 256–261.

Cohen, B. D., Senf, R., & Huston, P. E. Perceptual accuracy in schizophrenia, depression and neurosis, and effects of amytal. *Journal of Abnormal and Social Psychology,* 1956, **52,** 363–367.

Crookes, T. G. Size constancy and literalness in Rorschach Test. *British Journal of Medical Psychology,* 1957, **30,** 99–106.

Dahl, M. A singular distortion of temporal orientation. *American Journal of Psychiatry,* 1958, **115,** 146–149.

Darby, J. A. Alteration of some body image indexes in schizophrenics. *Journal of Consulting and Clinical Psychology,* 1970, **35,** 116–121.

Davids, A. A research design for studying maternal emotionality before childbirth and after social interaction with the child. *Merrill–Palmer Quarterly,* 1968, **14,** 344–354.

Davis, D., Cromwell, R., & Held, J. Size estimation in emotionally disturbed children and schizophrenic adults. *Journal of Abnormal Psychology,* 1967, **72,** 395–401.

Décarie, T. G. *Intelligence and affectivity in early childhood.* New York: International Universities Press, 1965.

De La Garza, C. O., & Worchel, P. Time and space orientation in schizophrenics. *Journal of Abnormal and Social Psychology,* 1956, **52,** 191–194.

Des Lauriers, A. M. *The experience of reality in childhood schizophrenia.* New York: International Universities Press, 1962.

Dobson, W. R. An investigation of various factors involved in time perception as manifested by different nosological groups. *Journal of General Psychology,* 1954, **50,** 277-298.

Draguns, J. G. Responses to cognitive and perceptual ambiguity in chronic and acute schizophrenics. *Journal of Abnormal and Social Psychology,* 1963, **66,** 24-30.

Ehrentheil, O. F., & Jenney, P. B. Does time stand still for some psychotics? *Archives of General Psychiatry,* 1960, **3,** 1-3.

Epstein, S. Overinclusive thinking in a schizophrenic and a control group. *Journal of Consulting Psychology,* 1953, **17,** 384-388.

Erikson, E. Identity and the life cycle: Selected papers. *Psychological Issues,* 1959, **1,** 1-171.

Escalona, S. Emotional development in the first year of life. In M. J. E. Senn (Ed.), *Transactions of the sixth conference on problems of infancy and childhood.* New York: Josiah Macy, Jr. Foundation, 1953. Pp. 11-92.

Fairbanks, H. Studies in language behavior, II. The quantitative differentiation of samples of spoken language. *Psychological Monographs,* 1944, **56,** (Whole No. 255), 19-38.

Fantz, R. L. Pattern vision in newborn infants. *Science,* 1963, **140,** 296-297.

Fantz, R. L. Pattern discrimination and selective attention as determinants of perceptual development from birth. In A. H. Kidd & J. L. Rivoire (Eds.), *Perceptual development in children.* New York: International Universities Press, 1966. Pp. 143-173.

Fantz, R. L., & Nevis, S. Pattern preferences and perceptual-cognitive development in early infancy. *Merrill-Palmer Quarterly,* 1967, **13,** 77-108.

Farina, A. Patterns of role dominance and conflict in parents of schizophrenic patients. *Journal of Abnormal and Social Psychology,* 1960, **61,** 31-38.

Federn, P. *Ego psychology and the psychoses.* New York: Basic Books, Inc., 1952.

Fenichel, O. *The psychoanalytic theory of neurosis.* New York: Norton, 1945.

Fish, B., & Alpert, M. S. Abnormal states of consciousness and muscle tone in infants born to schizophrenic mothers. *American Journal of Psychiatry,* 1962, **119,** 439-445.

Fish, B., & Hagin, R. Visual-motor disorders in infants at risk for schizophrenia. *Archives of General Psychiatry,* 1973, **28,** 900-904.

Fish, B., Shapiro, T., Halpern, F., & Wile, R. The prediction of schizophrenia in infancy: III. A ten-year follow-up report of neurological and psychological development. *American Journal of Psychiatry,* 1965, **121,** 768-775.

Fish, B., Wile, R., Shapiro, T. & Halpern, F. The prediction of schizophrenia in infancy: II. A ten-year follow-up report of predictions made at one month of age. In P. H. Hoch & J. Zubin (Eds.), *Psychopathology of schizophrenia.* New York: Grune & Stratton, 1966. Pp. 335-353.

Fisher, S. Body image and psychopathology. *Archives of General Psychiatry,* 1964, **10,** 519-529.

Fisher, S. Body image in neurotic and schizophrenic patients. *Archives of General Psychiatry,* 1966, **15,** 90-101.

Fisher, S., & Cleveland, S. E. *Body image and personality.* New York: Van Nostrand, 1958.

Fisher, S., & Renik, O. D. Induction of body-image boundary changes. *Journal of Projective Techniques and Personality Assessment,* 1966, **30,** 429-434.

Flavell, J. H. *The developmental psychology of Jean Piaget.* Princeton, New Jersey: Van Nostrand, 1963.

Fleming, P., & Ricks, D. F. Emotions of children before schizophrenia and before character disorder. In M. Roff and D. F. Ricks, (Eds.), *Life history research in psychopathology.* Minneapolis: University of Minnesota Press, 1970. Pp. 240-264.

Fraiberg, S. Libidinal object constancy and mental representation. *Psychoanalytic Study of the Child,* 1969, **24,** 9-47.

Freeman, T., Cameron, J. L., & McGhie, A. *Studies on psychosis.* New York: International Universities Press, 1966.

Freud, A. The mutual influences in the development of the ego and the id: Introduction to the discussion. *Psychoanalytic Study of the Child,* 1952, **7,** 42–50.

Freud, A. & Burlingham, D. *Infants without families.* New York: International Universities Press, 1944.

Freud, S. *The interpretation of dreams* (1900). Standard edition, Vols. IV & V. London: Hogarth Press, 1958.

Freud, S. *Psycho–analytic notes on an autobiographical account of a case of paranoia* (1911). Standard edition, Vol. XII. London: Hogarth Press, 1958, 3–82.

Freud, S. *On narcissism, an introduction* (1914). Standard edition, Vol. XIV. London: Hogarth Press, 1957, 73–102.

Freud, S. *Instincts and their vicissitudes* (1915). Standard edition, Vol. XIV. London: Hogarth Press, 1957, 117–140.

Freud, S. *Negation* (1925). Standard edition, Vol. XIX. London: Hogarth Press, 1961, 235–239.

Freud, S. *Civilization and its discontents* (1930). Standard edition, Vol. XXI. London: Hogarth Press, 1961, 57–145.

Gardner, G. G. Role of maternal psychopathology in male and female schizophrenics. *Journal of Consulting Psychology,* 1967, **31,** 411–413.

Garmezy, N. Children at risk: The search for the antecedents of schizophrenia. Part 1. Conceptual models and research methods. *Schizophrenia Bulletin,* 1974, **8,** 14–90. (a)

Garmezy, N. Children at risk: The search for the antecedents of schizophrenia. Part 2. Ongoing research programs, issues and intervention. *Schizophrenia Bulletin,* 1974, **9,** 55–125.(b)

Gibson, J. J. The perception of visual surfaces. *American Journal of Psychology,* 1950, **63,** 367–384.

Gill, M. M. The primary process. In R. R. Holt (Ed.), Motives and thought: Psychoanalytic essays in honor of David Rapaport. *Psychological Issues,* 1967, **18/19,** 259–298.

Goldberg, S., & Lewis, M. Play behavior in the year-old infant: Early sex differences. *Child Development,* 1969, **40,** 21–31.

Goldstein, K. Methodological approach to the study of schizophrenic thought disorder. In J. S. Kasanin (Ed.), *Language and thought in schizophrenia.* Berkeley: Univ. of California Press, 1944. Pp. 17–39.

Goldstein, K., & Scheerer, M. Abstract and concrete behavior; an experimental study with special tests. *Psychological Monographs,* 1941, **53,** 2.

Gordon, I. J. Early child stimulation through parent education. A final report to the Children's Bureau, Dept. of Health, Education, and Welfare, June, 1969.

Gottesman, I. I., & Shields, J. *Schizophrenia and genetics—a twin study vantage point.* New York: Academic Press, 1972.

Gottesman, L., & Chapman, L. Syllogistic reasoning errors in schizophrenia. *Journal of Consulting Psychology,* 1960, **24,** 250–255.

Grand, S., Freedman, N., & Steingart, I. A study of the representation of objects in schizophrenia. *Journal of the American Psychoanalytic Association,* 1973, **21,** 399–434.

Grunebaum, H., Weiss, J. L., Gallant, D., & Cohler, B. J. Attention in young children of psychotic mothers. *American Journal of Psychiatry,* 1974, **131,** 887–891.

Haith, M. M. Response of the human newborn to visual movement. *Journal of Experimental Child Psychology,* 1966, **3,** 235–243.

Hamilton, V. Size constancy and cue responsiveness in psychosis. *British Journal of Psychology,* 1963, **54,** 25–39.

Harrington, R., & Ehrmann, J. C. Complexity of response as a factor in the vocabulary performance of schizophrenics. *Journal of Abnormal and Social Psychology,* 1954, **49,** 362–

364. Harris, J. Size estimation of pictures as a function of thematic content for schizophrenic and normal subjects. *Journal of Personality,* 1957, **25,** 651–671.

Hartman, A. M. Apparent size of after-images in delusional and nondelusional schizophrenics. *American Journal of Psychology,* 1962, **75,** 587–595.

Hartmann, H., Kris, E., & Lowenstein, R. M. Notes on the theory of aggression. *Psychoanalytic Study of the Child,* 1949, **3–4,** 9–36.

Harway, N. I., & Salzman, L. F. Size constancy in psychopathology. *Journal of Abnormal and Social Psychology,* 1964, **69,** 606–613.

Heinstein, M. I. Behavioral correlates of breast-bottle regimes under varying parent-infant relationships. *Child Development Publications of the Society for Research in Child Development,* 1963, **28,** (4, Whole No. 88).

Heston, L. L. Psychiatric disorders in foster home reared children of schizophrenic mothers. *British Journal of Psychiatry,* 1966, **112,** 819–825.

Heston, L. L., & Denney, D. Interactions between early life experience and biological factors in schizophrenia. In D. Rosenthal, & S. S. Kety, (Eds.), *The transmission of schizophrenia.* Oxford: Pergamon Press, 1968. Pp. 363–376.

Hill, L. B. *Psychotherapeutic intervention in schizophrenia.* Chicago: Univ. of Chicago Press, 1955.

Holt, R. R. *Manual for the scoring of primary process manifestations in Rorschach responses.* Unpublished 9th draft. New York Univ. Research Center for Mental Health, 1963.

Holt, R. R. The development of the primary process: A structural view. In R. R. Holt (Ed.), Motives and thought: Psychoanalytic essays in honor of David Rapaport. *Psychological Issues,* 1967, **18/19,** 345–383.

Holt, R. R., & Havel, J. A method for assessing primary and secondary process in the Rorschach. In M. A. Rickers-Ovsiankina (Ed.), *Rorschach psychology.* New York: Wiley, 1960. Pp. 263–315.

Holtzman, W. H., Gorham, D. R., & Moran, L. J. A factor-analytic study of schizophrenic thought processes. *Journal of Abnormal and Social Psychology,* 1964, **69,** 355–364.

Holtzman, W. H., Thorpe, J. S., Swartz, J. D., & Herron, E. W. *Inkblot perception and personality.* Austin, Texas: Univ. of Texas Press, 1961.

Holzman, P. S. Perceptual dysfunction in the schizophrenic syndrome. In R. Cancro (Ed.), *The schizophrenic reactions.* New York: Brunner/Mazel, 1970, 216–232.

Hozier, A. Q. On the breakdown of the sense of reality: A study of spatial perception in schizophrenia. *Journal of Consulting Psychology,* 1959, **23,** 185–194.

Hubel, D. H., & Wiesel, T. N. Receptive fields of single neurones in the cat's striate cortex. *Journal of Physiology,* 1959, **148,** 574–591.

Hubel, D. H., & Wiesel, T. N. Receptive fields, binocular interaction, and the functional architecture in the cat's visual cortex. *Journal of Physiology,* 1962, **160,** 106–154.

Jacobson, E. *The self and the object world.* New York: International Universities Press, 1964.

Jannucci, G. I. Size constancy in schizophrenia: A study of subgroup differences. *Dissertation Abstracts,* 1965, **26,** 503.

Johannsen, W. J., Friedman, S. H., & Liccione, J. V. Visual perception as a function of chronicity in schizophrenia. *British Journal of Psychiatry,* 1964, **110,** 561–570.

Jortner, S. An investigation of certain cognitive aspects of schizophrenia. *Journal of Projective Techniques and Personality Assessment,* 1966, **30,** 559–568.

Kagan, J. *Change and continuity in infancy.* New York: Wiley, 1971.

Kantor, R. E., & Herron, W. G. *Reactive and process schizophrenia.* Palo Alto, California: Science and Behavior Books, 1966.

Karlsson, J. L. Genealogic studies of schizophrenia. In D. Rosenthal & S. S. Kety, (Eds.), *The transmission of schizophrenia.* Oxford: Pergamon Press, 1968. Pp. 85–94.

Karmel, B. Z. Complexity, amounts of contour, and visually dependent behavior in hooded rats, domestic chicks, and human infants. *Journal of Comparative and Physiological Psychology*, 1969, 69, 649 661.

Karmel, B. Z., Hoffman, R. F., & Fegy, M. J. Processing of contour information by human infants evidenced by pattern-dependent evoked potentials. *Child Development*, 1974, **45**, 39–48.

Kelly, P. *The effects of infant temperament and maternal psychiatric status on patterns of mother,-infant interaction.* Doctoral dissertation, University of Rochester, 1974.

Kernberg, O. Structural derivatives of object relationships. *International Journal of Psychoanalysis*, 1966, **47**, 236–253.

Kernberg, O. Early ego integration and object relations. *Annals of the New York Academy of Sciences*, 1972, **193**, 233–247.

Kety, S. S., Rosenthal, D., Wender, P. H., & Schulsinger, F. The types and prevalence of mental illness in the biological and adoptive families of adopted schizophrenics. In D. Rosenthal & S. S. Kety (Eds.), *The transmission of schizophrenia.* Oxford: Pergamon Press, 1968. Pp. 345–362.

Kidd, K. K., & Cavalli-Sjorza, L. L. An analysis of the genetics of schizophrenia. *Social Biology*, 1973, **20**, 254–265.

Klein, G. S. Consciousness in psychoanalytic theory—some implications for current research in perception. *Journal of the American Psychoanalytic Association*, 1959, **7**, 5–34.

Kuffler, S. W. Neurons in the retina: Organization, inhibition, and excitation problems. *Cold Spring Harbor Symposium in Quantitative Biology*, 1952, **17**, 281–292.

Kuffler, S. W. Discharge patterns and functional organization of mammalian retina. *Journal of Neurophysiology*, 1953, **16**, 37–68.

Laing, R. D. *The self and others.* Chicago: Quadrangle Books, 1962.

Laing, R. D., & Esterson, A. *Sanity, madness and the family.* New York: Basic Books, 1964.

Lakin, M. Personality factors in mothers of excessively crying (colicky) infants. *Monograph of the Society for Research in Child Development*, 1957, **22**, (1, Whole No. 64).

Landis, B. Ego boundaries. *Psychological Issues*, 1970, **6**, 1–172.

Landis, C. *Varieties of psychopathological experience.* New York: Holt, 1964.

Lang, P. J., & Buss, A. H. Psychological deficit in schizophrenia: II. Interference and activation. *Journal of Abnormal Psychology*, 1965, **70**, 77–106.

Lanzkron, J., & Wolfson, W. Prognostic value of perceptual distortion of temporal orientation in chronic schizophrenics. *American Journal of Psychiatry*, 1958, **114**, 744–746.

Lehmann, H. E. The influence of different psychoactive drugs on cognitive and memory tests in schizophrenic and geriatric psychotics. In H. Brill (Ed.), *Neuro-psycho-pharmacology.* Amsterdam: Excerpta Medica, 1967, 221–229.

Leibowitz, H. W., & Pishkin, V. Perceptual size constancy in chronic schizophrenia. *Journal of Consulting Psychology*, 1961, **25**, 196–199.

Lennard, H. L., Beaulieu, M., & Embrey, N. G. Interaction in families with a schizophrenic child. *Archives of General Psychiatry*, 1965, **12**, 166–184.

Lennard, H. L., & Bernstein, A. *Patterns in human interaction.* San Francisco: Jossey-Bass, 1969.

Lewis, H. *Deprived children.* London: Oxford University Press, 1954.

Lewis, M., & Goldberg, S. Perceptual-cognitive development in infancy: A generalized expectancy model as a function of the mother-infant interaction. *Merrill-Palmer Quarterly*, 1969, **15**, 81–100.

Lewis, M. and Rosenbaum, L. A. (Eds.), *The effect of the infant on its caregiver.* New York: Wiley, 1974.

Lidz, R.W., & Lidz, T. Therapeutic considerations arising from the intense symbiotic needs of schizophrenic patients. In E. B. Brody & F. C. Redlich (Eds.), *Psychotherapy with schizophrenics.* New York: International Universities Press, 1952. Pp. 168–178.

Lidz, T. The family, language, and the transmission of schizophrenia. In D. Rosenthal and S. S. Kety (Eds.), *The transmission of schizophrenia.* Oxford: Pergamon Press, 1968. Pp. 175–184.

Lidz, T. The influence of family studies on the treatment of schizophrenia. *Psychiatry,* 1969, **32,** 237–251.

Lidz, T. *The origin and treatment of schizophrenic disorders.* New York: Basic Books, 1973.

Lidz, T., Cornelison, A., Terry, D.,& Fleck, S. Intrafamilial environment of the schizophrenic patient: VI. The transmission of irrationality. *Archives of Neurology and Psychiatry,* 1958, **79,** 305–316.

Lidz, T., Fleck, S., & Cornelison, A. *Schizophrenia and the family.* New York International Universities Press, 1965.

Liem, J. H. Effects of verbal communications of parents and children: A comparison of normal and schizophrenic families. *Journal of Consulting and Clinical Psychology,* 1974, **42,** 438–450.

Livingston, P. B., & Blum, R. A. Attention and speech in acute schizophrenia: An experimental study. *Archives of General Psychiatry,* 1968, **18,** 373–381.

Loewald, H. Ego and reality. *International Journal of Psycho-analysis,* 1951, **32,** 10–18.

Loewald, H. On the therapeutic action of psycho-analysis. *International Journal of Psycho-analysis,* 1960, **41,** 16–33.

Loewald, H. On internalization. *International Journal of Psycho-analysis,* 1973, **54,** 9–17.

Lorenz, M. & Cobb, S. Language patterns in psychotic and psychoneurotic patients. *Archives of Neurology and Psychiatry,* 1954, **72,** 665–673.

Loveland, N. The relation Rorschach: A technique for studying interaction. *Journal of Nervous and Mental Disease,* 1967, **145,** 93–105.

Lovinger, E. Perceptual contact with reality in schizophrenia. *Journal of Abnormal and Social Psychology,* 1956, **52,** 87–91.

MacDorman, C. F., Rivoire, J. L., Gallagher, P. J., & MacDorman, C. F. Size constancy of adolescent schizophrenics. *Journal of Abnormal and Social Psychology,* 1964, **69,** 258–263.

Maher, B. *Principles of Psychopathology: An experimental approach.* New York: McGraw-Hill, 1966.

Maher, B. The language of schizophrenia: A review and integration. *British Journal of Psychiatry,* 1972, **120,** 3–17.

Maher, B. Thought disorder in schizophrenia. Paper presented at Yale University, February, 1975.

Maher, B. A., McKean, K. O., & McLaughlin, B. Studies in psychotic language. In P. Stone, D.C. Dunphy, M.S. Smith, & D.M. Ogilive (Eds.), *The General Inquirer.* Cambridge, Massachusetts: MIT Press, 1966.

Mahler, M. S. On child psychosis and schizophrenia. *Psychoanalytic Study of the Child,* 1952, **7,** 286–305.

Mahler, M. S. Thoughts about development and individuation. *Psychoanalytic Study of the Child,* 1963, **18,** 307–324.

Mahler, M. S. *On human symbiosis and the vicissitudes of individuation.* New York: International Universities Press, 1968.

Mahler, M. S., & Elkisch, P. Some observations on disturbances of the ego in a case of infantile psychosis. *Psychoanalytic Study of the Child,* 1953, **8,** 252–261.

Mann, M. B. Studies in language behavior. III. The quantitative differentiation of samples of written language. *Psychological Monographs,* 1944, **56,** (Whole No. 255), 41–74.

Maslow, A. H. Cognition of being in the peak experience. *Journal of Genetic Psychology,* 1959, **94,** 43–66.

McDonough, J. M. Critical flicker frequency and the spiral after-effect with process and reactive schizophrenics. *Journal of Consulting Psychology,* 1960, **24,** 150–155.

McOllio, A. Iryotholingimil simiilies of schizophrenia. *British Journal of Medical Psychology,* 1966, **39,** 281–288.

McGhie, A. Attention and perception in schizophrenia. In B. Maher (Ed.), *Progress in experimental personality research, Vol. 5.* New York: Academic Press, 1970. Pp. 1–35.

McGhie, A., & Chapman, J. Disorders of attention and perception in early schizophrenia. *British Journal of Medical Psychology,* 1961, **34,** 103–116.

McGhie, A., Chapman, J., & Lawson, J. The effect of distraction on schizophrenic performance: I. Perception and immediate memory. *British Journal of Psychiatry,* 1965, 3, 383–390.

Mednick, S. A. Breakdown in individuals at high risk for schizophrenia: Possible predispositional perinatal factors. *Mental Hygiene,* 1970, **54,** 50–63.

Mednick, S. A., & Schulsinger, F. Some premorbid characteristics related to breakdown in children with schizophrenic mothers. In D. Rosenthal & S. S. Kety (Eds.), *The transmission of schizophrenia.* Oxford: Pergamon Press, 1968. Pp. 267–291.

Mednick, S. A., & Schulsinger, F. Factors related to breakdown in children at high risk for schizophrenia. In M. Roff & D. F. Ricks (Eds.), *Life history research in psychopathology, Vol. I.* Minneapolis: Univ. of Minnesota Press, 1970. Pp. 51–93.

Milner, E. A study of the relationship between reading readiness in grade one school children and patterns of parent-child interaction. *Child Development,* 1951, **22,** 95–112.

Mishler, E. G., & Waxler, N. E. Family interaction processes and schizophrenia: A review of current theories. *International Journal of Psychiatry,* 1966, **2,** 375–413.

Mishler, E. G., & Waxler, N. E. *Interaction in families.* New York: Wiley, 1968.

Morris, G. O., & Wynne, L. C. Schizophrenic offspring and parental styles of communication. *Psychiatry,* 1965, **28,** 19–44.

Nameche, G. *Life patterns of children who became adult schizophrenics.* Doctoral dissertation, Brandeis University, 1965.

Oberndorf, C. P. Time—its relation to reality and purpose. *Psychoanalytic Review,* 1941, **28,** 139–155.

Orme, J. E. Personality, time estimation and time experience. *Acta Psychologia,* 1965, **22,** 430–440.

Orme, J. E. Time estimation and the nosology of schizophrenia. *British Journal of Psychiatry,* 1966, **112,** 37–39.

Osgood, C. *Method and theory in experimental psychology.* New York: Oxford Univ. Press, 1953.

Parens, H. A contribution of separation–individuation to the development of psychic structures. In J. B. McDevitt & C. F. Settlage (Eds.), *Separation–individuation: Essays in honor of Margaret S. Mahler.* New York: International Universities Press, 1971. Pp. 100–112.

Parsons, T., & Bales, R. F. *Family, socialization and interaction process.* Glencoe, Illinois: Free Press, 1955.

Payne, R. W. Cognitive abnormalities. In H. J. Eysenck (Ed.), *Handbook of abnormal psychology.* New York: Basic Books, 1961. Pp. 193–261.

Payne, R. W. The measurement and significance of overinclusive thinking and retardation in schizophrenic patients. In P. H. Hoch & J. Zubin (Eds.), *Psychopathology of schizophrenia.* New York: Grune & Stratton, 1966. Pp. 77–97.

Payne, R. W., & Caird, W. K. Reaction time, distractibility, and overinclusive thinking in psychotics. *Journal of Abnormal Psychology,* 1967, **72,** 112–121.

Payne, R. W., Hochberg, A. C., & Hawks, D. V. Dichotic stimulation as a method of assessing disorder of attention in overinclusive schizophrenic patients. *Journal of Abnormal Psychology,* 1970, **76,** 185–193.

Payne, R. W., Matussek, P., & George, E. I. An experimental study of schizophrenic thought disorder. *Journal of Mental Science,* 1959, **105,** 627–652.

Pearl, D., & Berg, P. S. Time perception and conflict arousal in schizophrenia. *Journal of Abnormal and Social Psychology,* 1963, **66,** 332–338.

Perez, P. Size constancy in normals and schizophrenics. In W. H. Ittelson & S. B. Kutash (Eds.), *Perceptual changes in psychopathology.* New Brunswick, New Jersey: Rutgers Univ. Press, 1961. Pp. 39–55.

Phillips, L. Case history data and prognosis in schizophrenia. *Journal of Nervous and Mental Disease,* 1953, **117,** 515–525.

Phillips, L. S. Social competence, the process-reactive distinction and the nature of mental disorder. In P. Hoch and J. Zubin (Eds.), *Psychopathology of schizophrenia.* New York: Grune & Stratton, 1966. Pp. 471–481.

Piaget, J. *The construction of reality in the child.* (M. Cook, Transl.) New York: Basic Books, 1954.

Piaget, J. *The child's conception of time.* (A.J.Pomerans,Transl.)New York:Basic Books,1969.

Pious, W. L. Obsessive-compulsive symptoms in an incipient schizophrenic. *Psychoanalytic Quarterly,* 1950, **19,** 327–351.

Pious, W. L. A hypothesis about the nature of schizophrenic behavior. In A. Burton (Ed.), *Psychotherapy of the psychoses.* New York: Basic Books, 1961. Pp. 43–68.

Pishkin, V., Smith, T. L., & Leibowitz, H. W. The influence of symbolic stimulus value on perceived size in chronic schizophrenia. *Journal of Consulting Psychology,* 1962, **26,** 323–330.

Pollin, W., & Stabenau, J. R. Biological, psychological and historical differences in a series of monozygotic twins discordant for schizophrenia. In D. Rosenthal & S. S. Kety (Eds.), *The transmission of schizophrenia.* Oxford: Pergamon Press, 1968. Pp. 317–332.

Pollock, G. H. On symbiosis and symbiotic neurosis. *International Journal of Psycho-analysis,* 1964, **46,** 1–30.

Provence, S., & Lipton, R. C. *Infants in institutions.* New York: International Universities Press, 1962.

Quinlan, D. M., & Harrow, M. Boundary disturbances in schizophrenia. *Journal of Abnormal Psychology,* 1974, **83,** 533–541.

Quinlan, D. M., Harrow, M., Tucker, G., & Carlson, K. Varieties of "disordered" thinking on the Rorschach. *Journal of Abnormal Psychology,* 1972, **79,** 47–53.

Rabin, A. I. Time estimation of schizophrenics and non-psychotics. *Journal of Clinical Psychology,* 1957, **13,** 88–90.

Rabin, A. I., King, G. F., & Ehrmann, J. C. Vocabulary performance of short-term and long-term schizophrenics. *Journal of Abnormal and Social Psychology,* 1955, **50,** 255–258.

Ramey, C. T., Heigar, L., & Klisz, D. K. Synchronous reinforcement of vocal responses in failure-to-thrive infants. *Child Development,* 1972, **43,** 1449–1455.

Rapaport, D.,.Gill, M. M., & Schafer, R. *Diagnostic psychological testing. Vol. I.* Chicago: Year Book, 1945.

Rapaport, D., Gill, M. M., & Schafer, R. *Diagnostic psychological testing. Vol. II.* Chicago: Year Book, 1946.

Rappaport, M., Rogers, N., Reynolds, S., & Weinmann, R. Comparative ability of normal and chronic schizophrenic subjects to attend to competing voice messages: Effects of method of presentation, message load and drugs. *Journal of Nervous and Mental Disease,* 1966, **143,** 16–27.

Raush, H. L. Perceptual constancy in schizophrenia. I. Size constancy. *Journal of Personality,* 1952, **21,** 176–187.

Raush, H. L. Object constancy in schizophrenia: The enhancement of symbolic objects and conceptual stability. *Journal of Abnormal and Social Psychology,* 1956, **53,** 231–234.

Reichard, S., & Tillman, C. Patterns of parent-child relationships in schizophrenia. *Psychiatry*, 1950, **13**, 247–257.

Reitman, E., & Cleveland, S. E. Changes in body image following sensory deprivation in schizophrenic and control groups. Doctoral dissertation, Univ. of Houston, 1962.

Reitman, E. E., & Cleveland, S. E. Changes in body image following sensory deprivation in schizophrenic and control groups. *Journal of Abnormal and Social Psychology*, 1964, **68**, 168–176.

Renik, O. D., & Fisher, S. Induction of body-image boundary changes in male subjects. *Journal of Projective Techniques and Personality Assessment*, 1968, **32**, 45–48.

Reynolds, G. A. *Perceptual constancy in "schizophrenics" and "normals"*. Doctoral dissertation. Purdue Univ., 1953.

Ricks, D. F., & Berry, J. C. Family and symptom patterns that precede schizophrenia. In M. Roff & D. F. Ricks (Eds.), *Life history research in psychopathology*. Minneapolis: Univ. of Minnesota Press, 1970. Pp. 31–50.

Ricks, D. F., & Nameche, G. F. Symbiosis, sacrifice and schizophrenia. *Mental Hygiene*, 1966, **50**, 541–551.

Rieder, R. O. The offspring of schizophrenic parents: A review. *Journal of Nervous and Mental Disease*, 1973, **157**, 179–190.

Robins, L. N. *Deviant children grown up*. Baltimore, Maryland: Williams & Wilkins, 1966.

Rorschach, H. *Psychodiagnostics*. (5th Ed.) Berne: Hans Huber, 1942.

Rose, G. Narcissistic fusion states and creativity. In M. Kanzer (Ed.), *The unconscious today: Essays in honor of Max Schur*. New York: International Universities Press, 1971. Pp. 495–505.

Rosenbaum, G. Feedback mechanisms in schizophrenia. In G. Tourney & J. S. Gottlieb (Eds.), *Lafayette clinic studies in schizophrenia*. Detroit: Wayne State Univ. Press, 1971.

Rosenbaum, G., Flenning, F., & Rosen, H. Effects of weight intensity on discrimination thresholds of normals and schizophrenics. *Journal of Abnormal Psychology*, 1965, **70**, 446–450.

Rosenfeld, S. *Notes on self and object differentiation and communication in borderline children*. Unpublished manuscript, Hampstead Child-Therapy Clinic, 1972.

Rosenfeld, S., & Sprince, M. An attempt to formulate the meaning of the concept "Borderline." *Psychoanalytic Study of the Child*, 1963, **18**, 603–635.

Rosenfeld, S., & Sprince, M. Some thoughts on the technical handling of borderline children. *Psychoanalytic Study of the Child*, 1965, **20**, 495–517.

Rosenthal, D. The heredity-environment issue in schizophrenia. In D. Rosenthal & S. S. Kety (Eds.), *The transmission of schizophrenia*. Oxford: Pergamon Press, 1968. Pp. 413–427.

Rosenthal, D. *Genetic theory and abnormal behavior*. New York: McGraw-Hill, 1970.

Rosenthal, D., Wender, P. H., Kety, S. S., Schulsinger, F., Welner, J. & Ostergaard, L. Schizophrenics' offspring reared in adoptive homes. In D. Rosenthal & S. S. Kety (Eds.), *The transmission of schizophrenia*. Oxford: Pergamon Press, 1968. Pp. 377–391.

Roth, D. Unit transfer: An exploratory study. *Archives of General Psychiatry*, 1961, **4**, 171–181.

Roth, D., & Blatt, S. J. Psychopathology of adolescence. *Archives of General Psychiatry*, 1961, **4**, 289–298.

Roth, D. & Blatt, S. J. Spatial representations and psychopathology. *Journal of the American Psychoanalytic Association*, 1974, **22**, 854–872.

Rutter, M. *Children of sick parents: An environmental and psychiatric study*. London: Oxford Univ. Press, 1966.

Salapatek, P. Visual scanning of geometric figures by the human newborn. *Journal of Comparative and Physiological Psychology*, 1968, **66**, 247–258.

Salapatek, P., & Kessen, W. Visual scanning of triangles by the human newborn. *Journal of Experimental Child Psychology*, 1966, **3**, 155–167.

Salzinger, K., Portnoy, S., Pisoni, D. B., & Feldman, R. S. The immediacy hypothesis and response-produced stimuli in schizophrenic speech. *Journal of Abnormal Psychology,* 1970, **76,** 258–264.

Sameroff, A. J., & Zax, M. Schizotaxia revisited: Model issues in the etiology of schizophrenia. *American Journal of Orthopsychiatry,* 1973, **43,** 744–754. (a)

Sameroff, A. J., & Zax, M. Perinatal characteristics of the offspring of schizophrenic women. *Journal of Nervous and Mental Disease,* 1973, **157,** 191–199. (b)

Sanders, R., & Pacht, A. R. Perceptual size constancy of known clinical groups. *Journal of Consulting Psychology,* 1952, **16,** 440–444.

Saucer, R. T. A further study of the perception of apparent motion by schizophrenics. *Journal of Consulting Psychology,* 1958, **22,** 256–258.

Saucer, R. T. Chlorpromazine and apparent motion perception by schizophrenics. *Journal of Consulting Psychology,* 1959, **23,** 134–136.

Saucer, R. T., & Sweetbaum, H. Perception of the shortest noticeable dark time by schizophrenics. *Science,* 1958, **127,** 698–699.

Schafer, R. Regression in the service of the ego. In G. Lindzey (Ed.), *Assessment of human motives.* New York: Holt, 1958. Pp. 119–148.

Schafer, R. Generative empathy in the treatment situation. *Psychoanalytic Quarterly,* 1959, **28,** 342–373.

Schafer, R. Bodies in schizophrenic Rorschach responses. *Journal of Projective Techniques,* 1960, **24,** 267–281.

Schafer, R. *Aspects of internalization.* New York: International Universities, 1968.

Schaffer, H. R. & Emerson, P. E. Patterns of response to physical contact in early human development. *Journal of Child Psychology and Psychiatry and Allied Disciplines,* 1964, **5,** 1–13.

Schopler, E., & Loftin, J. Thought disorders in parents of psychotic children: A function of test anxiety. *Archives of General Psychiatry,* 1969, **20,** 174–181.

Searles, H. F. *The nonhuman environment in normal development and in schizophrenia.* New York: International Universities Press, 1960.

Searles, H. F. *Collected papers on schizophrenia and related subjects.* New York: International Universities Press, 1965.

Sedman, G. "Inner Voices": Phenomenological and clinical aspects. *British Journal of Psychiatry,* 1966, **112,** 485–490. (a)

Sedman, G. A comparative study of pseudohallucinations, imagery and true hallucinations. *British Journal of Psychiatry,* 1966, **112,** 9–17. (b)

Senden, M. von. *Raum-und Gestaltauffassung.* Leipzig: Barth, 1932. Cited by C. Osgood, *Method and theory in experimental psychology.* New York: Oxford Univ. Press, 1953.

Shakow, D. Some psychological features of schizophrenia. In M. L. Reymert (Ed.), *Feelings and emotions: The Mooseheart symposium.* New York: McGraw-Hill, 1950. Pp. 383–390.

Shakow, D. Segmental set: A theory of the formal psychological deficit in schizophrenia. *Archives of General Psychiatry,* 1962, **6,** 1–17.

Shakow, D. Psychological deficit in schizophrenia. *Behavioral Science,* 1963, **8,** 275–305.

Silverman, J. Scanning-control mechanism and "cognitive-filtering" in paranoid and nonparanoid schizophrenia. *Journal of Consulting Psychology,* 1964, **28,** 385–393.

Silverman, J. The problem of attention in research and theory in schizophrenia. In P. Bakan (Ed.), *Attention: An enduring problem in psychology.* Princeton: Van Nostrand-Reinhold, 1966. Pp. 134–178.

Silverman, L. H. Further experimental studies of dynamic propositions in psychoanalysis. *Journal of the American Psychoanalytic Association,* 1970, **18,** 102–124.

Singer, M. T. Family transactions and schizophrenia: I. Recent research findings. In J. Romano (Ed.), *The origins of schizophrenia,*   *Excerpta Medica International Congress Series,* 1967, No. 151, 147–164. (Proceedings of the First Rochester International Conference).

Singer, M. T., & Wynne, L. C. Thought disorder and family relations of schizophrenics: III. Methodology using projective techniques. *Archives of General Psychiatry,* 1963, 12, 187–200. (a)

Singer, M. T., & Wynne, L. C. Thought disorder and family relations of schizophrenics: IV. Results and implications. *Archives of General Psychiatry,* 1965, 12, 201–212. (b)

Singer, M. T., & Wynne, L. C. Communication styles in parents of normals, neurotics and schizophrenics. In I. M. Cohen (Ed.), *Family structure, dynamics and therapy.* Washington, D.C.: American Psychiatric Association, 1966. Pp. 25–38.

Slepian, H. *A developmental study of inner versus external speech in normals and schizophrenics.* Doctoral dissertation, Clark Univ., 1959.

Small, S. M. Paranoia: An historical overview with a twenty-five year continuous case study. *Behavioral Neuropsychiatry,* 1971, 3, 2–11.

Snyder, S. Perceptual closure in acute paranoid schizophrenics. *Archives of General Psychiatry,* 1961, 5, 406–410.

Snyder, S., Rosenthal, D., & Taylor, I. R. Perceptual closure in schizophrenia. *Journal of Abnormal & Social Psychology,* 1961, 63, 131–136.

Spitz, R. A. Hospitalism: A follow-up report. *Psychoanalytic Study of the Child,* 1946, 2, 113–117.

Spitz, R. A. The psychogenic diseases in infancy. *Psychoanalytic Study of the Child,* 1951, 6, 255–275.

Spitz, R. A. & Wolf, K. M. Anaclitic depression. *Psychoanalytic Study of the Child,* 1946, 2, 313–342.

Stein, K. B., & Craik, K. H. Relationship between motoric and ideational activity preference and time perspective in neurotics and schizophrenics. *Journal of Consulting Psychology,* 1965, 29, 460–467.

Steingart, I., & Freedman, N. A language construction approach to the examination of self/ object representation in varying clinical states. *Psychoanalysis and Contempory Science,* 1972, 1, 132–178.

Stern, G. G., Caldwell, B. M., Hersher, L., Lipton, E. L., & Richmond, J. B. A factor analytic study of the mother-infant dyad. *Child Development,* 1969, 40, 163–181.

Stierlin, H. The adaptation to the "stronger" person's reality: Some aspects of the symbiotic relationship of the schizophrenic. *Psychiatry,* 1959, 22, 143–152.

Strauss, J. Hallucinations and delusions as points on Continua Function. *Archives of General Psychiatry,* 1969, 21, 581–586.

Tausk, V. On the origin of the "influencing machine" in schizophrenia (1919). In R. Fliess (Ed.), *The psychoanalytic reader.* New York: International Universities Press, 1948, 31–64.

Thomas, A., Chess, S. & Birch, H. *Temperament and behavior disorders in children.* New York: New York Univ. Press, 1968.

Thomas, R. Comments on some aspects of self and object representation in a group of psychotic children. *Psychoanalytic Study of the Child,* 1966, 21, 527–580.

Trunnell, T. L. Thought disturbance in schizophrenia: Replication study utilizing Piaget's theories. *Archives of General Psychiatry,* 1965, 13, 9–18.

Venables, P. H. Input dysfunction in schizophrenia. In B. A. Maher (Ed.), *Progress in experimental personality research, Vol. I.* New York: Academic Press, 1964. Pp. 1–47.

Von Domarus, E. The specific laws of logic in schizophrenia. In J. S. Kasanin (Ed.), *Language and thought in schizophrenia.* Berkeley: Univ. of California Press, 1944. Pp. 104–113.

Vygotsky, L. S. *Thought and language.* (Transl. by E. Hanfmann & G. Vakar). Cambridge, Massachusetts: MIT Press, 1962.

Wallace, M. B. Future time perspective in schizophrenia. *Journal of Abnormal and Social Psychology,* 1956, **52,** 240–245.

Waxler, N. E. Parent and child effects on cognitive performance: An experimental approach to the etiological and responsive theories of schizophrenia. *Family Process,* 1974, **13,** 1–21.

Webb, W., Davis, D. & Cromwell, R. Size estimation in schizophrenics as a function of thematic content of stimuli. *Journal of Nervous and Mental Disease,* 1966, **143,** 252–255.

Weckowicz, T. E. Size constancy in schizophrenic patients. *Journal of Mental Science,* 1957, **103,** 475–486.

Weckowicz, T. E. Perception of hidden pictures by schizophrenic patients. *Archives of General Psychiatry,* 1960, **2,** 521–527.

Weckowicz, T. E. Shape constancy in schizophrenic patients. *Journal of Abnormal and Social Psychology,* 1964, **68,** 177–183.

Weckowicz, T. E., & Blewett, D. B. Size constancy and abstract thinking in schizophrenic patients. *Journal of Mental Science,* 1959, **105,** 909–934.

Weckowicz, T. E., & Hall, R. Distance constancy in schizophrenic and nonschizophrenic mental patients. *Journal of Clinical Psychology,* 1960, **16,** 272–276.

Weckowicz, T. E., Sommer, R., & Hall, R. Distance constancy in schizophrenic patients. *Journal of Mental Science,* 1958, **104,** 1174–1182.

Weiner, I. B. *Psychodiagnosis in schizophrenia.* New York: Wiley, 1966.

Weinstein, A. D., Goldstone, S., & Boardman, W. K. The effect of recent and remote frames of reference on temporal judgments of schizophrenic patients. *Journal of Abnormal and Social Psychology,* 1958, **57,** 241–244.

Wender, P. H., Rosenthal, D., & Kety, S. S. A psychiatric assessment of the adoptive parents of schizophrenics. In D. Rosenthal & S. S. Kety (Eds.), *The transmission of schizophrenia.* Oxford: Pergamon Press, 1968. Pp. 235–250.

Werner, H. *Comparative psychology of mental development.* New York: International Universities Press, 1948.

Werner, H., & Kaplan, B. *Symbol formation: An organismic-developmental approach to language and the expression of thought.* New York: Wiley, 1963.

Whiteman, M. The performance of schizophrenics on social concepts. *Journal of Abnormal and Social Psychology,* 1954, **49,** 266–271.

Wilcox, B. M. Visual preferences of human infants for representations of the human face. *Journal of Experimental Child Psychology,* 1969, **7,** 10–20.

Wild, C., Singer, M., Rosman, B., Ricci, J., & Lidz, T. Measuring disordered styles of thinking. *Archives of General Psychiatry,* 1965, **13,** 471–476.

Williams, E. B. Deductive reasoning in schizophrenia. *Journal of Abnormal and Social Psychology,* 1964, **69,** 47–61.

Witkin, H. A. Psychological differentiation and forms of pathology. *Journal of Abnormal Psychology,* 1965, **70,** 317–336.

Wolff, P. H. Cognitive considerations for a psychoanalytic theory of language acquisition. In R. R. Holt (Ed.), Motives and thought: Psychoanalytic essays in honor of David Rapaport. *Psychological Issues,* 1967, **18/19,** 300–343.

Wynne, L. C. Family transactions and schizophrenia: II. Conceptual considerations for a research strategy. In J. Romano (Ed.), *The origins of schizophrenia, Excerpta Medica International Congress Series,* 1967, No. 151, 165–178. (Proceeding of the First Rochester International Conference).

Wynne, L. C., Ryckoff, I., Day, J., & Hirsch, S. Pseudo-mutuality in the family relations of schizophrenics. *Psychiatry,* 1958, **21,** 205–220.

Wynne, L. C., & Singer, M. T. Thought disorder and family relations of schizophrenics: I. A research strategy. *Archives of General Psychiatry,* 1963, **9,** 191–198. (a)

Wynne, L. C., & Singer, M. T. Thought disorder and family relations of schizophrenics: II. A classification of forms of thinking. *Archives of General Psychiatry*, 1963, **9**, 199–206.(b)

Yarrow, L. J. Research in dimensions of early maternal care. *Merrill-Palmer Quarterly*, 1963, **9**, 101–114.

Yates, A. J. Data-processing levels and thought disorder in schizophrenia. *Australian Journal of Psychology*, 1966, **18**, 103–129.

Zahn, T. P. Acquired and symbolic affective value as determinants of size estimation in schizophrenic and normal subjects. *Journal of Abnormal and Social Psychology*, 1959, **58**, 39–47.

Zigler, E., & Phillips, L. Social competence and the process-reactive distinction in psychopathology. *Journal of Abnormal Psychology*, 1962, **65**, 215–222.

Zucker, L. *Ego structure in paranoid schizophrenia: A new method of evaluating projective material*. Springfield, Illinois: Thomas, 1958.

Author Index

H

Harin, R. 212, 252
Haith, M.M. 5, 253
Haley, J. 102, 249
Hall, R. 33, 262
Halpern, F. 10, 243, 252
Hamilton, V. 33, 253
Harrington, R. 44, 253
Harris, J. 34, 254
Harrow, M. 59, 258
Hartman, A.M. 33, 254
Hartmann, H. 4, 254
Harway, N.I. 33, 34, 254
Havel, J.A. 54, 57, 254
Hawks, D.V. 42, 257
Heigar, L. 82, 258
Heinstein, M.I. 82, 254
Held, J. 34, 251
Herron, E. W. 25, 254
Herron, W.G. 36, 254
Hersher, L. 82, 261
Heston, L.L. 10, 245, 246, 254
Hill, L.B. 78, 85, 254
Himmel, S. 33, 250
Hirsch, S. 94-95, 102-103, 104, 105, 262
Hochberg, A.C. 42, 257
Hoffman, R.F. 5, 255
Holt, R.R. 51, 54, 55, 56, 57-58, 254
Holtzman, W.H. 23, 25, 254
Holzman, P.S. 26, 254
Hooks, W. 105, 249
Hozier, A.Q. 24, 26, 254
Hubel, D.H. 5, 254
Hurvich, M. 235, 250
Huston, P.E. 32, 251

J

Jackson, D. 102, 249
Jacobson, E. 3, 4, 13, 63, 65, 71, 72, 79,
    83, 86, 108, 227, 254
Jannucci, G.I. 33, 254
Jenney, P.B. 31, 252
Johannsen, W.J. 32, 34, 254
Jortner, S. 43, 59, 229, 230, 254

K

Kagan, J. 5, 10, 15, 65, 82, 226, 254

Kantor, R.E. 36, 254
Kaplan, B. 6, 7, 41, 47, 49, 53, 54, 226,
    262
Karlsson, J.L. 246, 254
Karmel, B.Z. 5, 255
Kelly, P. 240, 255
Kernberg, O. 4, 255
Kessen, W. 5, 259
Kety, S.S. 10, 242, 245, 259, 262
Kidd, K.K. 10, 245, 255
King, G.F. 44, 258
Klein, G.S. 36, 255
Klisz, D.K. 82, 258
Koslowski, B. 240, 250
Kris, E. 4, 254
Kuffler, S.W. 5, 255

L

Laing, R.D. 98-99, 255
Lakin, M. 82, 255
Landis, B. 3, 23, 24, 226, 227, 255
Landis, C. 19, 255
Lang, P.J. 38, 226, 255
Lanzkron, J. 31, 255
Lawson, J. 38, 257
Lehmann, H.E. 38, 255
Leibowitz, H.W. 33, 36, 255, 258
Lennard, H.L. 96, 99, 103-104, 255
Lewis, H. 82, 255
Lewis, M. 82, 240, 253, 255
Liccione, J.V. 32, 34, 254
Lidz, R.W. 3, 78, 85, 226, 255
Lidz, T. 3, 9, 40, 43, 45, 48-49, 78, 79, 85,
    89, 92, 94-95, 98, 99, 100, 102, 226,
    231, 255, 256, 262
Liem, J.H. 106-107, 256
Lipton, E.L. 82, 261
Lipton, R.C. 7, 82, 238, 258
Livington, P.B. 38, 256
Loewald, H. 4, 17, 227, 256
Loftkin, J. 107, 260
Lorenz, M. 52, 256
Loveland, N. 101, 256
Lovinger, E. 33, 34, 36, 256
Lowenstein, R.M. 4, 254

M

MacDorman, C.F. 33, 256

Subject Index